Refugees

hopefully they'll fade away –
these sighs of fear
life bereft of poetry
road paved with anguish
repulsive, barren heart

it is time to depart
for lasting peace
freedom fulfilled
along the paths of ancient truths
in this citadel of sublime soaring

From 'Road to Freedom' by Diangitukwa Fweley

Refugees

Perspectives on the Experience of Forced Migration

Edited by Alastair Ager

PINTER

London and New York

Cassell
Wellington House, 125 Strand, London WC2R 0BB
370 Lexington Avenue, New York, NY 10017–6550

First published 1999
© Alastair Ager and the contributors 1999

British Library Cataloguing-in-Publication Data
A catalogue record for this book is available from the British Library.

ISBN 0-304-33922-9 (hardback)
      0-304-33923-7 (paperback)

Library of Congress Cataloging-in-Publication Data
Refugees: perspectives on the experience of forced migration/edited
   by Alastair Ager.
      p.   cm.
   Includes bibliographical references and index.
   ISBN 0–304–33922–9. — ISBN 0–304–33923–7 (pbk.)
   1. Refugees.   2. Forced migration.   I. Ager, Alastair.
HV640. R437   1998
362.87—dc21   98–35943
                                                                             CIP

Typeset by BookEns Ltd., Royston, Herts
Printed and bound in Great Britain by Biddles Ltd, Guildford and King's Lynn

Contents

Contributors

Howard Adelman has been Professor of Philosophy at York University in Toronto since 1966. He was founder of the Centre for Refugee Studies, and served as its Director and editor of the periodical *Refuge* until 1993. He has served in many university positions, including Acting Dean of Atkinson College and two terms as director of the graduate programme in philosophy at York University. In 1996–97, he headed the research unit on Prevention/Early Warning at York University. Professor Adelman has been the recipient of numerous awards and grants. He has written eighteen monographs, over eighty journal articles and chapters and has edited books and special editions of journals. In addition to his philosophical writings, he has written extensively on the Middle East, humanitarian intervention, membership rights, ethics, refugee policy and early warning. Recent publications include the co-edited volume *Immigration and Refugee Policy: Australia and Canada Compared* and the study – co-authored with Astri Suhrke – *Early Warning and Conflict Management: The Genocide in Rwanda*.

Alastair Ager is Director of the Centre for International Health Studies and Professor of Applied Psychology at Queen Margaret College, Edinburgh, and a Research Associate of the Refugee Studies Programme, University of Oxford. He is a graduate of the universities of Keele, Wales and Birmingham. He has over fifty publications spanning the fields of disability, community integration and refugee studies. His work in the latter area has included research studies of the experience of Mozambican refugees in Malawi and, more recently, analysis of the social integration of refugees in Scotland. He is a member of the Editorial Board of the *Journal of Refugee Studies* and a regular contributor to the education programme at the Refugee Studies Programme, University of Oxford. He has worked with a number of agencies involved in refugee assistance, including UNHCR, MSF-Holland and Oxfam, with field experience across Southern Africa, South Asia and Eastern Europe.

Frederick L. Ahearn, Jr, is Professor and former Dean of Social Service at the Catholic University of America in Washington, DC, and is affiliated as a Tutor at the Refugee Studies Programme, University of Oxford. He received his doctorate in social work from Columbia University. He has had extensive experience in

Latin America and the Philippines working in the aftermath of disasters: conducting needs assessments, designing programmes and researching the experience of displaced persons and their families. He is co-author of the *Handbook of Mental Health Care of Disaster Victims* and *Refugee Children: Theory, Research and Services*.

John W. Berry is Professor of Psychology at Queen's University, Kingston, Ontario. He received his PhD from the University of Edinburgh in 1966. He has been a lecturer at the University of Sydney, a fellow of the Netherlands Institute for Advanced Study, and a Visiting Professor at the universities of Nice, Geneva, Bergen and Oxford. He is a Fellow of the Canadian Psychological Association, and Fellow and Past President of the Inter-national Association for Cross-Cultural Psychology. He specializes in the areas of cross-cultural, multicultural, social and cognitive psychology.

Agnès Callamard holds a PhD in Political Science from the New School for Social Research, New York. She was awarded a doctoral and post-doctoral fellowship at the Centre for Refugee Studies of York University in Toronto, where she conducted research on international and African refugee movements, and refugee women. She has taught at Atkinson College, York University, worked as a consultant for the United Nations, and conducted extensive fieldwork in Eastern and Southern Africa. She is the author of many articles on refugee movements and is currently the Research Policy Co-ordinator at the International Secretariat of Amnesty International in London.

Giorgia Doná was, at the time of writing her chapter, working in Rwanda as Lecturer and Regional Director for the Child Studies Unit, Department of Applied Psychology, University College Cork. She has a master's in Anthropology from Cambridge University and a master's and a doctorate in Psychology from Queen's University, Kingston, Ontario. Her research interests include acculturation and mental health, refugees, psychosocial needs of children in difficult circumstances, and humanitarian assistance. She has conducted research in Central and North America, and in Africa.

Barbara Harrell-Bond was founding Director of the University of Oxford Refugee Studies Programme (1982–96) and is now Visiting Professor, Makerere University, Uganda. Her research has increasingly focused on the delivery of humanitarian assistance, particularly by the UN and its agencies, and international and human rights law, especially as this affects refugees, asylum-seekers and other displaced population groups. Principal publications include *Imposing Aid: Emergency Assistance to Refugees* (Oxford University Press, 1986), *Community Leadership and the Transformation of Freetown (1801–1976)* (with D. Skinner and A. Howard, Mouton, 1977) and *Modern Marriage in Sierra Leone: A Study of the Professional Group* (Mouton, 1975). In addition, she has acted as a consultant to governments, non-governmental organizations such as Oxfam and Norwegian People's Aid, and intergovernmental organizations such as the International Federation of Red Cross and Red Crescent Societies, the European Union, the Food and Agriculture Organisation and the World Food Programme. In 1996 she was awarded the Distinguished Service Award by the American Anthropological Association.

Susan Levy is a South African clinical psychologist with specialist interest in the area of trauma. She was part of the first group of mental health workers in South Africa to begin working with ex-detainees and their families. She spent six years working at the Medical Foundation for the Care of Victims of Torture in London. Currently she works in the Adult Mental Health Unit at Chelsea and Westminster Hospital, London. She lectures and teaches on a range of programmes, including work with the Minster Psychotherapy Centre and the Tavistock Centre.

Maryanne Loughry is Pedro Arupe Tutor at the Refugee Studies Programme at the University of Oxford. She is a psychologist with research interests in the field of health psychology and the effects of conflict and detention on children. She has worked in refugee camps in Hong Kong and the Philippines and has trained refugee workers in Vietnam, Gaza and the West Bank. She is currently involved in the development of educational materials in support of training to address psychosocial issues in refugee and forced migration settings.

Derek Summerfield is a medical doctor with experience of war zones in Zimbabwe, Nicaragua and Gaza. He works as a psychiatrist with the Medical Foundation for the Care of Victims of Torture, London, and is Honorary Senior Lecturer in Community Psychiatry at St George's Hospital Medical School, London. He has been a consultant to Oxfam and is a Research Associate at the Refugee Studies Programme, Queen Elizabeth House, University of Oxford.

Charles Westin, a social psychologist, is Chair of Migration and Ethnicity Studies and Director of the Centre for Research in International Migration and Ethnic Relations at the University of Stockholm. He has led several national surveys of the Swedish people's attitudes towards migration-related issues, and written widely on discrimination, identity, torture and multiculturalism. Currently he is working on a 25-year follow-up of the Ugandan Asians in Europe as a transnational diaspora, and leads the Swedish team in the International Comparative Studies of Ethnocultural Youth (ICSEY) programme. He is also currently co-ordinating the UNESCO project 'Management of Cultural Pluralism in Europe'.

Roger Zetter is Professor and Deputy Head of the School of Planning at Oxford Brookes University, founding editor of the *Journal of Refugee Studies* and a Research Associate of the Refugee Studies Programme, University of Oxford. The main focus of his research is the institutional and policy dimensions of refugee aid and the impact of humanitarian assistance on refugees. From 1988 to 1992 he co-ordinated a large-scale research project on humanitarian assistance to Mozambican refugees in Malawi and Zimbabwe, funded by ESRC (UK)/Pew Charitable Trust. He prepared a state-of-the-art paper on refugee shelter provision and settlement policies for the first UNHCR Workshop on Improved Shelter Response and Environment for Refugees, published in 1995. In 1997–98 he was a consultant to Oxfam, co-ordinating the evaluation of its Great Lakes Programme following the emergency in Rwanda. Currently, he is directing a study of social housing provision for refugees and asylum-seekers in the UK funded by the Housing Corporation.

Acknowledgements

I am deeply grateful to all contributors for the commitment, enthusiasm and scholarship that they brought to bear in producing this volume. I am particularly thankful to Barbara Harrell-Bond, whose zeal, intellect and – to be frank – persistent belligerence played such a part in drawing me, and indeed many others, into the field of refugee studies. My deepest debt, however, is to Juana Gabriele and the many others who provided such moving insight into the experience of refugees in the course of fieldwork by Wendy Ager and myself in Malawi at the beginning of this decade.

I do not know whether the fact that I have outlived two editors at Cassell is more a testament to mobility in the publishing industry or the demands of this particular project, but I am grateful for the support and encouragement of both Lara Burns and Petra Recter, as well as Sandra Margolies, who has brought the book through to the finishing post. Thanks are also due to Fiona Sutherland at CIHS for assistance in the preparation of this manuscript.

Finally, I am grateful to Wendy, Charlie and Joe Ager, who have contributed in a number of ways to the production of this volume, not least in their tolerance of my distraction from responsibilities towards them over the past two years. The following text gives consistent testimony to the preciousness of a supportive social world which respects personal vision, and I thank them for their part in creating such an environment for facilitating this contribution to the understanding of the refugee experience.

The permission of Random House and Guilo Einaudi for use of Primo Levi's poem 'If This Is a Man' is gratefully acknowledged.

Five Leaves Publications, Nottingham, are thanked for permission to use part of 'Road to Freedom' by Diangitukwa Fweley, published in *The Bend in the Road: Refugees Writing*, edited by J. Langer (1997).

Abbreviations

ANC	African National Congress
CIREFCA	International Conference on Refugees, Displaced and Repatriates of Central America
DAC	Development Assistance Committee (of the Organisation for Economic Co-operation and Development)
DHA	Department of Humanitarian Affairs (of the United Nations)
DP	displaced person
EU	European Union
FRG	Federal Republic of Germany
GDR	(former) German Democratic Republic
GP	general practitioner
IDP	internally displaced person
IRO	International Refugee Organization
MAA	mutual assistance agency
NARV	Nordic Assistance to Repatriated Vietnamese
NATO	North Atlantic Treaty Organization
NGO	non-governmental organization
NNGO	'Northern-based' non-governmental organization
OAS	Organization of American States
OAU	Organization of African Unity
OECD	Organisation for Economic Co-operation and Development
POP	People Oriented Planning
PTSD	post-traumatic stress disorder
QIP	quick-impact project
RPA	Rwanda Patriotic Army
RPF	Rwanda Patriotic Front
RSP	Refugee Studies Programme
SWAPO	South-West Africa People's Organization
UNDP	United Nations Development Programme
UNHCHR	United Nations High Commissioner for Human Rights
UNHCR	United Nations High Commissioner for Refugees
UNICEF	United Nations Children's Fund
UNRWA	UN Relief and Works Agency for Palestine Refugees in the Near East
WFP	World Food Programme

1

Perspectives on the refugee experience

Alastair Ager

The growth of global refugee numbers through the past three decades has established an increasingly high profile for the issue of forced migration within political and public debate. Flows of refugees have brought major political, economic, social, cultural and personal consequences across all continents. Palestinians displaced to neighbouring states by Israeli military action in 1948 (Hudson, 1997) and those fleeing contemporary conflicts across such regions as the Balkans, West Africa and South Asia demarcate fifty years of experience of uprooting, displacement and long- or short-term resettlement as a result of political or military action. Statistics – for instance, the fact that the current global population of over 50 million refugees and displaced persons represents approaching 1 per cent of the world's population – tell something of this story. The concern of this volume, however, is the human experience behind such figures and the complex forces – political, social, psychological, etc. – which serve to shape it.

While refugees, in common parlance, constitute those forced from their homes as a result of war or political oppression, in terms of the Geneva Convention of 1951 the term *refugee* has a narrower definition, in referring to a person

> who, owing to a well-founded fear of being persecuted ... is outside [their] country of nationality. (Article 1, Geneva Convention, 1951)

Such a definition – discussed in greater detail in Chapters 2 and 3 – thus excludes those displaced within the borders of their home country. While such *internally displaced persons* (IDPs) are not afforded protection under the Geneva Convention, many may – in humanitarian terms – have similar needs to those meeting the Convention's definition for refugees. With the majority of current conflicts involving internal disputes between political, ethnic or regional groupings (rather than conflict between sovereign states), relocation with respect to internal 'boundaries' imposed by military action is a common migratory pattern. The global population of internally displaced persons is, indeed, broadly equivalent to the global population seeking refuge across national borders.

The Geneva Convention provides the core basis with respect to which a forced migrant may claim refugee status from another state. Before the determination of their status – based on appraisal of individual claims by authorities of the receiving state – such persons are most appropriately referred to as *asylum-seekers*. In practice, however, agencies such as the United Nations High Commissioner for Refugees (UNHCR) frequently consider as refugees those displaced across borders as a result of conflict – often in large numbers in the context of 'complex emergencies' (see Chapter 3) – without formal legal determination of refugee status under the terms of the Geneva Convention.

In consequence, in the following analyses, while the terms *internally displaced person* and *asylum-seeker* will be used in a manner consistent with the criteria above, the term *refugee* will often be used in a more generic sense to cover all classes of *forced migrants* (i.e. excluding economic and other 'voluntary' migrants). In any situations where this usage may lead to ambiguity, such terms as 'Convention refugee' may be used to define those fulfilling the narrower conditions of the Geneva Convention.

The refugee experience

'The refugee experience' is a term which has been widely used in the field of refugee studies to denote the human consequences – personal, social, economic, cultural and political – of forced migration. While a range of theories and concepts may be employed in attempts to map the impact of forced migration, the use of this term emphasizes the centrality of refugees themselves to the attempted analysis. It is the impact of forced migration on refugee communities and the individuals within them – and the forces that have shaped their experience – which are the key concerns here. In addition to more local circumstance, the political and social history of regions (see Chapter 2), the policy and actions of the humanitarian regime (see Chapter 3), trends in political philosophy (see Chapter 4) and gender awareness (see Chapter 8) are all crucially relevant to comprehensive analysis of the experience of refugees.

The 'lived experience' of refugees is also clearly of relevance to such analysis, but is not the focus of the current volume. Documentation of the subjective experience of uprooting and refuge is an important component of refugee studies, with recent compilations of refugees' writing and testimony (Agger, 1994; Langer, 1997) providing moving insight into the personal construction of events and meanings. Such sources not only appropriately empower refugee voices within the discourse of refugee studies, but frequently provide challenging and critical insight into the receipt of refugee assistance. In this volume Chapters 6 and 10, in particular, make use of refugee narratives to build and validate their analyses.

However, the focus of the current volume is not the 'lived experience' of refugees *per se*, but rather analyses from the social sciences which provide a potential bridge between such accounts and macro-analyses of political conflict, migration and emergency and development policy. The volume seeks to link political, social and cultural forces with the experience of forced migrants. Indeed, a central premise of the volume is the complex linkage between individual experience and social behaviour and trends in such realms as political philosophy, gender relations and national identity. This first chapter offers frameworks with respect to which such influences on the experience of forced migration may be mapped, providing a foundation for elaboration in subsequent chapters.

The phases of the refugee experience

A common framework for consideration of the refugee experience is that which identifies discrete phases within forced migration (see Desjarlais *et al.*, 1995). Typically, such phases are identified as pre-flight, flight, temporary settlement and resettlement (or repatriation). What are the common experiences of refugees through these phases? And what consequences do such events have on the well-being of refugees?[1]

Pre-flight

ECONOMIC HARDSHIP AND SOCIAL DISRUPTION

> When the war began our livestock was taken away by the soldiers ... at first we carried our produce at night to avoid confiscation by the troops ... all the shops closed down for fear of looting by soldiers ... the conflict completely disrupted trade in the area ... we began to hide in the hills away from the village at night.[2]

In the period leading up to flight, many households experience serious economic hardship as the result of disruption of income-generating activity and/or shortage of food (Ager *et al.*, 1991). Such hardships may relate to the more frequently recognized factors of political persecution or armed conflict, but they can also serve in their own right as major threats to well-being. A comprehensive study of Indochinese refugees in the USA (Rumbaut, 1991) which examined the relationship between present well-being and reported motives for migration indicated escape from harsh living conditions (famine, poor economic conditions, inability to make a living, etc.) as a significant predictor of psychological distress. Economic repression and increasing landlessness have been a precipitating feature of displacement within many states of Central America (Farias, 1994).

Social disruption also impacts the refugee experience pre-flight both directly and, by reducing resources which may buffer the impact of other events, indirectly. Concern with the direct experience of persecution or violence can blind appreciation of the profound consequences that such chronic factors as restricted mobility or school closure can have on the experience of a community. The impact of such disruption of civil society has received little empirical attention in the refugee literature, despite numerous studies having demonstrated the significant impact of social disruption on well-being in the context of natural disasters (e.g. Gueri and Perez, 1986; Lima, 1992; Revel, 1996).

The fragmentation of families is the only factor to have been considered with any vigour in the context of refugees, and here primarily with respect again to the direct impact of military conflict (e.g. Ressler *et al.*, 1988; Richman, 1993). In a study of a sample of 373 East European refugees resettled in Australia prior to 1955, Krupinski *et al.* (1973) found that 43 per cent had had a close relative die during the military occupation of their homelands. Rumbaut (1991) reports that approaching 50 per cent of the US-resettled Indochinese refugees sampled in his study had lost a family member in the immediate pre-flight period, with nearly 20 per cent reporting imprisonment of a family member during the same period. McCallin (1996) observed that 24 per cent of a sample of 109 Mozambican refugee women had been separated from their children prior to their flight to Zambia. In Rumbaut's (1991) study, analysis established that family loss was a significant predictor of distress in the resettlement environment. Such effects would clearly be anticipated, but have as yet seldom been unequivocally demonstrated – partly reflecting methodological constraints on study in the pre-flight period. Further study of this phase in refugee experience is clearly warranted, however, with Ben-Porath (1991) signalling, for example, the potential influence of factors such as familial conflict over the decision to flee – a key issue with respect to which there are few meaningful data.

Data from Croatia and Bosnia-Herzegovina indicating that approximately 50 per cent of respondents (beneficiaries of assistance projects) had experienced 'betrayal by neighbours and acquaintances' during the course of conflict in the region (Agger and Mimica, 1996) exemplify other dimensions of social disruption that may shape the experience of forced migrants.

PHYSICAL VIOLENCE

> I told them to run away with us ... but they refused ... and stayed and hid in a hole. It was two aunts and one of my uncles with his son and one brother of mine. They stabbed my brother here in the front ... they killed my brother with a knife. And one of my brother's cousins ... they opened the stomach and they put the intestines on the chest of my aunt. They cut the arms, the legs and they cut the head off.

> I see it like it is happening now. I see the images exactly like I saw the day the people were killed. And sometimes I become deaf because hearing sounds like guns and shooting my ears become closed. When I remember that ... I used to cry sometimes ... and I can't eat ... sometimes I sleep without eating because of what I think I saw ... I have never seen things like that.[3]

While there are few data on the impact of economic deprivation and social disruption on the well-being of refugees, there are a considerable number of studies which have attempted to relate exposure to violent events to levels of emotional distress (Agger and Mimica, 1996; Beiser *et al.*, 1989; Boothby, 1994; Kinzie *et al.*, 1990; Mollica *et al.*, 1987). Although such events can have major impacts, there is concern that an overemphasis on discrete experiences of trauma can encourage an acutely individualized and decontextualized view of the refugee experience (Bracken *et al.*, 1995; Muecke, 1992). It is not in question that such events are highly salient in understanding the processes influencing the adjustment of refugees, but there must be a concern to conceptualize such events within the full breadth of the refugee experience. Individuals' 'trauma stories' repeatedly emerge in presentation of clinical case material and anthropological case study alike, with a clear implication that such narratives have a key role in refugees' own understandings of their experience. Mollica (1989, p. 109) indeed asserts:

> Each and every refugee patient has at least one traumatic experience that figures prominently as an essential aspect of his or her life history. It is not uncommon for a refugee patient to respond to the question, 'when did your problem begin?' by stating, 'On April 20, 1975, at 6 p.m., the Communist troops ...'

This phenomenon asserts the key role of the 'trauma story' in refugee self-understanding. But there is a danger that the vividness and drama of such events – which promotes their centrality in the attributions of distress made by refugees and assistance workers alike – can encourage inattention to other, less tangible aspects of the refugee experience which may be equally powerful in influencing well-being. In this vein Muecke (1992, p. 520) relates the pre-existing focus on traumatic experiences to reductionist dangers in the widespread use of the diagnostic label 'post-traumatic stress disorder' (PTSD):

> Whilst having PTSD as a diagnostic assist no doubt has empowered clinicians by giving them the sense that they know what they are dealing with clinically, the label has yet to lead to cure or even palliation of the profound distress with which many refugees live. The widespread utilisation of the PTSD diagnosis ... sanctions continuing neglect of refugee suffering, suffering that is associated not only with the experience of persecution and trauma, but with ... stigma, isolation and rejection.

The early classic study of war trauma by Freud and Burlingham (1943) firmly established the role of family support in individuals' interpretation of, and response to, violent events. Subsequent studies have not always been so thorough in identifying the social context of experienced trauma. Clinical case studies of traumatized refugees are generally incapable of drawing out the function of such social factors, constrained as they are by a lack of a non-clinical comparison population who may have experienced similar events.

Such reports have nonetheless served to highlight specific trauma-related symptomology (flashbacks, memory disturbance, panic, sleeplessness, etc.) in a significant proportion of refugees. In a prospective study of admissions over a six-month period to their Indochinese Psychiatry Clinic, Mollica *et al.* (1987) reported 92 per cent of Hmong/Laotian patients to be meeting PTSD diagnostic criteria. Petroska Beška *et al.* (1995) report 22 per cent of Bosnian children in refugee camps in Macedonia as meeting this criterion, although a larger number displayed elevated levels of anxiety, introversion and depression. A meta-analysis of studies of the survivors of torture (Goldfeld *et al.*, 1988) – while showing wide variation across studies and contexts – indicated extreme levels of anxiety and insomnia persisting for considerable periods after such experience.

It is population-based studies that are required to put these findings in perspective. Murphy (1955) studied rates of mental illness for refugees resettling in the UK after World War II, and demonstrated a positive correlation with the degree of persecution and trauma experienced during the war. Krupinski *et al.*'s (1973) study of postwar resettlement of East European refugees in Australia also established a clear relationship between rates of psychiatric illness and the severity of war experiences, though this relationship was significantly modulated by the refugees' sociocultural background. Garcia-Peltoniemi (1987) notes the difficulties in conducting similar studies with contemporary refugee influxes, but they clearly are vital. The context of the clinical work of Kinzie and associates in Oregon is clarified considerably, for example, by their non-clinical population study demonstrating that as many as 50 per cent of the Cambodian refugees attending a Portland high school evidenced symptoms consistent with a diagnosis of PTSD (Kinzie and Sack, 1991). The broader social experience of such refugees must not be occluded through over-reliance on such a diagnostic label. Nonetheless, such data argue for sensitivity to the potential needs of those exposed to extreme violence prior to flight.

POLITICAL OPPRESSION

> Her husband left as usual for work but did not return home that night. Finally, she called his mother and sister to tell them she thought that he had been detained. As for herself, she said that she had been afraid yet did not cry. She began to worry about what would happen to her four children if she too were arrested. Toward midnight, the oldest child began to cry. The mother told her children, 'Pack a suitcase. We have to go.' She left the house alone to check whether someone was watching them.[4]

While political oppression may manifest itself in terms of economic hardship, social disruption and/or physical violence, lack of rights of assembly, freedom of expression, etc. clearly have a direct impact too on the refugee experience (Zwi and Ugalde, 1991). Powerlessness has a major influence on perceived well-being, and, to the extent that it may produce an established pattern of attribution regarding self-esteem and personal potency, may have a long-term influence on mental health.

Punamäki's work with Palestinian women experiencing military occupation has demonstrated the clear – if complex – linkages between the experience of political oppression and well-being (Punamäki, 1990). With displaced populations the relevance of such linkage has perhaps been acknowledged most clearly in work with refugees from Central America. Subsequent to an analysis of the emotional distress evidenced in a clinical sample of individuals displaced from El Salvador, Farias has argued that the analysis of the refugee experience needs increasingly to 'take into account the dialectical relation between the sociopolitical processes of terror and intimidation, the social conditions of marginality and illegality, and the emotional responses of individuals' (Farias, 1991, cited in Muecke, 1992). The work of Punamäki (1990) provides a model – presently unemulated – of how such political factors may be integrated within an empirical analysis of well-being.

Flight

SEPARATION

Flight from one's homeland clearly represents an event which – even if accomplished swiftly and in safety – is likely to prompt major emotional and cognitive turmoil (Ager, 1993). Across samples of Cambodian refugees resettled within Australia and the USA, Eisenbruch (1990) found anger regarding separation from homeland to be one of the strongest and most widespread responses. For those leaving family members behind in Cambodia, separation had had a clearly tangible focus. Even those who did not experience family separation, however, commonly reported a sense of 'unfinished business' in Cambodia and a wish to return. It is the strength of such reactions to separation from one's home society which has led Eisenbruch (1990, 1992) to propose recognition of the phenomenon of 'cultural bereavement' in refugee populations. For resettling refugees, further consequences of separation from one's homeland are subsequently considered in the context of readjustment to a new culture.

PASSAGE

> Ms A left Vietnam in a boat with 32 people, nine of whom were female. A few days after they set out to sea they were met by five pirate boats. All nine females were abducted. They were separated into three boats. Ms A was raped for five consecutive nights. Each night she was raped by seven pirates. She attempted to commit suicide by jumping into the sea, but she was grabbed by her hair and rescued. On the sixth day, the pirates abandoned her on a beach by a refugee camp.[5]

The emotional burden of flight is frequently further exacerbated by the experience of extreme danger. Women are particularly vulnerable to sexual abuse during this phase (Agger, 1994; Forbes-Martin, 1992; Goldfeld *et al.*, 1988; Mollica *et al.*, 1987). Empirical studies of refugee adaptation shortly after arrival in a country of first asylum (e.g. Felsman *et al.*, 1990) have, however, generally not attempted to separate out the discrete impact of passage from that of the pre-flight period. Given evidence of the extreme experiences of many refugees during passage to countries of first asylum – and their salience in individuals' personal accounts of flight (Mollica, 1989) – greater sensitivity to the discrete consequences of passage is called for.

Reception

FIRST ARRIVAL

> A refugee arrives in Hong Kong numbed, disoriented, vulnerable, sometimes half alive – living a nightmare of Kafkaesque proportions. He is hanging by a thread to both external and internal life. He is immediately interviewed by immigration officials and later by UNHCR representatives, given a number and assigned to a camp ... where a hut and bed number are designated. Bewildered and isolated in his confusion ... the refugee's first inclination is to preserve what remains of his identity by burying it. Faced by uniformed authority asking questions, giving him numbers, talking about camps, he feels sufficient reverberations of Vietnam ... to immediately distrust camp officials and camp regulations.[6]

On arrival in the country of first asylum refugees are generally faced with some form of registration procedure. Establishment of status as a refugee may be crucial with regard to receipt of food assistance and other support. The experience of new arrivals at reception centres can frequently be harrowing (Harrell-Bond, 1986). Refugees may go through an extensive period when they have justifiable fear of being forced to return to their home to once again face war and/or persecution. Especially when there are large influxes of refugees – when treatment can be especially impersonal and threatening (see Mitchell and Slim, 1990) – refugees may assume roles of dependency and helplessness (see Chapter 6 for a fuller discussion of this issue).

Settlement

It is important to acknowledge that a significant proportion of the world's refugees do not reside in camps on arrival in the country of first asylum. Throughout Africa large numbers of refugees have 'self-settled' among the indigenous population (Kibreab, 1991). This pattern seems especially prevalent where there are close kinship ties between the refugee group and the local population (see Ager *et al.*, 1995). Studies of 'self-settled' refugees – who will frequently have avoided the registration process indicated above – are far fewer in number than those examining the experience of refugees in established camps. Such studies as have been conducted have indicated significant advantages to self-settlement, despite the fact that such refugees will generally receive less (or nothing) in the way of assistance from governmental and non-governmental agencies and may – in some contexts – appropriately fear action by the authorities with regard to their 'informal' status (Hansen, 1990). Compensations appear to include greater opportunity for income generation (Ager *et al.*, 1995; Zetter, 1996), increased socialization (Ager *et al.*, 1995), and a greater sense of belonging and independence (Hansen, 1990).

> Then one becomes aware of the ongoing psychological catastrophe: almost everybody is silent, even children, apart from some sore, persistent crying. People's faces wear a dazed, distant or constantly distressed look. People sit motionless, staring ahead, or with their faces covered, as if trying to hide within themselves. Children sit as close up to their mother or father as possible, they do not play. They do not smile or giggle shyly, but look at you with large, serious, anxious eyes.[7]

> Well, we are refugees and have to put up with things. But we do need to know what our fate is to be. We need help to get out of the camp. I don't think we shall manage it soon. That is the worst of living here, you never know a thing. You must just hope to be told to go – but you never know a thing.[8]

For many refugees, however, camp life represents an extended period (Chan and Loveridge, 1987; Muecke, 1992) of their refugee experience. Studies within camp settings frequently confound the impacts of the camp environment and pre-refuge experience (Felsman *et al.*, 1990). A study by Beiser *et al.* (1989) partially isolated the impact of camp experiences by comparison across three settings which varied in the harshness of their regime. Stressful camp conditions led to an increase in depressive symptoms, though the effect was transient; differences between those interned in the harsh and less harsh camps decreased on subsequent resettlement in Canada. In the setting of long-term refugee camps on the Thailand–Cambodia border (see Mollica *et al.*, 1993; Mollica, 1994) increases in attempted suicide, domestic violence, apathy, hopelessness and depression were linked to camp conditions. A number of writers have noted how conditions within camps approximate the form of 'total institution' identified by Goffman (1961) as encouraging authoritarianism in those with power and dependence in those without it. To the extent that camps facilitate an attitude of 'learned helplessness' (Seligman, 1975) among refugees, they may also significantly increase the likelihood of depression (Chan and Loveridge, 1987).

Resettlement

CULTURE CONFLICT

Resettlement in the developed world involves a significant minority of the world's refugees. The experience of this group has, however, received considerably greater attention (see Chapter 7) than the majority resettling in the developing world (through either repatriation to their homeland or settlement in a neighbouring state). Analysis in terms of the 'social distance' involved in resettlement would question the generalizability of findings regarding resettlement within the developed world to the situation facing most refugees (Fisher and Cooper, 1990). The work of Lin (1986) with Southeast Asian refugees would support this contention, evidencing the greater problems of those resettling into Western settings compared to those remaining within the region. Nonetheless, the considerable heterogeneity of cultures within developing nations ensures that settlement in a neighbouring state – or indeed displacement within one's home country – can also involve transition across a very significant social distance.

The model proposed by Berry (1991; see also Chapter 7) with regard to the acculturation strategies available to refugee groups has won wide currency. The model essentially proposes that refugee and host country attitudes towards both refugees' cultural identity and their relationship with other groups determine the mode of acculturation adopted by resettlers. Refugees valuing both will tend to pursue 'integration', for instance, while governmental policy encouraging only the latter would foster 'assimilation'. Although Berry notes some evidence that refugee adaptation may be better in societies encouraging the pluralist, integration strategy rather than assimilation, the linkage between acculturation strategy and well-being appears to be dependent upon a broad range of personal, social and political factors (Berry and Kim, 1988). Krupinski *et al.* (1973) noted a significant relationship between intensity of refugees' social contacts and their psychiatric status, which was interestingly modulated by refugee country of origin. A prospective study of Hmong refugees resettled in the Minnesota area (Westermeyer *et al.*, 1983) indicated that refugees sponsored by religious organizations with explicit assimilationist goals were more vulnerable to psychiatric difficulties. A number of other variables plausibly linked with the process of acculturation (including proximity of household to other Hmong households, change of residence since arriving in the USA, and access to an individual with knowledge of both Hmong and American societies) bore no apparent relationship to adjustment (Westermeyer *et al.*, 1983). A study by Nicassio and Pate (1984, cited in Ben-Porath 1991) of 1638 Indochinese refugees resettled in the USA noted more adjustment difficulties in refugees who were more advanced in age, who had less education and income, who were unemployed, and had resided in the USA for shorter periods of time. This latter finding reinforces the conclusions of Berry (1991), Garcia-Peltoniemi (1987) and Rumbaut (1991) with regard to the initial period of resettlement evidencing the greatest psychological distress. Nonetheless, for a significant minority of refugees being in an alien culture appears to present chronic adjustment difficulties (Eisenbruch, 1990).

EMPLOYMENT DIFFICULTIES

Problems in gaining appropriate employment can provide an additional long-term difficulty. Without employment, financial and personal pressures may be considerable (McSpadden, 1987). Rumbaut's major study of Indochinese refugees (1991) found those not in the labour force to report significantly higher levels of distress. Among US-resettled Hmong refugees, those in receipt of welfare payments were found by Westermeyer *et al.* (1983) to be significantly more likely to present with mental health problems. Even those successful in gaining employment typically experience substantial downward mobility (Garcia-Peltoniemi, 1987; Krupinski *et al.*, 1973; Stein, 1979), with consequential threats to self-esteem as well as standard of living (Ben-Porath, 1991).

Intergenerational conflict

> A Hmong family was referred from the emergency room after the mother had attempted suicide by swallowing pills. The family crisis was precipitated unknowingly by their eldest 14-year-old daughter, who had allowed a 14-year-old Hmong boy to carry her books home from school. When she introduced the boy to her mother at the door, her mother began weeping, tearing at her clothes, and later ingested pills. The mother had assumed that the girl had become sexually active and was trying to force a marriage on her parents (neither of which was the case).[9]

Differential rates and/or strategies of acculturation within families clearly create major stresses (Westermeyer, 1991). Children typically acculturate faster than adults as a result of school socialization. Women and the elderly – with a greater likelihood of isolation at home – may commonly adjust behaviour and expectations far more slowly, if at all (Krupinski *et al.*, 1967; Westermeyer, 1986). Intergenerational conflict is, in consequence, generally a phenomenon which is likely to *increase* rather than *decrease* over time from resettlement. Acute difficulties may arise after many years in the new setting, long after specific sponsorship supports have been withdrawn. Crises can occur precipitously and outside the expectation of the host community, as in the case (cited by Westermeyer, 1991) of a Hmong father who hanged himself when his son – with money that the youth had himself earned – bought a car without first seeking his father's permission. Role reversals within families – children assuming adult roles as consequence of their relative facility with language and procedure within the host culture – can produce powerfully destructive dynamics within families. Schools, as a major agent for socialization of refugee youth into the mores of a host society (Ready, 1992), hold a key role in monitoring potential conflicts within families as a result of such acculturation.

The above discussion reflects the bias of the existing literature in focusing on resettlement which involves movement from the country of temporary asylum to some third country. Given trends within the global refugee population, however, adjustment required on repatriation – resettlement within one's country of origin – has become an increasingly important issue. While some of the issues identified above clearly apply to repatriating refugees, recent studies (e.g. Doná, 1993; Loughry and Nguyen, 1997) have begun to explore the unique problems faced in these circumstances. Chapters 7 and 9 explore these issues in further detail.

Danger of reinforcing a discourse of refugee vulnerability

While the above framework of the phases of the refugee experience gives insight into the range of issues commonly experienced by forced migrants, there is a danger that such a focus unduly 'pathologizes' the experience of refugees. For instance, the narratives that have been used to illustrate the analysis may be seen as reinforcing a discourse regarding the 'vulnerability' (Bracken *et al.*, 1995; see also Chapter 5) and potential 'dependency' (Harrell-Bond, 1986; Harrell-Bond *et al.*, 1992; see also Chapter 6) of refugees. Such discourse needs to be balanced with an appreciation of the common resilience of refugee communities, and the considerable resources within them for responding to the challenges of forced migration. Failure of assistance agencies to acknowledge such capacities appropriately is, indeed, an important theme within many chapters in this volume (see Chapters 3, 5, 6 and 9, in particular).

The conceptualization of the refugee experience afforded by the above analysis of the phases of forced migration, while providing insight into common elements of refugee experience, clearly requires extension. In particular there is a need for a more comprehensive appraisal of the historical, political, social and psychological forces shaping the experience of forced migration in differing settings and in response to differing circumstances. The following section lays the foundation for such analysis by identifying issues then elaborated upon in subsequent chapters.

Forces shaping the experience of forced migration

Dimensions of influence

The forces which shape the refugee experience range from global trends in policy, politics and philosophy, through more local social and cultural processes, to personal characteristics and capacities. Such categorizations are neither robust nor exclusive but do serve to emphasize the breadth of analysis, from macro to micro level, required when considering factors influencing the experience of forced migration. Conceptualization of factors operative at global, social and personal levels also facilitates understanding of the interaction and interrelationship between forces at such differing levels of analysis.

For example, as considered previously, it is clear that the experience of forced migration is crucially shaped by personal factors, such as the beliefs and values of the displaced. Hudson's (1997) appraisal of the situation of Palestinian refugees, for example, notes the salience of personal and family histories in refugees' construction of their current circumstances. Lina Kostarova-Unkovska's report of a displaced Balkan mother cradling her son as she calls him her 'little avenger of Kosovo' (personal communication, 1995) gives vivid insight into the personal constructions of ethnic conflict.

However, critique of analysis at this personal level comes, appropriately, when such histories, beliefs and values are not linked to the social processes which have served to shape them. Summerfield (1995; see also Chapter 5) notes the decontextualized and overtly individualistic conceptualizations of the refugee experience that can arise from too narrow a focus on the personal circumstances and characteristics.

Understandings of the personal experience of refugees are thus, in the case of the above examples, valuably informed by the relevant social histories regarding the development of ethnic identity (Hudson, 1997; Murdzeva-Skaric, 1993). This is in no way to deny the influence of personal characteristics, nor indeed to propose a social determinism in which all personal experience is 'caused by' broader social influences (a tendency which Harrell-Bond (1986) notes as reflecting an 'oversocialised concept of man'). The interaction is inevitably two-way, with personal values both reflected in and reflecting social trends (with power relations crucially shaping the precise nature of their relationship).

Similarly, one can argue that appreciation of global geopolitical trends may provide valuable insight into the forces shaping the social experience of communities. Of relevance to the above examples, the social histories of local nationalisms may be valuably informed by appraisal of the political forces which have served to foster the global growth of ethnonationalisms in the late twentieth century (see Chapters 3 and 5). This is not to reduce the social forces shaping local national identities to the inevitable consequence of global trends in identity and nationhood. Again, the social both reflects and constructs the global.

The current volume

Given the above, chapters in this volume appropriately span global, social and personal perspectives on the experience of forced migration. Chapters 2, 3 and 4 pay particular attention to global trends and developments, while acknowledging their interaction with social and personal dimensions of the refugee experience.

In Chapter 2, Charles Westin illustrates global forces shaping patterns of forced migration by regional analysis of sub-Saharan Africa and Europe. Westin argues that in both continents the process and history of political development is key to understanding both origins of, and response to, population flows. To the extent that such political developments frequently reflect global trends and pressures, the issue of forced migration has to be addressed by concerted actions of the international community at large, rather than individual states in isolation. Indeed, Westin argues that it is generally actions seeking to protect current notions of the nation-state that result in infringement of human rights, and subsequent forced migration. In these terms, refugee flows may be seen as symptoms of unfinished nation-building and state formation.

Chapter 3 provides an overview of the humanitarian regime for refugee assistance, and in so doing identifies forces which have shaped international humanitarian policy over the past fifty years. Roger Zetter traces the evolution of legal understandings of international obligations to refugees since the establishment of the Geneva Convention relating to the status of refugees in 1951. A significant factor in such evaluation has been the recognition that refugees are generally members of threatened social or cultural groups, with protection policy increasingly having to consider the needs of displaced communities rather than those of individual asylum-seekers. Zetter then considers the roles and interests of the UNHCR, non-governmental organizations (NGOs) and host governments within the international humanitarian relief regime, and relates these to the interests of refugees themselves.

In Chapter 4, Howard Adelman provides a broad conceptual analysis of philosophical, political and cultural trends which profoundly shape the context of forced migration in the twentieth century. Adelman locates the development of both refugee policy and local understandings of conflict and separation of peoples to the global phenomena of modernity and globalization. These phenomena have underpinned the establishment of abstract principles of individual rights and self-determination, and perceptions of a mandate to act on behalf of others denied such rights and autonomy. Adelman also notes the development of the nation-state as key in this process. He argues that the twentieth century has been the century of refugees not because it has been extraordinary in forcing refugees to flee, but because of the division of the world into nation-states with the potential not only to abuse or protect rights but also to determine the right of entry of non-citizens. While acknowledging the role of the international community in shaping the actions of states, Adelman suggests that recent evidence points to the resolution of refugee crises stemming less from international agencies and abstract principles than from local actions and concrete pragmatic solutions.

While Chapters 5, 6 and 7 focus on key social and cultural aspects of the experience of refugee communities, each locates its analysis with respect to broader global issues. In Chapter 5, Derek Summerfield's concern is with the social disruption caused by conflict and displacement and mechanisms by which communities may rebuild social structures and meanings. The context for such analysis is the clear global trend for the targeting of civilians – and the structures of society with respect to which their lives have previously been ordered – within contemporary warfare. Summerfield argues that the refugee experience must be understood in terms of the meanings and constructions of displaced communities themselves, with humanitarian assistance responding to their expressed priorities, not least calls for reparation and justice.

Barbara Harrell-Bond develops a related theme in Chapter 6 in examining the consequences of power differentials between refugees and those engaged in their assistance. As in Chapter 5, the analysis of the relationship between refugees and their 'helpers' in specific settings is developed with respect to the broader issue of the disempowerment and marginalization of refugee communities, and the potential stereotyping of the refugee 'role'. Harrell-Bond demonstrates how the experienced well-being of individual refugees is located within a social context critically influenced by access to political and economic resources. With international humanitarian assistance agencies frequently the 'gatekeepers' of significant political and economic resources, Harrell-Bond calls for greater emphasis on the 'self-management' of refugee communities.

In Chapter 7, Giorgia Doná and John Berry consider the issues faced by refugees in adjusting to life in a country of refuge or on repatriation to their country of origin. Their analysis is developed with respect to the specific circumstances of Guatemalan refugees living in settlements in Mexico and, subsequently, returning to Guatemala. Refugees are seen to be active 'constructors' of their identity, balancing continuity with cultural tradition with the demands and opportunities of their current environment. Doná and Berry link this work to a broader analysis of the strategies which individual refugees and refugee communities (and, indeed, other migratory groups) adopt in the management of acculturation.

Chapters 8 and 9 consider forces shaping the experience of specific categories of refugee. In Chapter 8, Agnès Callamard provides a gendered and political analysis of the experience of refugee women. Callamard's analysis is grounded in the individual experience by refugee women of sexual violence and disenfranchisement from decision-making. She develops analysis of such experience within the context of the culture of the refugee camp, demonstrating how roles are legitimized or constrained by the 'constructors' of that culture (governments, agencies and refugees themselves) and thereby are open to challenge and change. Callamard also links the construction of individual women's experience with global debates regarding refugee assistance policy and the bases of human rights protection.

In Chapter 9, Fred Ahearn, Maryanne Loughry and Alastair Ager identify the key forces shaping the experience of refugee children. They note the role of direct experience and that mediated by family and broader society in shaping a child's understanding of conflict and displacement, and identify how individual characteristics, history of socialization, availability of family and community support, etc. influence coping capacity. The social understandings provided by family and community are argued to be key in supporting the resilience of refugee children. Chapters 7, 8 and 9 thus all reinforce the principle of the individual experience of refugees being structured by the social roles and under-standings available within the refugee community.

In providing a psychodynamic perspective on the refugee experience, Chapter 10 develops such analysis of the 'constructed world' of the refugee. Through the vehicle of case histories of victims of torture, Susan Levy demonstrates how the personal and the political interact in the shaping of the refugee's experience. The manner in which torture affects not just the mental resilience of the individual, but the fabric of entire communities is demonstrated. Echoing an earlier theme from Chapter 5, Levy argues that the acknowledgement and validation of experience – the sharing of pain and injustice – is key for the well-being both of survivors of torture and of war-affected communities.

Modernism vs. postmodernism

The above sketches the analysis pursued in subsequent chapters. While a broad range of issues are addressed in the course of such study, one recurrent theme is the tension between modern and postmodern forms of discourse in the analysis of the refugee experience. This may seem a very abstract issue with which to conclude, but is, in practice, at the core not only of analysis of the refugee experience, but also of determining appropriate *response* to such experience.

As a system of thought, postmodernism may be defined as 'a response to the accumulating signs of the limits ... of modernity. Postmodernity is a way of living with the doubts, uncertainties and anxieties which seem increasingly to be a corollary of modernity' (Smart, 1993, p. 12). Postmodernism makes no claim on the rationality which underpins modernist thought. Bracken *et al.* (1997) note the tensions between modernist and postmodernist frameworks in providing a basis for ethical responsibility. Modernist frameworks support a '*responsibility to act* in the world in ways which are justifiable ... with an obligation to acquire reliable knowledge to guide one's actions' (Bracken *et al.*, 1997, p. 435; original emphasis). Postmodernist frameworks, in contrast, support 'a *responsibility to otherness* ... a concern not to impose order on the world but instead to allow the emergence of other voices and visions, even where this involves increasing complexity and ambivalence' (Bracken *et al.*, 1997, p. 436; original emphasis).

The alternative discourses prompted by these two frameworks may be traced at many points in the current volume. Earlier within this chapter, for instance, analysis which may support a 'discourse of vulnerability' was noted. Such analysis both fosters and reflects the notion of responsibility to act or intervene on the part of humanitarian agencies. On the other hand, focus on the responsibility to otherness leads to emphasis on refugee voices and visions, reflecting rather more a 'discourse of resilience'. The analyses of Harrell-Bond, Summerfield, Zetter and Callamard may all be seen to stress the importance of valuing the indigenous perspective and resources of refugee communities in the face of the modernist agenda of the international humanitarian regime.

This is not, however, to champion postmodern analysis exclusively. There is a danger that in valuing plural interpretations of value and experience, all constructions are credited with equal validity, and one account has little power to challenge another. The postmodernist framework serves refugees well when it fosters the valuing of their perspective as an otherwise devalued 'other'. It serves them less well if the moral claim of their experience on the world community – very much a modernist, if not premodernist, conception – is rendered impotent.

Notes

1   An earlier version of the subsequent analysis was first presented in an unpublished working paper produced on behalf of the Harvard Medical School Project on International Mental and Behavioral Health.
2   Statements of Mozambican refugees interviewed in the course of the UNHCR-funded study reported by Ager *et al.* (1991, 1995).
3   Statements of Mozambican children reported by Dodge and Raundalen (1991).
4   Statement of Chilean woman reported by Gonsalves (1990).
5   Quotation from US State Department report (Cheung, 1984) cited by Mollica *et al.* (1987).
6   Reported by Chan and Loveridge (1987).
7   Quotation from Jareg (1987).
8   Reported by Chan and Loveridge (1987).
9   Clinical report by Westermeyer (1991).

References

Ager, A. (1993) Mental health issues in refugee populations: a review. Working Paper for the Project on International Mental and Behavioral Health, Harvard Medical School, Department of Social Medicine.

Ager, A., Ager, W. and Long, L. (1991) A case study of refugee women in Malawi. Report to UNHCR. Zomba: Centre for Social Research.

Ager, A., Ager, W. and Long, L. (1995) The differential experience of Mozambican refugee women and men. *Journal of Refugee Studies*, 8 (3), 263–87.

Agger, I. (1994) *The Blue Room: Trauma and Testimony among Refugee Women.* London: Zed Books.

Agger, I. and Mimica, J. (1996) *Psychosocial Assistance to Victims of War in Bosnia-Herzegovina and Croatia: An Evaluation.* Brussels: European Community Humanitarian Organisation.

Beiser, M., Turner, R.J. and Ganesan, S. (1989) Catastrophic stress and factors affecting its consequences among Southeast Asian refugees. *Social Science and Medicine*, 28, 183–95.

Ben-Porath, Y. (1991) The psycho-social adjustment. In *Mental Health Services for Refugees, Refugee Mental Health Program, US Dept. of Health and Human Services*, pp. 1–23. Bethesda, MD: National Institute of Mental Health.

Berry, J.W. (1991) Refugee adaptation in settlement countries: an overview with an emphasis on primary prevention. In F.L. Ahearn and J.L. Athey (eds), *Refugee Children: Theory, Research, and Services*, pp. 20–38. Baltimore: Johns Hopkins University Press.

Berry, J.W. and Kim, U. (1988) Acculturation and mental health. In P. Dasen, J.W. Berry and N. Sartorius (eds), *Health and Cross-cultural Psychology: Towards Applications*, pp. 207–36. London: Sage.

Boothby, N. (1994) Trauma and violence among refugee children. In A. Marsella, T. Bornemann, S. Ekblad and J. Orley (eds), *Amidst Peril and Pain: The Mental Health and Well-being of the World's Refugees.* Washington, DC: American Psychological Association.

Bracken, P., Giller, J. and Summerfield, D. (1995) Psychological responses to war and atrocity: the limitations of current concepts. *Social Science and Medicine*, 40, 1073–82.

Bracken, P., Giller, J. and Summerfield, D. (1997) Rethinking mental health work with survivors of wartime violence and refugees. *Journal of Refugee Studies*, 10 (4), 431–42.

Chan, K.B. and Loveridge, D. (1987) Refugees 'in transit': Vietnamese in a refugee camp in Hong Kong. *International Migration Review*, 21, 745–59.

Desjarlais, R., Eisenberg, L., Good, B. and Kleinman, A. (1995) *World Mental Health: Problems and Priorities in Low-Income Countries.* Oxford: Oxford University Press.

Dodge, C.P. and Raundalen, M. (1991) *Reaching Children in War: Sudan, Uganda and Mozambique.* Bergen: Sigma Forlag/Scandinavian Institute of African Studies.

Doná, G. (1993) Acculturation and mental health of Guatemalan refugees living in settlements in Mexico. Unpublished doctoral thesis, Queen's University, Kingston, Ontario.

Eisenbruch, M. (1990) Cultural bereavement and homesickness. In S. Fisher and C. Cooper (eds), *On the Move: The Psychology of Change and Transition*. Chichester: Wiley.

Eisenbruch, M. (1992) Toward a culturally sensitive DSM: cultural bereavement in Cambodian refugees and the traditional healer as taxonomist. *Journal of Nervous and Mental Disease*, 180, 8–10.

Farias, P. (1994) Central and South American refugees: some mental health challenges. In A. Marsella, T. Bornemann, S. Ekblad and J. Orley (eds), *Amidst Peril and Pain: The Mental Health and Well-being of the World's Refugees*, pp. 101–14. Washington, DC: American Psychological Association.

Felsman, J.K., Leong, F.T.L., Johnson, M.C. and Felsman, I.C. (1990) Estimates of psychological distress among Vietnamese refugees: adolescents, unaccompanied minors and young adults. *Social Science and Medicine*, 31, 1251–6.

Fisher, S. and Cooper, C.L. (1990) *On the Move: The Psychology of Change and Transition*. Chichester: Wiley.

Forbes-Martin, S. (1992) *Women Refugees*. London: Zed Books.

Freud, A. and Burlingham, D.T. (1943) *War and Children*. New York: Ernst Willard.

Garcia-Peltoniemi, R.E. (1987) Psychopathology in refugees. Prepared for the National Institute of Mental Health's Refugee Assistance Program – Mental Health Technical Assistance Center of the University of Minnesota.

Goffman, I. (1961) *Asylums*. Chicago: Aldine.

Goldfeld, A.E., Mollica, R.F., Pesavento, B.H. and Faroane, S.V. (1988) The physical and psychological sequelae of torture. *Journal of the American Medical Association*, 259, 2725–9.

Gonsalves, C.J. (1990) The psychological effects of political repression on Chilean exiles in the U.S. *American Journal of Orthopsychiatry*, 60, 143–53.

Gueri, M. and Perez, A.L. (1986) Medical aspects of the 'El Ruiz' avalanche disaster, Colombia. *Disasters*, 10, 150–7.

Hansen, A. (1990) Long-term consequences of two African refugee settlement strategies. Paper presented at the Annual Meeting of the Society for Applied Anthropology (USA), York, England, March 1990.

Harrell-Bond, B. (1986) *Imposing Aid*. Oxford: Oxford University Press.

Harrell-Bond, B., Voutira, E. and Leopold, M. (1992) Counting the refugees: Gifts, givers, patrons and clients. *Journal of Refugee Studies*, 5 (3/4), 205–25.

Hudson, M.C. (1997) Palestinians and Lebanon: the common story. *Journal of Refugee Studies*, 10 (3), 243–60.

Jareg, E. (1987) *Psychosocial Factors in Relief Work during Famine and Rehabilitation.* Oslo: Redd Barna.

Kibreab, G. (1991) *The State of the Art Review of Refugee Studies in Africa.* Uppsala Papers in Economic History, Research Report 26, Uppsala.

Kinzie, J.D., Boehnlein, J.K., Leung, P.K., Moore, L.J., Riley, C. and Smith, D. (1990) The prevalence of posttraumatic stress disorder and its clinical significance among Southeast Asian refugees. *American Journal of Psychiatry,* 147, 913–7.

Kinzie, J.D. and Sack, W. (1991) Severely traumatized Cambodian children: research findings and clinical implications. In F.L. Ahearn and J.L. Athey (eds), *Refugee Children: Theory, Research, and Services,* pp. 92–105. Baltimore: Johns Hopkins University Press.

Krupinski, J., Stoller, A. and Wallace, L. (1973) Psychiatric disorders in East European refugees now in Australia. *Social Science and Medicine,* 7, 31–49.

Langer, J. (1997) *The Bend in the Road.* Nottingham: Four Leaves.

Lima, B.R. (1992) Psychosocial consequences of natural disasters: implications for informing action with refugee communities. In M. McCallin (ed.), *The Psychological Well-being of Refugee Children: Research, Practice and Policy Issues,* pp. 46–67. Geneva: International Catholic Child Bureau.

Lin, K.M. (1986) Psychopathology and social disruption in refugees. In C.L. Williams and J. Westermeyer (eds), *Refugee Mental Health in Resettlement Countries,* pp. 61–73. Washington, DC: Hemisphere.

Loughry, M. and Nguyen, X.N. (1997) *The Reintegration of Unaccompanied Returnee Children in Thua Thien Hue Province.* A Report for the Norwegian Refugee Council, Oslo, Norway.

McCallin, M. (1996) *The Psychological Well-being of Refugee Children: Research, Practice and Policy Issues,* 2nd edition. Geneva: International Catholic Child Bureau.

McSpadden, L.A. (1987) Ethiopian refugee resettlement in the western United States: social context and psychological well-being. *International Migration Review,* 21, 796–819.

Mitchell, J. and Slim, H. (1990) *Registration in Emergencies.* Oxfam Practical Health Guide No. 6. Oxford: Oxfam.

Mollica, R.F. (1989) Developing effective mental health policies and services for traumatised refugee patients. In D.R. Koslow and E.P. Salett (eds), *Crossing Cultures in Mental Health,* pp. 101–15. Washington, DC: International Counselling Center.

Mollica, R. [F.] (1994) Southeast Asian refugees: migration history and mental health issues. In A. Marsella, T. Bornemann, S. Ekblad and J. Orley (eds), *Amidst Peril and Pain: The Mental Health and Well-being of the World's Refugees.* Washington, DC: American Psychological Association.

Mollica, R.F., Donelan, K., Tor, S., Lavelle, J., Alias, C., Frankel, M. *et al.* (1993) The effect of trauma and confinement on functional health and mental health status of Cambodians living in Thailand–Cambodia border camps. *Journal of the American Medical Association*, 270 (5), 581–6.

Mollica, R.F., Wyshak, G. and Lavelle, J. (1987) The psychosocial impact of war trauma and torture on Southeast Asian refugees. *American Journal of Psychiatry*, 144, 1567–72.

Muecke, M.A. (1992) New paradigms for refugee health problems. *Social Science and Medicine*, 35, 515–23.

Murdzeva-Skaric, O. (1993) National identity and patriotism. In L. Kostarova-Unkovska (ed.), *Children Hurt by War*. Skopje: General Children's Consulate of the Republic of Macedonia.

Murphy, H.B.M. (1955) Refugee psychoses in Great Britain: admissions to mental hospitals. In H.B.M. Murphy (ed.), *Flight and Resettlement*, pp. 173–94. Paris: UNESCO.

Petroska-Beška, V., Kostarova-Unkovska, L. and Simouska, V. (1995) *Risk and Resilience in Refugee Children and Their Adaptation to the New Environment*. Skopje: Institute of Psychology.

Punamäki, R.-L. (1990) *Political Violence and Psychological Responses: A Study of Palestinian Women, Children and Ex-prisoners*. Tampere: Tampere Peace Research Institute Research Reports 41.

Ready, T. (1992) School and the passage of refugee youth from adolescence to adulthood. In M. McCallin (ed.), *The Psychological Well-Being of Refugee Children: Research, Practice and Policy Issues*, pp. 181–200. Geneva: International Catholic Child Bureau.

Ressler, E.M., Boothby, N. and Steinbock, D.J. (1988) *Unaccompanied Children*. New York: Oxford University Press.

Revel, J.P. (1996) Natural disasters and other accidents: provisions of psychological support. In Y. Danieli, N.S. Rodley and L. Weisaeth (eds), *International Responses to Traumatic Stress*. New York: Baywood.

Richman, N. (1993) Annotation: children in situations of political violence. *Journal of Child Psychology and Psychiatry*, 34 (8), 1286–302.

Rumbaut, R.G. (1991) The agony of exile: a study of the migration and adaptation of Indochinese refugee adults and children. In F.L. Ahearn and J.L. Athey (eds), *Refugee Children: Theory, Research, and Services*, pp. 53–91. Baltimore: Johns Hopkins University Press.

Seligman, M.E.P. (1975) *Helplessness: On Depression, Development, and Death*. San Francisco: Freeman.

Smart, P. (1993) *Postmodernity*. London: Routledge.

Stein, B.N. (1979) Occupational adjustment of refugees: the Vietnamese in the United States. *International Migration Review*, 13, 25–45.

'psychosocial' issues for NGO workers. *Development in Practice*, 5, 352–6.

Westermeyer, J. (1986) Migration and psychopathology. In C.L. Williams and J. Westermeyer (eds), *Refugee Mental Health in Resettlement Countries*, pp. 39–59. Washington, DC: Hemisphere.

Westermeyer, J. (1991) Psychiatric services for refugee children. In F.L. Ahearn and J.L. Athey (eds), *Refugee Children: Theory, Research, and Services*, pp. 127–62. Baltimore: Johns Hopkins University Press.

Westermeyer, J., Vang, T.F. and Neider, J. (1983) Refugees who do and do not seek psychiatric care: an analysis of premigratory and postmigratory characteristics. *Journal of Nervous and Mental Disease*, 171, 86–91.

Zetter, R. (1996) Refugee survival and NGO project assistance for Mozambican refugees in Malawi. *Community Development Journal*, 31 (3), 214–29.

Zwi, A. and Ugalde, A. (1991) Political violence in the Third World: a public health issue. *Health Policy and Planning*, 6, 203–17.

2

Regional analysis of refugee movements: origins and response

Charles Westin

In keeping with a somewhat broader definition than one based upon a strict interpretation of the 1951 Geneva Convention, the UNHCR currently recognizes 27 million persons as refugees who have *crossed international borders* in search of protection (United Nations, 1995). These are people who have been forced to leave their homes owing to war, ethnic conflict or persecution for reasons of race, religion or ethnicity. In addition to these recognized refugees, another 26 million persons are *internally displaced*. Of these, close to 5 million are defined as the concern of the UNHCR. The total number of refugees and displaced persons is considerable by any standard of comparison, almost equalling the population of large nations such as France, Italy or the United Kingdom.

Regional analysis

Most of the world's refugees and displaced persons are found in Africa and Asia, and, more recently, since the war in Bosnia-Herzegovina and the conflicts in the Caucasus region, also in Europe. In Africa more than 9 million are seeking refuge, mainly in neighbouring countries. Rwanda, Liberia and Somalia are presently the principal countries of origin. Close to 8 million refugees are of Asian origin, with Afghanistan, Iraq, Iran and Palestine as the major countries of origin. Approximately 8 million refugees are of European origin. The most important sources are the successor states of former Yugoslavia, primarily Bosnia-Herzegovina, the independent Caucasian states of Armenia and Georgia and the semi-autonomous republic of Chechenya within the Russian Federation. The situation in South America forms a sharp contrast, with the total number of refugees in the region currently amounting to only slightly more than 200,000. The figures are higher for North America (close to 1.5 million refugees). Some major 'refugee-producing' countries (for example Iran,

Ethiopia, Sudan, Congo and the Federal Republic of Yugoslavia) are major recipients of refugees from other countries at the same time.

The vast majority of refugees and displaced persons either are within their country of origin or have crossed the border into a neighbouring country. A smaller percentage have made their way to a third country within the region. In relation to the magnitude of the global refugee population the numbers who have sought refuge in other continents are comparatively insignificant.

Regional analysis of refugee movements can serve to illustrate both the contrasts and commonalities across settings differing in terms of economic development, population size, availability of land, efficiency of territorial and boundary control, and ethnopolitical context. I will begin my analysis by considering trends applying to refugee flows within the developing world. I will concentrate this review – for the purposes of illustration – on the situation in sub-Saharan Africa, acknowledging that differences of culture, environment and political context influence the playing out of trends in such other regions as South Asia. I will then turn to analyse the situation in Europe in the wake of the war in Bosnia-Herzegovina and the ongoing conflicts in the Caucasian region. I will also comment upon the flows of refugees from the developing to the developed world, rather insignificant in terms of numbers but highly significant in terms of reactions and policy.

Origins of refugee movements in sub-Saharan Africa

One cannot really discuss trends in refugee policy that apply to the African situation without saying something about the historical, social and political context. The extraordinarily large flows of refugees in sub-Saharan Africa have been triggered by a combination of factors relating to environmental conditions, demographic structure and population development, economic resources and ethnopolitical conflicts. The desertification of the Sahel belt in the interior of West Africa, caused by overgrazing, population increase and a series of severe droughts, has given rise to an increasing migration pressure towards the coastal regions in the west and south. Environmental refugees are projected to increase in numbers throughout Africa in the foreseeable future (Oucho, 1996). During the most recent decades, however, the really large flows of refugees have been prompted by ethnic and political conflict, initially between liberation movements and colonial powers, and thereafter between different ethnopolitical factions *within* the boundaries of given states. Only a few instances of controversy have led to a state of armed conflict or war *between* states (Gurr, 1993).

Africanists in general agree that one root cause of the severe conflicts haunting the continent dates back to the arbitrarily drawn boundaries settled by the European imperial powers at the Berlin Conference in 1878. These boundaries were inherited by the independent successor states that formed in the wake of colonialism from the end of the 1950s to the mid-1970s. The transition of power was itself a destabilizing factor. Practically all sub-Saharan state boundaries are artificial in the sense that they do not coincide with ethnic, cultural, linguistic, religious or national groupings that have developed out of Africa's own historical experiences. These boundaries are at the same time *permeable* (people cross them back and forth without being intercepted by border control authorities) and *permanent* in the sense that no state is prepared voluntarily to concede part of its sovereign territory to a neighbouring state for reasons of creating ethnic, linguistic or national homogeneity (Gurr, 1993). Most states, then, are multiethnic. Boundaries divide one and the same ethnic community between different states but also place different ethnic groups together within the confines of one multiethnic state formation. Some states are bi-ethnic, Rwanda and Burundi being the most typical cases. Somalia is one of the very few mono-ethnic states in sub-Saharan Africa (Oucho, 1996).

Authoritarian rule and disregard for human rights by governing élites, breakdown of the state in Somalia and Liberia, harsh material conditions and widespread poverty, social inequality and widening gaps between the poor and rich, limited educational and professional opportunities, far-reaching illiteracy, demographic imbalances, famines, epidemics, etc. are all factors that have had aggravating effects upon underlying social and ethnic conflicts in the region (Bariagaber, 1995).

Some refugee movements evolved out of the turmoil in conjunction with independence and the transition of power, and the ensuing struggles between different ethnic factions over political control. The shift to independence was particularly chaotic in former Belgian Congo (present-day Democratic Republic of Congo) and in Rwanda and Burundi in the early 1960s. Refugee mobility as from the late 1960s and on through the 1970s was mainly concentrated in the southern parts of the continent, although the Nigerian civil war of 1967–70 set off a major refugee emergency (Horowitz, 1985). Large population segments were displaced as a result of the wars of liberation that were fought against the remaining colonial powers in Angola, Mozambique and Namibia, and within the bastions of white supremacy in Rhodesia and South Africa (Allen and Morsink, 1994). In the 1980s new types of conflict began to emerge at the same time as many old tensions remained unresolved.

Several times during the past decades the two territorially small but densely populated states of Rwanda and Burundi have been the scenes of genocide, population displacements, massive material destruction and forced migrations to neighbouring countries. The most recent outburst of violence, leading to a new emergency, flared up during the spring and summer of 1994. Most analysts attribute the root causes of the endemic violence in these two states to the distinctive bi-ethnic set up of Hutus and Tutsis. In both Rwanda and Burundi hostility between these two peoples has been exploited by both sides in the quest for power (Kuper, 1977; Lemarchand, 1994; Reyntjens, 1996).

Large-scale refugee movements across state boundaries have continued to take place throughout the postcolonial era, adding to the many earlier displaced persons from previous emergencies, many of whom remain in a state of limbo, having neither repatriated themselves nor resettled in the country of asylum. The total number of refugees and displaced persons, then, has increased significantly over the years. Moreover, each new outburst of ethnic violence and each *coup d'état* has tended to bring out even greater numbers of displaced persons than in previous crises. In round figures, the refugee flows of the 1960s were of a magnitude of tens of thousands of persons. By the 1970s the volumes had risen to hundreds of thousands, and since the 1980s we are speaking literally of millions. More than 1 million persons of Mozambican origin fled to Malawi at the end of the 1980s (Hussein, 1995). The 1994 crisis in Rwanda triggered a flow to Zaire[1] and Tanzania of between 1 million and 1.5 million persons within a matter of weeks (Rutinwa, 1996a). By the end of 1994 a total of 2.5 million Rwandan refugees had sought asylum in neighbouring states (Anacleti, 1996).

The areas hardest hit by armed conflict have generally been located in the eastern and southern parts of Africa, the Great Lakes region being affected most severely of all. However, in West Africa, Nigeria suffered enormously during the four years of civil war, and in recent years the political chaos in Liberia has generated large refugee flows to neighbouring countries (Oucho, 1996).

Responses to refugee movements in sub-Saharan Africa

In the African context, as elsewhere, there have essentially been three approaches to dealing with refugee influxes:

- settlement in the first country of asylum;
- resettlement in a third country (second country of reception); and
- voluntary repatriation.

These approaches are not necessarily mutually exclusive. Initial settlement in the first country of asylum may be followed by resettlement elsewhere and eventually by repatriation. However, for African refugees, resettlement overseas has seldom been an option (Oucho, 1995), and even resettlement in third countries within the region is unusual. Settlement in the first country of asylum or repatriation have been the available solutions. In the country of settlement options have either been to integrate into local communities on a self-settlement basis, or through government, international or NGO-sponsored schemes, usually requiring time spent in organized camps (Hussein, 1995; Kibreab, 1995; von Bernuth, 1996).

Settlement and integration

In earlier movements, refugees from Rwanda and Burundi settled fairly successfully along the border regions in Tanzania. These refugees were welcomed by the Tanzanian authorities as well as by locals, and they were absorbed into Tanzanian society without any very obvious adjustment problems (van der Meeren, 1996). One facilitating factor was the availability of vacant land that the Tanzanian government wanted to settle. Moreover, the cultural and ethnic affinity between the Rwandan refugees and the local Tanzanian communities close to the Rwandan border generally prevented manifestations of conflict. Local Tanzanian villagers, as so often in Africa, gave evidence of genuine solidarity with those seeking protection (Rutinwa, 1996a). It is reported that Tutsi refugees who crossed the border into Uganda brought their herds of cattle with them without running into any problems (van der Meeren, 1996). In Uganda about half of the 200,000 Rwandan refugees settled among the local population; the rest were registered in camps. In numbers these earlier influxes of refugees were modest compared to the magnitude of the most recent one.

On the basis of an empirical study of Angolan refugees in Zambia, Hansen (1990) argues that self-settled rural refugees were more successfully integrated into Zambian society, although economically worse off than scheme-settled refugees. Almost all scheme-settled refugees wished to return to Angola whereas none of the self-settled was inclined to do so. In the recent Rwandan emergency, Goyens *et al.* (1996) claim that Rwandan refugees to Zaire who mixed with the local population beyond the vicinity of the camp at Goma fared much better than those who remained in the large camps. Ager *et al.* (1995) report that programmes in integrated settlements for the Mozambican refugees in Malawi aimed at supporting women's integration were more beneficial than programmes that were camp based.

On the basis of these and numerous other reports, *self-settlement and integration* into local communities when possible seems to have been the least problematic alternative with regard to a number of different points of evaluation. *Organized resettlement* in Tanzania and Zambia, on the other hand, has implied the relocating of refugees from border regions, the natural points of entry, to more distant parts of the host country where free land has been available. However, these resettlements have not always been successful (Christensen, 1985). The virtues of both self-settlement and organized resettlement are being reconsidered. Over time the availability of vacant land to settle has run low, partly owing to increasing populations in the host countries, but mainly as a result of governments' policies of holding vacant land in trust for their own citizens (Anacleti, 1996).

The general impression given by the literature is that local populations in receiving countries have shown remarkable signs of tolerance and solidarity with fleeing victims of colonial oppression in earlier decades and of ethnopolitical violence in the most recent ones. One explanation for this is that state borders do not coincide with the much older ethnic and tribal boundaries. Refugees from one country will generally be treated kindly by ethnic or tribal compatriots on the other side of the border. So while the deviation of state boundaries from ethnocultural boundaries is part of the problem, it has, to date, also been part of the solution.

As long as the influxes were of a moderate size the cost of harbouring refugees was not too much of a strain upon the receiving country's economy. This positive attitude to refugee admission is reflected in the 1969 Organization of African Unity (OAU) Refugee Convention, which goes considerably further in general acceptance of refugee claims than the 1951 Geneva Convention and the 1967 Protocol on the Status of Refugees. Aggression, foreign occupation or foreign domination are recognized as grounds for seeking protection abroad.

However, owing to the rapidly increasing numbers of refugees in recent years, the pressures upon the economic resources of the receiving societies have become painfully obvious. This is all the more noticeable in several cases in which refugee-producing countries coping with disrupting internal conflict are themselves hosting refugee populations from other countries. In countries where government control is weak refugee populations may be at great risk (van der Meeren, 1996). In Zaire severe tension built up between local populations and the Rwandan refugees (Goyens *et al.*, 1996). Tanzania, previously a country internationally recognized for its generous attitude to incoming refugees, has now enacted a law restricting the admission of refugees (Rutinwa, 1996a). Refugees will be admitted only on the condition that the international community will share the economic burden.

Temporary refuge and repatriation

Integration into the host society used to be considered a durable solution. The early experiences showed that long-term settlement and integration were manageable (Oucho, 1996). Today, however, long-term settlement is possible only if the international community is willing to share the economic burden. Regrettably, this has not been the case, so even the optimal conditions provided in Tanzania have not proved effective in the long run (van der Meeren, 1996). And as Hansen (1990) remarks, agricultural settlement schemes allowing a certain degree of self-sufficiency are in themselves not durable solutions if refugee influxes continue. These schemes are rather cost-effective ways of *holding* refugee populations for extended periods.

Voluntary repatriation has been regarded as the best of the 'durable' solutions to the refugee dilemma. This policy was recommended by the international conferences that took place in Addis Ababa as early as 1967 and confirmed once more at the Arusha conference in 1979 (Rogge, 1994). Assisted land-settling in the host country was seen as the second-best alternative at the 1967 conference if repatriation was not a feasible option. Many millions of refugees in Africa have in fact been repatriated in recent years. Some examples of successful repatriations are Ugandans from Sudan and Zaire in the late 1980s and Namibians from Angola and Zambia in the early 1990s (Oucho, 1996). A more controversial example is the return of Tutsi refugees to Rwanda, accompanied by the militant Rwandan Popular Front (RPF), which was in a state of war with the Hutu-led regime since 1990. Before 1996 repatriation was not a viable option for the Tutsi refugees from the 1960s and on (van der Meeren, 1996). After the Hutu slaughter of Tutsi civilians in 1994 the RPF seized power. The Tutsi 'repatriation' by force then sparked off a surge of Hutu refugees into Zaire and Tanzania, twenty times the number of the previously exiled Tutsis. In November and December 1996 some 600,000 Hutu refugees from Rwanda located in eastern Zaire set off back home. This spontaneous return was triggered by skirmishes in the unstable Goma region between Zairean and irregular Rwandan forces.

Long-term solutions

Despite the Addis Ababa, Arusha and Oslo recommendations, and despite evidence from some cases where it has been operational, voluntary repatriation has not proved to be a durable solution for the majority of Africa's refugees. Voluntary repatriation has worked in some cases, but not in others. Reports of successful integration into the host country generally refer to earlier refugee flows (Rutinwa, 1996b). With growing population pressures and an increasing unwillingness on the part of host countries to make land available for settlement by refugees, this option will be less realistic in the future. In view of the most recent Rwandan crisis and its repercussions upon Zaire and Tanzania, there is a greater need than ever to work out genuinely durable solutions.

The refugee problem in Africa has reached such proportions that it may be solved only through the concerted efforts of the international community. The only realistic long-term approach seems to be to address the root causes of the conflicts and conditions that generate refugee flows, and then to find appropriate solutions to them. This requires rethinking the entire problem. In the final analysis it means coming to grips with the problems of democratization, equality, justice, rule of law and economic development. It will have to involve the implementation of literacy and civic education programmes, and, in a more utopian vein, the devising of institutionalized forms of dealing with ethnic or tribal conflict. The efforts of the international community need to be directed towards finding diplomatic solutions to acute conflicts, and in the long term to secure peaceful coexistence between conflicting factions and groups. Finding solutions to the refugee crisis, then, will involve much more than finding ways to handle refugee flows once they are on the move, or of directing aid to concentrations of refugees (von Bernuth, 1996). The crucial issue is to get at the causes of the refugee movements. These causes are complex to say the least.

Origins of refugee movements in Europe

For the past fifty years Africa has undergone a difficult transformation from a colonial order, characterized by authoritarian European minority rule in practically every country, to political independence and African majority rule. This has been an ongoing process of emancipation, affecting different parts of the continent with the full force of social and political convulsions at different periods of time. In most states democracy is yet to be achieved. During the same period the European scene, on the other hand, was dominated for more than forty years by the stalemate of the Cold War. By and large, the theoretical, political and legal discourse on refugees has been fashioned by the European, not the African or Asian, experiences, and more specifically by the early postwar/Cold War period.[2]

As a result of the talks at Yalta and Potsdam in 1945 concerning the political outcome of World War II, the boundaries between the Soviet Union and several central European states were redrawn. The Soviet Union expanded its territory at the expense of Finland, Germany, Poland, Czechoslovakia, Hungary and Romania. It annexed Estonia, Latvia and Lithuania. Poland was partly compensated by territory that had been

German before the war (Holsti, 1991). These boundary revisions gave rise to immense shifts of population during the years immediately following the war.

The advancing Red Army not only had forced the German forces to retreat, but also had pushed hundreds of thousands of civilians in front of it. Those on the wrong side of what appeared to be new borders – homeless people who had been on the move away from the front during the final months of the war, slave labour that had been brought by force to Germany from the east, along with survivors from the death camps, mainly Jews from all corners of Europe – added up to millions of displaced persons who were in need of food, shelter, medical aid and resettlement when peace was restored in May 1945. Most of the Jews who survived the purges and the death camps eventually left for Israel or the USA. Displaced persons from Western Europe were repatriated in due course. The situation was more complex for East and Central Europeans owing to the harsher conditions of the occupation and the Nazi population policies that had been employed. For many of the displaced and uprooted from Europe east of Germany 'return' was out of the question (Zolberg *et al.*, 1989).

Refugees from the Soviet bloc

Within less than a year after the conclusion of the war friction between the Western powers and the Soviet Union developed into a major rift. This created a new refugee context of people escaping from the communist-run countries. Initially there were passages through the Iron Curtain. In time, however, they were closed one by one. When the Berlin Wall was erected in 1961 the barrier to the West was finally sealed. Nonetheless, attempts were made by the really desperate to cross over to the West. Many lost their lives doing so. There were also defectors from the East – persons representing their countries in various diplomatic and economic capacities as well as in exchange in the fields of sport, culture, education, etc. – who took their chances while visiting Western countries.

On rare occasions certain borders to the West opened up temporarily. In 1956 200,000 Hungarians fled when the Soviet Union repressed the freedom movement. A similar outflow of refugees took place from Czechoslovakia in 1968 when the Soviet forces put an end to the liberal reform policies initiated by the Czech leadership. Then again, after the 1981 *coup d'état* in Poland temporarily put a stop to Solidarity, a new wave of refugees made their way to Western countries (Zolberg *et al.*, 1989). For most of this period it was somewhat easier for Yugoslav dissidents to escape to the West as Yugoslavia was never controlled by the Soviet Union. Indeed, from the mid-1960s the government of Yugoslavia encouraged labour migration to Western countries as a way of coping with the country's economic problems. Some Yugoslavs claimed refugee status, but generally this was not necessary in the 1960s since states readily accepted them as labour migrants.

The *coup d'état* led by the Greek colonels in 1967 gave rise to a further outflow of refugees. Since many Greeks by this time had emigrated to Western countries to help ease labour shortages a similar situation prevailed: for labourers there was little need to claim refugee status (Rose, 1969).

During the early stages of the Cold War, Western Europe was generously committed to refugee reception. It was only natural in view of the horrors, forced displacement and genocide that had taken place during World War II. This attitude was possible because the number of refugees escaping from Eastern Europe was small, apart from the outflows of 1956, 1968 and later during the 1980s. It was hard to get out from the communist countries. Borders, airports and communications were rigorously controlled. Those who did manage to reach the West were generally automatically granted asylum. Not only were they admitted and recognized, each single *émigré* was a propaganda triumph for the West (Young, 1991). In Europe refugees from developing countries were exceptional in the 1950s and 1960s.

Since most countries of Western Europe accepted large intakes of labour from peripheral regions of Europe and former colonies at this time, the small trickle of refugees was treated within the general labour migration framework. There were no specific integration policies. People were put to work with little or no preparation, usually in unqualified jobs within the industrial and service sectors. Repatriation was out of the question. Integration into first countries of asylum was sometimes an option. Germany, and Austria in particular, were the most obvious first countries for most Eastern refugees. Resettlement into a third country was normally the most favoured solution. For many years non-governmental organizations and the UNHCR (established in 1951) were involved in transferring displaced persons from refugee camps in central Europe to countries that would resettle them. A primary objective of the UNHCR was to work out durable solutions to the refugee problem that had been overshadowing Europe (Loescher, 1993).

Third World refugee migration

Since the early 1970s developing countries – the South – have become increasingly drawn into the global economic system. Growing out-migration is one of the consequences. Most of this migration has been regionally confined. Indian and Pakistani labour is imported to the Gulf states. Filipinos and Indonesians find unqualified jobs in the tiger economies of Southeast Asia. In Africa there are large regionally based movements of people. South Africa has been economically dependent upon in-migration of labour from neighbouring states for decades. Accurate assessments of the size of these movements between developing nations are seldom available owing to a lack of rigour and/or record-keeping at border controls. Interregional African migration may well be of a magnitude a hundred times larger than African out-migration to developed nations of the North. Nevertheless, a potential for migration from developing to developed nations gradually built up over the years as a consequence of the globalization of the economy (Castles and Miller, 1993).

In European migration history the early 1970s represents a turning point. Labour migration was stopped almost simultaneously across the whole of Western Europe as refugees from developing nations started to appear in Europe (Hammar, 1985). The first developing world refugee emergency to affect Western Europe was the expulsion of the 70,000 Ugandan Asians in 1972. A year later the *coup d'état* against the Allende regime prompted a flow of asylum-seekers to Europe from Chile and neighbouring states. In 1975 people fearing the Communist takeover in Vietnam, mostly of Chinese ethnic origin, fled in overcrowded vessels to Hong Kong, Thailand, Malaysia and Singapore. More than 1 million Vietnamese were eventually resettled in the USA, lesser numbers in Australia and Canada, and some also in various European countries. During the 1970s there was also a steady flow to Europe of asylum-seekers from the Middle East, notably Kurds and Syrian Christians (Zolberg *et al.*, 1989).

At this time the numbers reaching Europe were still small and the receiving countries could handle the situation quite easily. Initially the asylum regulation and resettlement policies that had developed as a response to the Cold War divide were applied to these new categories. As immigrant communities gradually became established in the receiving countries, networks between the receiving and sending countries evolved. Inevitably, as a logical consequence of the migration network dynamics, family reunifications started to increase during the early 1980s (Westin, 1996). Political refuge and family reunification were the only gates open to those who wanted to settle in Western countries. Since only refugees and family members were accepted in the West, it was asylum-seekers and family members who came.

The USA and Canada were favoured destinations (Simmons, 1996), but Western Europe, and Germany in particular, was also attractive. By international standards the constitution of the Federal Republic of Germany (West Germany) laid down an unusually liberal definition of refugee status. So did Austria and Sweden. For Germany and Austria the most important reason for doing so was their geographical location as first countries of asylum for East European refugees (Salomon, 1991). A second reason was that West Germany had committed itself to accept and resettle any person of German descent from the East. This included the entire population of the German Democratic Republic (East Germany). Anyone who could prove that they were of German descent was technically speaking entitled to German (FRG) citizenship. These 'ethnic Germans', *Volksdeutsche* or *Aussiedler*, many of whom no longer speak German as their native language, are believed to be descendants of German colonists from medieval times and later, who spread throughout Eastern Europe to the Volga and in the Balkans right the way to Turkey. Today, the *Aussiedler*, Russian Jews and Pontic Greeks represent the most important out-migrating categories from the successor states of the Soviet Union (Castles and Miller, 1993).

A third reason for the rather liberal postwar refugee definition in the German constitution and policies in Sweden of accepting *de facto* refugees (that is to say, seekers of asylum who would not qualify according to a strict interpretation of the Geneva Convention) may be seen as some form of compensation for the roles of these nations in World War II. Nazi Germany was responsible for the genocide of at least 6 million people, not to mention the massive displacement of people and enormous material destruction. Sweden and Switzerland managed to avoid being drawn into the war at the price of morally questionable concessions to Nazi Germany.

By the end of the 1980s all European governments had begun to tighten their asylum procedures. Humanitarian reasons were no longer accepted as grounds for asylum in Europe (Loescher, 1993). The aim of this change of practice and interpretation was primarily to reduce the influx of migrants from the developing world. The late 1980s, then, represents yet another milestone in the establishment of what has come to be referred to as 'Fortress Europe'.

The Bosnian refugee crisis

The frozen East–West divide came to an unexpected end in 1989. The fall of the Berlin Wall was brought about by the large-scale movement of GDR residents to West Germany once the restrictions imposed by the Communist governments upon out-migration had eased. By the end of 1989 all Moscow-controlled puppet regimes in Europe had been replaced. Quite a few analysts predicted that once the Soviet power bloc was crumbling there would be a general scramble to get to the West. Western governments therefore had an additional reason to tighten their rules of entry (Luciani, 1993). Two years later the Soviet Union itself collapsed. Its former republics claimed independence and international recognition. Unfortunately the prospects of future peaceful coexistence in Europe were soon thwarted by reports of brewing conflict in the Caucasus region and Yugoslavia.

The causes of the war between Croatia and Serbia, and then in Bosnia-Herzegovina, are complex. They pertain to age-old divisions of groups on religious, historical and ethnic grounds. They concern claims to contested territory, but also the long totalitarian hegemony of the Communist Party, which suppressed expressions of ethnic identities. It began with Slovenia's declaration of independence. This was followed by Croatia's bid for independence, and thereafter by that of Bosnia-Herzegovina and Macedonia. This was too much for the Belgrade regime. The war between Croatia and the Serbian–Montenegrin remains of Yugoslavia raged back and forth in eastern Slavonia. Villages and towns in the contested zones were razed. The war then spread into Bosnia-Herzegovina (Woodward, 1995).

A new term for an old practice was coined: *ethnic cleansing* (Bell-Fialkoff, 1996). Ethnic minority enclaves in the complex Bosnian ethnocultural mosaic were driven away from their quarters and villages. Bosnian Croats and Bosnian Serbs were the main perpetrators, Muslims being the principal targets. In this war, however, all three parties were both victims and offenders. Ethnic cleansing implied more than forced displacement. It was a strategy aimed at incapacitating the reproductive potentials of the targeted minority. Regular attacks were staged upon women and children. This involved the systematic 'spoiling' and dishonouring of young women through rape and sexual torture (Tison and Westin, 1997). Ethnic cleansing also led to mass executions of young men and women, whose only crimes were to belong to the wrong ethnic group, in the wrong place at the wrong time.

This escalating inferno set off a massive refugee emergency. Practically all Western Europe was affected. Germany received by far the largest number of refugees from ex-Yugoslavia. In Germany, as in Austria, Sweden and Switzerland, there were already comparatively large Yugoslav communities that had built up during the era of labour migration. These countries, plus Hungary and the Netherlands, have received the largest number of Bosnian refugees. Most of the displaced persons, however, remained in the region – in Bosnia, Croatia and Serbia. In Germany and Sweden, Albanians from Kosovo and Macedonia also represented a substantial proportion of asylum-seekers.

The Yugoslavian crisis led to a wave of refugees seeking asylum outside the war zones. Despite the well-documented atrocities involved in the ethnic cleansing policies, a majority of the displaced Bosnians are not regarded as Convention refugees. The majority of them have fled from *generalized violence* due to ethnic conflict (Dacyl, 1996) rather than from individualized persecution for the five reasons stipulated in the 1951 Geneva Convention. This means that they lack the formal legal grounds to be entitled to the same level of protection from the international community as Convention refugees. Hein (1995) maintains that only 10 per cent of the refugees currently residing in Western Europe are refugees as recognized by the Geneva Convention.

There have been different responses to the Bosnian refugee crisis. One much criticized response in almost all Western Europe was to demand visas of Bosnian citizens. Another reaction was for states with large intakes of refugees from Bosnia to call for international co-operation and *burden-sharing* (Dacyl, 1996). A third response has been to change policies of permanent settlement in countries of asylum in favour of temporary protection in anticipation of future repatriation. The changing conditions of asylum increasingly led people in need of protection to enter Western countries illegally. According to a report prepared by the International Centre for Migration Policy Development in Vienna (published in 1994), an average of 85 per cent of all asylum-seekers in Western Europe whose applications had been rejected managed to stay on in the country of refuge, in most cases as clandestine or illegal migrants. The problem is especially serious for Italy, geographically situated just across the narrow Adriatic from troubled Albania and the Yugoslav successor states.

Responses to refugee movements in Europe

European countries have followed different models for refugee reception. France and Germany have concentrated on short-term solutions, whereas the Netherlands and the Scandinavian countries in the 1970s developed mechanisms for refugees' long-term integration into society. The UK on the other hand has employed a rather *ad hoc* scheme for refugee resettlement (Joly, 1995). In Britain non-governmental organizations have played an essential role in the reception programmes, whereas the Scandinavian countries have largely depended upon services within the public sector. An overall assessment is that when numbers were small there were no intentional policies of counteracting local concentrations of specific groups. As numbers increased, dispersal policies were adopted by most West European states.

In view of current unemployment rates and strains upon national economies, receiving societies are increasingly experiencing refugee resettlement as an economic burden (Brochmann, 1996). The fact that refugee resettlement initially involves substantial costs for the state has been exploited by racist and right-wing organizations in anti-immigration propaganda.

Refugees come up against an increasingly critical public opinion, a proliferation of racist actions and a growing popular support for right-wing parties (Baumgartl and Favell, 1995). There has been a marked increase in the political activity of the extreme right and an upsurge of violence directed at immigrants, refugees, asylum-seekers and minorities in a number of European cities (Björgo and Witte, 1993). Networks of neo-Nazi and fascist organizations are establishing themselves across national boundaries. Nationalistic ideology is spreading through Europe, generating a vicious circle of social exclusion, intolerance and distrust in democratic solutions. Immigrants and ethnic minorities, however, increasingly resist the role of passive victims of racial violence, and seek to mobilize counter-forces. One way of describing these developments is in terms of increasing *polarization* (Willems, 1996).

During the past decade parties have formed, or been revived, that exploit public discontent with unemployment, tax burdens and above all immigration. Throughout Europe popular support for the radical right parties has grown dramatically. There has been a shift of the public debate towards exclusion and intolerance, with the traditional democratic parties in the centre of the political field revising their views on migration policy in an attempt not to lose political ground to right-wing extremists (Westin, 1997).

Managing the problems of mass flight emergencies and finding durable solutions to forced migration with its long-term consequences upon sending and receiving societies is clearly beyond the capacity of individual states. International solutions must be sought. In this context the European Union (EU) has become an increasingly important actor. The EU can promote political solutions to conflicts that generate forced migration. In theory it can pressurize potential applicant states to comply with the Declaration of Human Rights, and to solve their ethnic minority problems by just and democratic means. Along with other international organizations it can contribute to peacekeeping operations. It is mainly in another capacity, however, that the role of the EU is increasingly discussed. *Fortress Europe*, or Fortress European Union, is about abolishing borders between the member states of the union, thus encouraging internal labour force mobility and limiting in-migration from the South and East. It is in the interest of the EU to harmonize the migration policies of its member states. It is *not* in the interest of the EU to reinforce in-migration to Europe as a means of handling refugee emergencies (Muus, 1997).

The Schengen agreement on lifting all border controls between the signatory states explicitly requires co-ordination and integration of migration policies. The outer boundaries facing non-Schengen states will serve as the boundaries of the entire Schengen body. This means that there will be no regular or traditional legal means (passport control, customs, etc.) to prevent persons who have entered one Schengen state from moving around to other signatory states (Meijers *et al.*, 1992). In order to curb illegal immigration, the police authorities will have to heighten the level of control of internal aliens. Those whose skin colour, facial features and body characteristics depart from the somatic norm images of the majority population are likely to be subjected to increased control.

Various measures have also been introduced to reinforce external border control. Airlines are fined for bringing in passengers who are not eligible to enter member states. Immigration and police authorities in different countries impart information about illegal organizations involved in smuggling migrants to Europe. States in Central and Eastern Europe are now defined as 'safe', which means that they are considered to respect human rights and thus qualify as first asylum countries.

Visas and control of documents are required even of those who wish to seek asylum, a measure that has significantly brought down the number of asylum-seekers. The implication of these requirements is that *access to the asylum procedures is blocked* (Pentevold-Bø, 1995). The objective of introducing these restrictions is to direct asylum-seekers to countries within their own region. What may result is an increase in illegal migration and clandestine entries.

These far-reaching reactions on the part of refugee-receiving states within the EU show that the refugee issues in Europe are now being regarded as national security problems (Hein, 1995). It is not the life, security or protection of the individual victim of purges, pogroms, ethnic cleansing, low-intensity warfare or breakdown of the state that is of principal concern to the West European states. What is at stake, governments claim, is the economic vitality of the Western welfare state. The argument is that on its own the advanced welfare state cannot carry the burden of resettling large refugee populations – from the developing world or from Eastern Europe. Such emphasis on *burden*-sharing alludes to the depersonalization of refugees, and emphasizes how the evaluation of asylum and refugee questions in Europe has incrementally shifted from a focus on propaganda triumphs *vis-à-vis* the Soviet *bloc*, through humanitarian concern, to a preoccupation with national security issues.

Refugee movements and the crisis of the nation-state

The refugee situations in sub-Saharan Africa and Europe differ in many respects. On the whole the number of refugees has been considerably larger in Africa for a much longer period of time. Moreover, the conflicts generating refugee movements and massive displacements are spread across that continent, whereas in Europe the postwar conflicts have been confined to rather specific areas. During the Cold War it was the border areas between NATO and the Warsaw Pact countries (Hungary, Czechoslovakia, Poland) from which refugee movements emanated. Since then the areas of crisis have been located in the Balkans and Caucasus. The causes of mass migration have, however, been broadly similar: violations of human rights on a massive scale, ethnic cleansing, breakdown of the state and internal conflict.

In sub-Saharan Africa the most operational solution to refugee influxes has been integration on a self-settlement basis in local communities. These settlements have been mainly concentrated in the border areas of the first country of reception. During the Cold War period in Europe, the principal solution was to resettle refugees on a permanent basis in a third country. In Africa repatriation is now the politically 'preferred' strategy. In Europe the policy of granting permanent residence to facilitate long-term integration is being reconsidered. Temporary residence permits are being introduced in the context of temporary protection, thus implying that even in Europe repatriation is now the long-term objective for dealing with mass flight situations (Stein *et al.*, 1995). Repatriation, however, is not a durable solution as long as the conditions that bring about refugee movements are not addressed. The costs involved in refugee resettlement are higher in Europe than in Africa. On the other hand, European states have stronger economies than the majority of African states and have previously been capable of carrying these costs. In both Africa and Europe the number of refugees has increased to such levels that individual states are no longer able or willing to take on the costs of providing protection, food and shelter in mass flight situations. The conflicts that give rise to displacement and mass flight need to be solved. This can be achieved only through the concerted efforts of the international community.

At the core of the international refugee phenomenon is a basic asymmetry of power relationships. The Declaration of Human Rights pertains to individuals. When human rights are violated, the victims are individual human beings. Perpetrators are also individuals. The Nuremberg trials established that those found guilty of crimes against humanity are personally responsible for these offences and hence liable to punishment even in cases where the offender *only* followed orders issued by superior commanding officers. On the other hand, when we are speaking about violations of human rights it is also important to note that perpetrators act as *representatives of the state*, or of some organization or body controlled by the state. The conditions that produce massive displacements and refugee flows are invariably situations in which individuals are wronged by collectives, where the collective in most cases is the state, some of its bodies or organizations supported by the state. However, the OAU definition of refugees also recognizes non-state actors as perpetrators giving rise to legitimate refugee status. An increasing number of states are following this example.

On the international scene states are the principal actors. States are the actors that ultimately control territory and thus borders. States grant or refuse citizenship, and states hold large arsenals of weapons for mass destruction. States interact with each other, both in competition and in co-operation. The existence of a given state may be threatened by external forces, usually other states, or by the economic power of international capital. The existence of the state may also be threatened by internal forces, either by revolutionary movements aiming to take over power, a general weakening of state authority, often constituted in the rivalry over power between different élite groups, or through the secession of specific regions. It seems almost inevitable that whenever the government of a given state is threatened, violent forces of an enormous destructive potential are unleashed. The civilian population, consisting of individual human beings, is victimized. The state's interest of protecting itself against dissolution thus clashes with universal norms which aim to protect individual rights.

Nation-building and state formation are two different processes although they often tend to coincide. In English-language usage the terms *nation, country* and *state* often tend to be used interchangeably. However, *nation* may be considered as reflecting an orientation towards characteristics of a people (culture, language, religion, history), *country* towards territory (land, resources, economy, geography) and *state* towards governance (legislation, rule, administration, political control, power). In a very general sense, nation-building is about adjusting a given set of people with their diverse manners, norms and identities to a given territory and power structure. The nation-state ideal is one people, one territory, one state. In cases of dissonance – and dissonance always exists – there are two basic strategies: altering territory and borders to adjust the spatial extension of the state to the distribution of the nation-forming people or, alternatively, altering people to adjust them to the given territorial extension. It is only the state that has the full power to adjust borders and to suppress regional claims for autonomy. Nation-building thus is about forming one people, with one collective national identity, out of a multitude of regional or local identifications, ethnic, linguistic or whatever. History shows that nation-building has been accomplished through a wide range of internal and external processes.

The 'altering people' strategy often involves forced or voluntary assimilation as an essential element. Mass education has played an important role in the nation-building processes. It is a device to shape general standards, and at the same time a means to implant allegiance to the state. Political participation and citizenship, in many states implying compulsory national service, are also important in this context. Besides these *persuasive* means there are more coercive and brutal ones. Social exclusion, expulsion, 'ethnic cleansing' and genocide have also been elements of nation-building processes. Although the modern nation may carve its identity out of already existing ethnic and cultural elements, the nation-state itself is a fairly recent phenomenon. It is when nation-building processes combine with state formation, often involving élite groupings trying to mobilize people according to their perceived image of the nation – that is to say, when the full power of the state may be employed to homogenize cultures, languages and the identifications of its subjects – that problems of ethnic conflict have tended to occur.

The 'altering territory' strategy in the nation-building process may be a less attractive approach to the state in the sense that any readjustment of international borders will necessarily affect other states. This approach implies that national territory is either increased through territorial acquisition from other states, or decreased by conceding part of one's territory to other states. It usually takes war to change international boundaries. Europe has been through a long process of nation-building and state formation. In the Balkans and parts of Eastern Europe it is still far from being completed. It took three major wars (1870–1, 1914–18, 1939–45) to finally (?) settle the border between France and Germany, which had been contested ever since the time of Charlemagne. In Africa the state formation process started much later. The large number of refugees in Africa as well as in Eastern Europe and the Balkans may be seen as symptoms of *unfinished nation-building and state formation processes* (Zolberg, 1983). The root causes of mass flights, refugee movements and large-scale displacements pertain to the global crisis of the nation-state system in which internal conflicts (the 'altering people' approach) invariably have international consequences.

Notes

1   In May 1997 the name of Zaire was changed to the Democratic Republic of Congo. In this text the name Zaire will be used when referring to events taking place before May 1997.
2   See the 1951 Geneva Convention on Refugees, which specifically points to the European scene. This geographic clause was not altered until the 1967 Protocol on the Status of Refugees.

References

Ager, A., Ager, W. and Long, L. (1995) The differential experience of Mozambican refugee women and men. *Journal of Refugee Studies*, 8 (3), 265–87.

Allen, T. and Morsink, H. (eds) (1994) *When Refugees Go Home.* Trenton: Africa World Press.

Anacleti, O. (1996) Regional responses to the Rwandan emergency. *Journal of Refugee Studies,* 9 (3), 303–11.

Bariagaber, A. (1995) Linking political violence and refugee situations in the Horn of Africa: an empirical approach. *International Migration,* 33 (2), 155–74.

Baumgartl, B. and Favell, A. (eds) (1995) *New Xenophobia in Europe.* London: Kluwer Law International.

Bell-Fialkoff, A. (1996) *Ethnic Cleansing.* Basingstoke: Macmillan.

Bernuth, R. von (1996) The voluntary agency response and the challenge of co-ordination. *Journal of Refugee Studies,* 9 (1), 281–90.

Björgo, T. and Witte, R. (1993) *Racist Violence in Europe.* Basingstoke: Macmillan.

Brochmann, G. (1996) *European Integration and Immigration from Third Countries.* Oslo: Scandinavian University Press.

Castles, S. and Miller, M.J. (1993) *The Age of Migration: International Population Movements in the Modern World.* London: Macmillan.

Christensen, H. (1985) *Refugees and Pioneers: History and Field Study of a Burundian Settlement in Tanzania.* Geneva: United Nations Research Institute for Social Development.

Dacyl, J.W. (1996) International responses to refugee flows from former Yugoslavia. In *Temporary Protection: Problems and Prospects.* Report No. 22. Raoul Wallenberg Institute, University of Lund.

Goyens, P., Porignon, D., Soron'gane, E.M., Tonglet, R., Hennart, P. and Vis, H.L. (1996) Humanitarian aid and health services in eastern Kivu, Zaïre: collaboration or competition? *Journal of Refugee Studies,* 9 (3), 268–80.

Gurr, T. (1993) *Minorities at Risk: A Global View of Ethnopolitical Conflicts.* Washington, DC: United States Institute of Peace Press.

Hammar, T. (ed.) (1985) *European Immigration Policy: A Comparative Study.* Cambridge: Cambridge University Press.

Hansen, A. (1990) *Refugee Self-Settlement versus Settlement on Government Schemes: The Long-Term Consequences for Security, Integration and Economic Development of Angolan Refugees (1966–1989) in Zambia.* Geneva: UNRISD.

Hein, C. (1995) Refugees between rejection and integration: current asylum policies in Europe. In M. Delle Donne (ed.), *Avenues to Integration Refugees in Contemporary Europe.* Naples: Ipermedium.

Holsti, K.J. (1991) *Peace and War: Armed Conflicts and International Order 1648–1989.* Cambridge: Cambridge University Press.

Horowitz, D.L. (1985) *Ethnic Groups in Conflict.* Los Angeles: University of California Press.

Hussein, K. (1995) The nutrition crisis among Mozambican refugees in Malawi: an analysis of the response of international agencies. *Journal of Refugee Studies*, 8 (1), 26–47.

International Centre for Migration Policy Development (1994) *The Key to Europe: A Comparative Analysis of Entry and Asylum Policies in Western Countries*. Swedish Government Official Reports 1994: 135. Ministry of Culture, Stockholm.

Joly, D. (1995) Reception and settlement policies: a comparative study. In M. Delle Donne (ed.), *Avenues to Integration Refugees in Contemporary Europe*. Naples: Ipermedium.

Kibreab, G. (1995) Eritrean women refugees in Khartoum, Sudan, 1970–1990. *Journal of Refugee Studies*, 8 (1), 1–25.

Kuper, L. (1977) *The Pity of It All: Polarisation of Racial and Ethnic Relations*. London: Duckworth.

Lemarchand, R. (1994) *Burundi: Ethnocide as Discourse and Practice*. Cambridge: Cambridge University Press.

Loescher, G. (1993) *Beyond Charity: International Co-operation and the Global Refugee Crisis*. Oxford: Oxford University Press.

Luciani, G. (ed.) (1993) *Migration Policies in Europe and the United States*. Dordrecht: Kluwer Academic Publishers.

Meijers, H., Bolten, J.J., Cruz, A., Steenbergen, J.D.M., Hoogenboom, T., Swart, A.H.J., Verhey, L.F.M. and Boeles, P. (1992) *Schengen: Internationalisation of the Central Chapters of the Law on Aliens, Refugees, Privacy, Security and the Police*, second revised edition. Leiden: Stichting NJCM-Boekerij.

Muus, P. (ed.) (1997) *Exclusion and Inclusion of Refugees in Contemporary Europe*. Utrecht: European Research Centre on Migration and Ethnic Relations.

Oucho, J.O. (1995) International migration and sustainable human development in Eastern and Southern Africa. *International Migration*, 33 (1), 31–54.

Oucho, J.O. (1996) Refugees and displacement in sub-Saharan Africa: instability due to ethnic and political conflicts and ecological causes. In A. Adepoju and T. Hammar (eds), *International Migration in and from Africa: Dimensions, Challenges and Prospects*. Dakar: PHRDA.

Pentevold-Bø (1995) Moral dilemmas in the European asylum and immigration policies. In M. Delle Donne (ed.), *Avenues to Integration Refugees in Contemporary Europe*. Naples: Ipermedium.

Reyntjens, F. (1996) Rwanda: genocide and beyond. *Journal of Refugee Studies*, 9 (3), 240–51.

Rogge, J.R. (1994) Repatriation of refugees. In T. Allen and H. Morsink (eds), *When Refugees Go Home*. Trenton: Africa World Press.

Rose, A.M. (1969) *Migrants in Europe: Problems of Acceptance and Adjustment*. Minneapolis: University of Minnesota Press.

Rutinwa, B. (1996a) The Tanzanian government's response to the Rwandan emergency. *Journal of Refugee Studies*, **9** (3), 291–302.

Rutinwa, B. (1996b) Beyond durable solutions: an appraisal of the new proposals for prevention and solution of the refugee crisis in the Great Lakes region. *Journal of Refugee Studies*, **9** (3), 312–25.

Salomon, K. (1991) *Refugees in the Cold War*. Lund: University of Lund Press.

Simmons, A.B. (ed.) (1996) *International Migration, Refugee Flows, and Human Rights in North America*. New York: Center for Migration Studies.

Stein, B.N., Cuny, F.C. and Reed, P. (eds) (1995) *Refugee Repatriation during Conflict: A New Conventional Wisdom*. Dallas: Center for the Study of Societies in Crisis.

Tison, B. and Westin, C. (1997) Cultural and gender issues. In Task Force on Refugees and Forced Migration, *Final Report to European Federation of Professional Psychologists Associations*. EFPPA General Assembly, Dublin, June 1997.

United Nations (1995) *Review of Population Trends, Policies and Programmes: Monitoring of World Population Trends and Programmes*. Population Commission, 28th Session, 21 February–2 March 1995.

van der Meeren, R. (1996) Three decades in exile: Rwandan refugees 1960–1990. *Journal of Refugee Studies*, **9** (3), 252–67.

Westin, C. (1996) Migration patterns. In M. Haour-Knipe and R. Rector (eds), *Crossing Borders: Migration, Ethnicity and AIDS*. London: Taylor & Francis.

Westin, C. (1997) Xenophobia and the refugee issue in Europe. Paper presented at the International Conference on Xenophobia, 13–15 June 1997, University of Western Cape, Bellville, Cape Town.

Willems, H. (1996) Right-wing extremism, racism or youth violence? Explaining violence against foreigners in Germany. *New Community*, **21** (4), 501–23.

Woodward, S.L. (1995) *Balkan Tragedy. Chaos and Dissolution after the Cold War*. Washington, DC: Brookings Institution.

Young, J.W. (1991) *Cold War Europe, 1945–89: A Political History*. London: Arnold.

Zolberg, A.R. (1983) The formation of new states as a refugee generating process. *Annals of the American Academy of Political and Social Science*, **467** (May), 24–38.

Zolberg, A.R., Suhrke, A. and Aguayo, S. (1989) *Escape from Violence*. Oxford: Oxford University Press.

3

International perspectives on refugee assistance*

Roger Zetter

Introduction

The 1950 UN Statute establishing the Office of the United Nations High Commissioner for Refugees (UNHCR)[1] and the parallel legal instrument of the Geneva Convention Relating to the Status of Refugees in 1951 constitute a defining moment in the response of the international community to the global phenomenon of population movements and a particularly problematic category of people on the move: those subject to forced displacement. Although refugees had existed for centuries, these instruments created, for the first time, an internationally agreed 'universalistic' (Zolberg *et al.*, 1989) legal definition of a refugee, conceptualized in terms of persecution and defined in relation to the state. These instruments gave concrete international form to a set of philosophical and ethical challenges and an enduring humanitarian concern. Additionally, the international community imposed on itself, through these instruments, a set of state responsibilities for this specifically defined category of migrants: the entitlement to protection from forcible repatriation. A powerful, but often controversial, label was also created (Zetter, 1991).

Yet, in institutionalizing both a status and a responsibility, the UNHCR was conceived as an *ad hoc* body of the UN and given a mandate for only three years. Few of the original signatories could have envisaged the enduring significance of these instruments as the incidence of refugee crises has proliferated through the second half of the century. The UNHCR mandate has been continuously reaffirmed by the UN General

* I wish to acknowledge the assistance of Charles Parrack in the preparation of this chapter.

Assembly in the ensuing five decades. From the basic principles set out half a century ago, a vast international 'humanitarian industry' has been established. From expenditure of about $5 million in the mid-1960s, the budget of UNHCR alone has grown from $70 million in 1975, to an estimated $1.3 billion in 1995 (UNHCR, 1995a, d). For the same twenty-year period the number of refugees, though fluctuating, has grown from 2.4 million to between 13.2 million (UNHCR, 1997b,c) and 16.2 million (USCR, 1996), depending on most recent estimates, peaking at 18.2 million in 1993. If other, related categories such as returnees, 'others of concern' and internally displaced persons are added, the UNHCR estimate totals about 22.7 million (UNHCR, 1997b). If the 3.8 million Palestinian refugees protected by UNRWA, the UN Relief and Works Agency for Palestine Refugees in the Near East, are included, the total increases to 26.5 million, and it rises yet further to about 51 million if one accepts Deng's estimate of 30 million internally displaced people (Deng, 1995), rather than the 4.8 million of UNHCR. But even these figures do not include possibly millions more who seek refuge from persecution across the permeable borders of much of the developing world. A complementary estimate in 1996 suggested that some 40 million people were at risk in humanitarian emergencies.[2]

We live in a world of refugees. Directly or indirectly, few countries are immune from the effects of refugees (UNRISD, 1995). It is estimated that refugee populations in excess of 10,000 people can be found in over 70 countries (UNHCR, 1995a). Repeated and increasingly violent humanitarian catastrophes, genocide and mass exoduses are instantaneously transmitted to living-rooms across the world, demanding an 'international response'. Global mobility also brings more and more refugees to the doorstep of countries far removed from the zones of conflict seen on the television screens. Ironically, it is precisely those countries in the developed world that agreed the original Convention and subscribe to the humanitarian principles which underpin it that are now most exercised by this global phenomenon and wish to contain the direct and indirect impacts (Joly, 1996; Mortimer, 1997). Over 3 million asylum applications were received by the governments of West European countries and the USA in the first half of the present decade (UNHCR, 1995a).

The Convention and its evolution

The Convention and its inception

Both the universalistic definition and the right of protection enshrined in the 1951 Convention were fundamental departures from the preceding approaches implemented by intergovernmental organizations such as the League of Nations and the International Refugee Office (IRO), or the pragmatic responses of individual governments to refugee crises earlier in the century. In contrast, after 1951, identification of refugees was no longer constrained to a particular national or ethnic group which had to be internationally agreed in the aftermath of specific instances of war and exodus. Instead, international obligations, arguably minimal, were henceforth predetermined by international law, not reactive and *ad hoc*.

The Convention provides two enduring core principles, which define the status and the entitlements of a refugee. So far as the claim to refugee status is concerned, Article 1 of the 1951 Convention applies to

> any person who, owing to a well founded fear of being persecuted for reasons of race, religion, nationality, membership of a particular social group or political opinion, is outside his [*sic*] country of nationality and is unable ... or unwilling to avail himself of the protection of that country.

The Convention also accords a number of entitlements to refugees. The most important of these is the obligation of a host country to protect a refugee from forcible repatriation – the principle of *non-refoulement* (Article 33). During the past two decades, as refugee populations have escalated, voluntary repatriation has been increasingly promoted as the most desirable of the three 'solutions' to refugee influxes. However, the principles of protection and *non-refoulement* remain at the core of international legal instruments and indeed remain the *raison d'être* of UNHCR, although its scope of action now extends far beyond this.

Arguably, the Convention has been remarkably durable, yet flexible, in accommodating a growing and increasingly complex and turbulent international problem, far removed from conditions in 1951. Most significantly, the formula defining a refugee has not been altered since its origin, and is still the reference point for all interpretations.

However, not surprisingly there has been continuing and extensive debate about the validity and shortcomings of the refugee definition set out in the Convention and indeed the application of the Convention itself. Durability has been achieved at a price for those trying to claim refugee status. Vincent describes the Convention as defining the 'narrow band of unambiguous victims' – in effect, a *de minimis* definition on which states can agree (Vincent, 1989); the corollary is the exclusion of perhaps millions who, on broader humanitarian rather than legal grounds, could justifiably claim the status. In addition, experience in the past half-century (see Chapter 2) confirms that people become refugees for complex and multiple reasons which do not easily lend themselves to the circumscribed Convention definition. Yet, given the challenge of producing concerted international action in refugee crises even under existing instruments, it is difficult to conceive the international community being able to agree on even a *de minimis* definition in the present day if one did not already exist, let alone one based on broader humanitarian principles. Moreover, the Convention allows states considerable discretion in determining the status of refugees and the right to asylum, and in interpreting their responsibilities and obligations to refugees set out in the Convention. Thus, the Convention, while creating the status of a refugee, does not provide the right to asylum; that is the responsibility of the receiving state to determine. Governments in the developed world are becoming adept at refining their responsibilities and introducing discretionary powers. In effect, a process of restructuring eligibility is well under way (Collinson, 1994; Harvey, 1997; Thorburn, 1995). Forcible repatriation of asylum-seekers, as opposed to those who successfully claim refugee status, is on the increase. To this extent, it can be argued that those who successfully claim refugee status are the lucky ones.

The original Convention reflected the essentially European focus of the signatories and the concerns and experiences of European states in the aftermath of World War II. Included here is the USA, the major funder of UNHCR since its inception and the dominant force behind the operation of the Convention and the agency. In a general sense it was a reaction to the failure of the Allied countries in the war to respond to the persecution and genocide of the Jews in Germany. At a more practical level it dealt with the challenge of repatriating or resettling over 11 million people displaced during the war in Europe and outside their countries of origin.

The Convention also reflected the transformation and Cold War division of postwar Europe into the Eastern and Western blocs. Although the extent to which those fleeing the newly formed communist states of Eastern Europe qualified as refugees under the Convention was questionable, nonetheless it was a timely instrument with which to emphasize the contrasts between political freedom and democracy in the West and state control under communism. For these reasons none of the communist states were signatories to the Convention. On the other hand, given the Eurocentric focus of the Convention, it was not applied for example to the huge population displacements which took place outside Europe after World War II. Thus, for example, neither the 3.8 million Palestinians (as a result of the founding of Israel in 1948, for whom the international community made special *ad hoc* provision through UNRWA) nor millions displaced by the partition of India and Pakistan in 1947 came within the remit of the Convention.

More significantly, although widely accepted in international law, the definition of a refugee applies only to *individual* claims to a well-founded fear of persecution. This ignores the fact that in many countries, especially in the developing world, ethnic conflict, insurrection against colonial rule, systematic political oppression and the suppression and abuse of human rights have affected millions of people in the past five decades who have suffered similar consequences as refugees. But they have not been accorded the same rights either, because they may not have been displaced across an international border or, even if they have, they may not have been able to substantiate an 'individual' claim to refugee status. Recent examples of these phenomena are Kurds and Tamils in Europe, or the millions of Salvadoreans and Guatemalans fleeing to the USA in the 1970s and 1980s because of domestic violence, or the emergence of Fortress Europe with its increasingly restrictionist attitude to particular ethnic or national groups of asylum-seekers.

These examples all indicate that, in the last analysis, who is a refugee is as much a matter of pragmatic political interpretation as one based on international law or supranational humanitarian imperatives. This is because the core of the Convention is predicated on the principles of protecting state sovereignty and relationships between states. Some authors (e.g. Hathaway, 1991a, b) thus argue that a fundamental dilemma exists in the definition of refugees, their claim to refugee status, and the form of international legal responsibilities. Accordingly, the extensive literature on root causes of refugee exodus (see Chapters 2 and 4) includes recognition that the actions of governments frequently create refugees. But there is no notion of blame enshrined in international law dealing with the problem of refugees. States expelling dissidents, or indirectly generating conditions of forced displacement, are not directly accountable to the international community for the refugees they create. Until recently the inter-national community has not felt empowered to intervene in the affairs of states creating an international burden of refugees; such political intervention would infringe sovereignty principles. Indeed, Article 2 of the Convention expressly commits the work of the UNHCR to be 'entirely non-political' and to be 'humanitarian and social'. However, in former Yugoslavia and Rwanda, the international community has directly intervened through UN peacekeeping mandates which have 'bought space' for humanitarian assistance by UNHCR and NGOs.

De facto, the definition and the response is reactive, relying both on essentially neutral legal principles and on the responsibility of the receiving states to interpret the legitimacy of individual claims to refugee status against the Convention definition. In effect therefore, the apparent certainty of the 1951 Convention definition of a refugee conceals a highly malleable status. That, nonetheless, the Convention has been so effective pays tribute to the skill of the original drafters.

The Convention: adaptation and challenge

Beyond this *first phase* origin and application in Europe, the evolution of the Convention and the response of the international community to the refugee phenomenon can be considered in two further phases. But to review and explain the subsequent evolution of the Convention in the *second phase*, we have to turn to the growth of refugees in the developing world.

The European origins of the Convention still remain clear. To this extent it has served the interests of the developed world well since its inception, as a tool for postwar resettlement: then, more recently and increasingly, for restrictionism. However, from the 1960s onwards, new dynamics in the evolution of refugee flows and thus the Convention began to emerge. With stability restored in Europe, notwithstanding the continued exodus from the Eastern bloc, the major incidence of forced migration from the 1960s onwards was experienced in the developing world, notably Central America, sub-Saharan Africa and Southeast Asia. The complex reasons for this are dealt with elsewhere in this book (see Chapters 2 and 4).

An entirely new set of circumstances confronted the international refugee regime which challenged the efficacy and scope of the instruments and responses designed in 1951.

First, whereas the global number of refugees had been declining in the 1950s, these new conditions were reflected in the rapid rise of refugee populations. Second, the exodus of hundreds of thousands of refugees was characterized by unpredictability and causative factors seemingly more complex and varied than the European experience of war between states. The concept of individual persecution and status determination inadequately fitted these new conditions of mass exodus. Third, refugee exoduses occurred with rapid onset, resolution often seemed intractable and exile was protracted. Fourth, and as a result, the impoverishment and destitution of vast numbers of refugees presented unparalleled demands for humanitarian assistance. Finally, underpinning all these factors, the burden of assistance fell on the very poor countries in the developing world, those least able to sustain their own developmental aspirations.

These new conditions demanded fundamentally different responses, both in the interpretation of the Convention and in the form and scope of response, notably by UNHCR. Predicated on limited domain – applying only to Europe – and time – those who had become refugees before 1 January 1951 – a Protocol was added to the Convention in 1967 which removed both these limitations. There are now 126 states party to the Convention and/or the Protocol.

In practice, while not extending the scope of the Convention, the international community had extended the mandate of UNHCR operations beyond these original limits. The exodus of Chinese to Hong

Kong in the 1950s, Algerians as a result of the war of independence against France, and the dramatic population movements in Central America in the 1960s had already brought into play the 'good offices' of UNHCR. What these changes did was to regularize the *ad hoc* situation which had developed and anticipate, probably unwittingly, the explosion in refugee populations in the next thirty years.

Nevertheless, in these new circumstances, the conceptualization of a refugee was found wanting. Reflecting the historical and political experiences of the two continents, both the Organization of African Unity (OAU) and the Organization of American States (OAS) adopted rather similar, but much broader, definitions of a refugee. In the case of the OAU the Convention on Refugee Problems in Africa, in 1969, made significant additions to the definition to include

> every person who, owing to external aggression, occupation, foreign domination, or events seriously disturbing public order in either part or the whole of his country of origin ... is compelled to seek refuge ... outside his country of origin.

The Cartegena Declaration of the OAS in 1984 went rather further by adding the concept of the 'threat of generalized violence, internal aggression ... and massive violation of human rights'.

While the definitions contained in these regional instruments are neither binding nor accepted beyond their continents of origin, they highlight important aspects of the refugee phenomenon and the reality of refugee crises which were confronting the international community. They indicate the growing complexity of root causes and the political solidarity of Africa in its struggle against colonial rule. They reflect the collective concern at internal instability, especially in newly independent states, which in large measure was the outcome of external aggression and the battle for geostrategic hegemony in the Third World by the Eastern and Western blocs. In the Horn of Africa (Ethiopia and Somalia), much of Southern Africa (e.g. Angola and Mozambique), as well as much of Central America and in Afghanistan, a picture of superpower conflict lies at the heart of the turmoil which produced the exodus of millions of people in the two decades from the late 1960s to the late 1980s. Notable also in the regional instruments, the concept of individual persecution, central to the Convention definition, is made subservient to broader political, economic and historical explanations of why people become refugees. As a whole, the international community does not formally accept this more liberal interpretation. Yet, as much of the literature on refugee flows clearly indicates, these root causes lie at the core of a world of refugees.

It was anticipated that the end of the Cold War in the late 1980s would herald a decline in the generation of forced migration since, as we have seen, superpower conflict was a significant root cause of flows in the developing world. Instead, paradoxically, it introduced a *third phase* in the evolution of the refugee regime. In the last decade of this century, and despite the success of the UNHCR's decade of repatriation – especially, for example, in Mozambique, Namibia and Central America – the flow of refugees has accelerated again. Thus, in 1995 over 2.7 million people were receiving humanitarian assistance in Bosnia-Herzegovina alone (UNHCR, 1995a). Over 3.5 million people were displaced in the Rwandan emergency in 1994, 2.5 million of whom were refugees.

This phase presents a different paradigm with novel characteristics added to those already outlined. The term 'complex emergencies' is now deployed: these are emergencies which have 'a singular ability to erode cultural, economic and civil structures of a society' (Bennett, 1995b, p. xiv). Arguably, large-scale refugee emergencies have always been 'complex'. This contemporary phenomenon, however, presents many new challenges, not just to the Convention and its validity, but to the modalities of intervention and the configuration of humanitarian relief as well (Macrae and Zwi, 1994): what has been described as the problem of 'locating humanitarian values within a context of organized inhumanity' (Slim, 1997, p. 3).

Normally, UNHCR, within the terms of the Convention and Protocol, operated together with the NGO refugee relief agencies outside zones of conflict and where the moral imperative for humanitarian aid was relatively clear-cut. In former Yugoslavia, the Rwanda Emergency in the Great Lakes region of Central Africa, and to a lesser extent the wars in other states of the former Soviet Union (Azerbaijan, Armenia), the refugee crisis was at the epicentre of conflict and an intricate part of it. Humanitarian relief and the broader issues of political conflict and international intervention became inextricably linked as countries imploded in forms of civil war even more violent than those in early decades. The carefully crafted relationship between humanitarian objectives and non-political interests had broken down. Evidence on the role of UNHCR in former Yugoslavia illustrates the extent to which it was, perhaps unwittingly or inevitably, subjected to politicization by all parties in the conflict (Cunliffe and Pugh, 1997). In contrast to earlier experiences, the international community, although in diplomatic disarray and lacking coherence, nevertheless explicitly asserted the right to both political and military intervention in the sovereign interests of states, in Rwanda and former Yugoslavia, ostensibly to secure large-scale humanitarian programmes. These interventions extended far beyond the studiously neutral peacekeeping missions of the past. For future refugee crises and the application of Convention definitions, perhaps a new precedent has been established in which humanitarian and political concerns are interactive.

A further outcome of these two major crises, so far as the Convention is concerned, is to challenge further the definition of a refugee. The horror of genocide, the associated process of ethnic cleansing as the tool of mass persecution, the meaningless distinction between refugees and those internally displaced (since large numbers of the displaced had not crossed borders) and the fact that perpetrators of violence might also be victims rendered the Convention definition of refugees all but meaningless. The classic definition of the persecuted individual in the Convention inadequately describes the mass of refugees in the second and especially this third phase, who are involuntary victims of broader social, political and ethnic forces. In an ironic reflection of one of the original motives for the Convention – the genocide of the Jews in Europe – the international community failed to protect hundreds of thousands of victims of genocide in both former Yugoslavia and Rwanda. Yet it found itself protecting, indeed being exploited by, the perpetrators of genocide (relabelled as refugees under the Convention definition), notably in the case of the Rwandan exodus. The concept of neutrality, which underpins considera-tion of the entitlements of asylum-seekers and the determination of refugee status, is severely tested where the humanitarian imperative is so closely linked to political interests and military operations.

These recent experiences provide evidence of other changes in the way the Convention is being interpreted. Because the limitations of the Convention and the associated relief regime have been further exposed, it is possible to detect a fundamental reconceptualization, not so much about the existence of the Convention itself, but in its role and function in situations of complex instability. The model of the Convention as the central but essentially reactive tool to tackle the phenomenon of refugees is being refocused on the role of the international community to mitigate the onset of humanitarian disasters and to redefine the form of response when this is enacted. The Convention is now but one instrument within a much broader framework of strategies dealing with causes rather than symptoms. These include preventive measures and the monitoring of vulnerability to potential humanitarian disasters; securing improved conditions of govern-ance and development through aid conditionality; underpinning relief with other forms of interventions, such as military action and assertive peacekeeping; establishing closer links between relief, rehabilitation and development where major humanitarian interventions have to be mobilized; and developing the modalities of reconstructing civil society destroyed by conflict. Unfortunately, the Department of Humanitarian Affairs (DHA) established by the UN in 1991 to integrate this formidable agenda has not yet established an effective institutional role or response.

To sum up, millions of refugees have been protected by the Convention. The existence of refugees is both rooted in international law and recognized as a matter of international responsibility. And yet, the Convention manifestly has failed to protect many of the persecuted. Indeed, in a world of refugees, protection is under increasing threat and humane deterrence is a tool widely used by Northern governments. Still falling disproportionately on countries and communities least able to provide sustainable responses or solutions, the refugee burden expands while, at the same time, the burden of the world's peacekeeping bill more than doubled to $5.4 billion between 1990 and 1995 (Macrae, 1997).

These continuing challenges and the new humanitarian paradigm lead to the next topic of this chapter: the institutional framework and activities of the humanitarian assistance regime.

The international humanitarian relief regime

We have already seen the enormous growth in expenditure by UNHCR in the last three decades. But this is only one component. It is estimated that nearly 9 per cent of DAC (the Development Assistance Committee of the OECD) aid (which totalled $56 billion in 1994) was spent on emergency relief, having risen from 1.6 per cent a decade earlier (Randel and German, 1996). It has been estimated that the relief programme for Afghan refugees in Pakistan alone cost $300 million annually throughout the 1980s (Bennett, 1995a). International emergency assistance for the first nine months of the Rwandan crisis (from April to December 1994) cost in the order of $1.4 billion, 85 per cent of it from official (i.e. bilateral and multilateral) donors (Joint Evaluation, 1996). UNHCR had over 450 NGO operating partners in 1994 (UNHCR, 1994, 1995b), and the number of NGOs in OECD countries working in human rights, refugee migration and development was 1322 in 1993 (OECD, 1993). In the Rwanda emergency over 200 NGOs were operational. The humanitarian relief regime is big business, very specialized and highly institutionalized.

How is humanitarian aid organized, managed and delivered? Who are the main actors and what are their roles? Like refugee emergencies and the Convention itself, the aid regime has evolved and developed. It is possible to identify two generalized models of refugee relief and assistance. These models have developed over the past three decades with relatively well-defined characteristics and well-developed institutional apparatus.

In the case of the developed world, where the influx of refugees is small and highly regulated, the model emphasizes modes and mechanisms of integration, for example in employment and education. Access to a range of specialist support services and targeted material provision is made available, usually within the context of the national framework of welfare services. This response model is the counterpart of the Convention's individualistic conception of the refugee. It assumes permanency of settlement. It is managed and almost totally financed by the host country.

The rest of this section, however, deals with the second and fundamentally different model which exists, almost exclusively, in the developing world and countries of mass displacement. Evolved in an *ad hoc* fashion, operationalized in large-scale and uncontrolled mass forced displacement, this model seeks to ensure not just 'protection', but the very survival of hundreds of thousands of lives. Its focus is basic needs and its underlying assumption is temporary provision and repatriation. It is financed and managed by the international community and divides into two main phases: acute emergency and longer-term 'care and maintenance'. The phenomenon of complex emergencies and the exceptional severity of their impact on such large numbers of victims places this classic model under increasing stress (Macrae and Zwi, 1994).

The main actors and their interests

There are three main actors involved in refugee relief. The first two are UNHCR and NGOs, which form a mutually reinforcing partnership; the third is host governments and local communities. There is, of course, a fourth and most important interest group, the refugees themselves. Since it is their interests which the regime is designed to serve, some of the contradictions in and challenges to the role of the institutionalized actors are examined below.

THE UNITED NATIONS HIGH COMMISSIONER FOR REFUGEES
Mandated to provide protection and to ensure *non-refoulement* under the terms of the 1951 Convention, UNHCR still has these as its prime functions, together with the promotion of durable solutions to refugee problems. UNHCR employed about 5600 people in 1997. Its functions have expanded in line with the changing nature of refugee causes and flows discussed in the previous section – the so-called 'additional functions'. It operates in 'refugee-like situations' where displaced people have not crossed international borders. For example, at the special request of the then UN Secretary-General, UNHCR became involved in Cyprus from 1974 where 40 per cent of the population became, technically, internally displaced rather than refugees. More recently it assumed the lead agency role for humanitarian assistance to 2.3 million people internally displaced in Bosnia-Herzegovina. Additionally, in its self-proclaimed decade of repatriation, it has worked extensively in countries from where refugees poured in the past to ensure sustainable repatriation and reintegration. Thus in Mozambique it has played a lead role in a programme involving over 1.7 million repatrees costing over $145 million (UNHCR, 1997a, b).

Despite the increasingly wide mandate, the reality is that UNHCR has become synonymous with large-scale, international emergency relief programmes over the past three and half decades. In virtually every refugee crisis, under the auspices of the UN, it acts as the lead agency in the co-ordination and provision of refugee assistance. Its agenda is dominated by the response to emergencies in the 'acute phase' and developing the so-called 'care and maintenance' of refugees in exile, in the longer term. And since, as we have seen, the burden of refugees falls heavily on poor countries unable to sustain even their own development needs, the provision of massive amounts of material assistance forms the core of relief programmes. This reality is not without its critics who argue that the prime function of effective protection has been compromised and marginalized by the 'additional functions', especially the high-profile, expensive and increasingly political role of relief operations (Goodwin-Gill, 1997).

How a refugee crisis enters the international domain can vary greatly. The power of the media and the leverage of NGOs usually precipitate action. The international response is always reactive. Getting agreement for intervention through diplomatic channels is notoriously slow: vital time can be lost. What is unarguable is that, despite increasing the role of early warning and prevention, crisis response and the lack of effective preparedness and contingency planning always characterize the action of the international community in general and UNHCR in particular (UNHCR, 1989; Joint Evaluation, 1996).

The inception of UNHCR action requires a mandate or special request from the UN and the agreement of host countries. Yet while mandating UNHCR confers international 'recognition' for a refugee emergency, issues of sovereignty ensure that not all refugee-receiving countries (and obviously no refugee-generating countries) readily accede to UNHCR intervention. For example, neither Zimbabwe nor Malawi acknowledged the early influxes of Mozambican refugees in the mid-1980s, although for very different reasons.

After UNHCR has been mandated and protocols agreed with the host governments, typically UNHCR then mounts an assessment mission. This defines the scale of the emergency and its likely development, and assesses the distribution of refugees and their material needs for shelter, clothing, food and water, medical provision, health care and sanitation. Initial definition of the action plan and disposition of emergency response teams takes place. Speed is essential. In the case of exodus from Rwanda, for example, where 850,000 refugees swept into former Zaire in four days, about 80,000 refugees and internally displaced people died mainly from cholera and dysentery in the region. The acute emergency phase – the first few weeks of a mass exodus – is driven by basic life-saving interventions to reduce disease, starvation and mortality.

In mobilizing assistance in the acute phase, two interrelated activities dominate UNHCR's role. First, UNHCR itself is not an operational agency; it co-ordinates and monitors relief programmes, which are delivered and implemented by its operational partners, primarily NGOs and the host government, but also other intergovernmental agencies such as the World Food Programme (WFP) and United Nations Development Programme (UNDP). Also, in partnership, it acts as an important supplier of relief commodities, provides logistics, and professional staffing of relief programmes. To a greater or lesser degree, depending on the relative power of the main actors, UNHCR will also manage the relief programme.

The second activity is the corollary of the first: fundraising. UNHCR has only modest permanent funding and what is available is used for its general programmes and administrative activities; but even the budget for this sector substantially comprises pledges and donations rather than core funding from the UN regular budget. Its special programmes, in other words the bulk of its activities such as emergency relief and repatriation, are entirely funded from voluntary contributions by governments, the donor community – both bilateral and multilateral organizations – and by NGOs. Thus in 1995, the projected budget for special as opposed to general programmes was roughly in the ratio 2:1, $864 million to $429 million (UNHCR, 1995a). Each emergency therefore requires a separate appeal, which constitutes a major challenge to UNHCR. Since many potential actors – particularly NGOs – make their own appeals to fund programmes and projects, this accentuates UNHCR's challenge. To take again the case of the Rwandan emergency, about 50 per cent of the costs in the first nine months were incurred by international agencies – primarily UNHCR (Joint Evaluation, 1996). In the case of the budget for the Malawi programme, which during the early 1990s was one of UNHCR's largest relief operations, this was running at $110 million in 1991, approximately equivalent to 20 per cent of the Malawi government's revenue base. Again about 50 per cent of this expenditure was under the auspices of UNHCR and much of the rest, as food aid, supplied by WFP (Zetter, 1995a).

Clearly, the sources and extent of funding are major determinants of how a programme is mobilized, how lives are saved and how refugees' livelihood strategies and needs are supported. UNHCR's funding arrangements put a political and diplomatic price on the lives of refugees depending on the effectiveness of its appeals and the claim an emergency makes on the world's humanitarian conscience.

There is no methodology to determine when an acute emergency changes to the 'care and maintenance' phase. The cynical view is that this stage rationalizes the inevitable onset of donor fatigue as the crisis disappears from the international agenda or is replaced by the next. UNHCR usually takes a leading role in shifting its role to programme consolidation and the design and organization of assistance for what may be protracted exile. Here the main elements are intended to be developmental rather than relief oriented, concerned with income generation and skills development projects, social and community development programmes such as education for children and helping the displaced to rebuild shattered social structures and roles. The manifest objectives are to encourage self-sufficiency to build up local capacity, and – more limited – to prepare refugees for eventual return.

In recent years, this classic model of UNHCR's role has evolved in the face of new challenges. Two factors account for this. First, voluntary repatriation is now a high-profile activity, exemplified in Mozambique, Myanmar, former Yugoslavia and Guatemala. In part this reflects a re-emphasis of UNHCR's original mandate to seek durable solutions – and repatriation is often claimed to be the preferred of the three durable solutions to refugee displacement. In part, and quite simply, repatriation has been promoted by the international community and host countries to relieve the costs which protracted large-scale forced displacements impose. Since some 7 million refugees are estimated to have returned in the 1990s, some success has been achieved, at least at a utilitarian level. But is this mere expediency?

At issue, given the resource constraints on UNHCR's competing activities, is the extent to which this shift from protection and relief to repatriation and reintegration best serves the humanitarian interests and needs of refugees. Refugees return for complex reasons which bear little similarity to the interests and priorities of the international community (Allen and Morsink, 1994). Thus, the extent to which repatriation under these conditions is truly voluntary is always under scrutiny. The danger exists that UNHCR compromises its core function of protection by being so fully involved in the mechanics of repatriation and cross-border operations, for example in Somalia in 1992. In any case, more refugees return spontaneously than under UNHCR voluntary programmes (Larkin *et al.*, 1991). Return home remains the not so easy option (Rogge, 1991; Warner, 1994; Stepputat, 1994).

At the same time, the second challenge derives from new forms of forced displacement in complex emergencies, discussed in the first part of the chapter. Here again, alongside its classic function of co-ordinating the relief operation, UNHCR has become enmeshed in broader debates about the politicization and the militarization of its humanitarian functions. To an extent, UNHCR has always been compromised: impartiality was assumed as part of the 'rules of the game', but politics has always been part of the emergency aid agenda (Kent, 1990). What is different now in complex emergencies is that these uneasy compromises are explicitly in the public gaze, extremely dramatic and far more difficult to reconcile.

Finally, both in repatriation and in emergency conditions, UNHCR is increasingly being forced to operate much more closely, and to compete, with other international agencies in the UN family (e.g. UNDP, UNHCHR, DHA, UNICEF), other multilateral agencies and specially convened task forces. Again, it remains an open question whether these changes best defend and serve the needs of that particular category of people designated in 1951: refugees. With the globalization of refugees comes the globalization of international action – the question goes much wider, of course, than UNHCR.

To summarize, then, some overall judgements about the strengths and weaknesses of UNHCR's interests and role can be made. If there has been a diminution in UNHCR's core role in affording protection, this must be of fundamental concern. As states in the developed world devise new ways of limiting the spirit and operation of the Convention by repressive measures and policies of 'human deterrence', even the *de minimis* definition is devalued, but must be defended. Equally, the case can be made that UNHCR's 'additional powers' have increasingly compromised its scope and effectiveness as humanitarian crises become more intractable. Yet no other agency is better placed or experienced to co-ordinate the provision of life-saving assistance to hundreds of thousands of refugees. On the other hand, the more important questions in such an analysis are why the 'additional powers' are needed and how they have been acquired. Is it the case that UNHCR, in striving for institutional maintenance, has willingly promoted the extension of its territory? Or are the 'additional powers' the corollary of an infinitely more complex refugee phenomenon than when UNHCR came into existence in 1951? Or is the reality that refugees are the migrants whom nobody wants? The international community has created an elaborate legal and institutional structure in which UNHCR is the servant to the world's humanitarian conscience. This allows individual states – both host governments and those that generate forced displacement – to abdicate fundamental responsibility for structural and proactive responses to this global problem. In any event, the carefully crafted and enduring financial dependency of the UNHCR effectively inhibits its power and ensures that, behind its humanitarian *raison d'être*, the organization acknowledges the political interests it must serve.

NON-GOVERNMENTAL ORGANIZATIONS

NGOs comprise the second major set of actors. Together with UNHCR they constitute the international refugee relief regime. Inevitably, only a generalized picture can be provided, given the number of NGOs, their geographical distribution, operational specialization and the range of their affiliations and self-declared mandates.[3] Comprising mainly Northern-based NGOs and, to a lesser extent, indigenously based NGOs in the host countries themselves, they constitute the front line of delivery of emergency and longer-term assistance to refugees. In one sense, this essentially pragmatic configuration is shaped by accidental factors. Consistent with their charitable orientation and compassionate aims (many NGOs are the charitable arm of different religious denominations), NGOs provided assistance in the refugee crises in the first half of the twentieth century. Their work both supported the interventions of the international community and challenged it to improve future responses. The 1951 Convention and the establishment of UNHCR institutionalized this configuration. The international legal and definitional responsibilities relating to refugees were divided from the operational provision of care and assistance to the forcibly displaced.

From this initial division of labour, at first in Europe after World War II and then, increasingly, in the developing world from the 1960s as the refugee relief regime evolved, a substantial industry has been created. NGOs no longer just fill the gaps in the relief system. They are major actors in their own right, working according to their precepts, articulated to their independent donor bases, with varying operational capabilities and organizational cultures (Walkup, 1997). But they are also partners, or subcontractors depending on one's viewpoint, to the international community. Intergovernmental agencies such as UNHCR (whose own sphere of influence has grown, as we have seen, with expansion of its mandate), the European Union and bilateral donors together fund by far the greater proportion of refugee relief and assistance which is channelled through NGOs.

Following the structure of the preceding section, this section will first outline the operational activities and limitations of NGOs, then discuss more general issues.

Working with local communities at the grass roots, local NGOs are well placed both to anticipate refugee emergencies and then to respond in the preliminary stages. They have been more successful accomplishing the latter than the former, where in any case they have little power to act. Typically it is local community groups, mission stations, church-based NGOs and secular NGOs involved in development projects with rural communities in border areas that first respond to the arrival of refugees. The religious groups may appeal to the NGO arm of their parent organizations such as CARITAS, for example – one of the Catholic Relief Agency NGOs – for material support to accommodate, feed and provide medical assistance to the trickle of refugees starting to cross the border. Equally, the more formally constituted NGOs find themselves pressed to switch resources from developmental projects into relief aid distribution. As we have seen, at this stage there are often compelling reasons why neither host governments nor the international community wish to act. In any case, intergovernmental agencies cannot match the outreach capacity of this array of locally operating NGOs. By default, assistance is provided on an informal basis; the interests of refugees are last on the formal agenda. Paradoxically, and depending on the capacity of local agencies and the scale of the influx, locally based responses are likely to be more in sympathy with the needs and coping mechanisms of refugees than a dependency-creating, fully mobilized international relief programme (see Chapter 6).

More complex large-scale emergencies of recent years, generating the sudden movement of very large numbers of refugees, have shaped a rather different NGO response. Local communities and NGOs have been overwhelmed, thus the appeal to parent NGOs or the large-scale internationally based NGOs in the North takes place almost immediately.

Yet in either case, NGOs are often instrumental in stimulating international concern and the mobilization of a full-scale relief programme. Sometimes with local counterparts, but more usually by the rapid build-up of air-freighted supplies from contingency and pre-positioned stock and expatriate personnel, NGOs can react very quickly in the acute emergency phase. Their relatively small size and the operational flexibility which comes with small bureaucracies and simple decision-making structures permit rapid intervention and the provision of essential relief items such as shelter, water supply and sanitation systems, food and medical assistance. For example, Oxfam installed a water supply system for 800,000 refugees in 18 days after the influx of Rwandan Hutu to former Zaire.

The larger NGOs act closely with UNHCR assessment missions and collaborate on initial programme design. But to further position themselves, they also conduct their own emergency assessments which may lead to very rapid deployments in advance of the main programme, as discussed above. The response capability of the large NGOs is now so well institutionalized and their competitive character so well established that the UNHCR often resorts to a sectoral and territorial division of the relief programme. This applies especially to larger NGOs which take the lead in supplying and implementing the major capital items of the relief programme itemized above. Smaller NGOs then fill gaps, usually in the 'softer' areas such as health education, specialist health care, social support and counselling. This pragmatic allocation of responsibilities is a managerial response which subsequently avoided the worst excesses of duplication experienced in Sudan, where over 150 NGOs operated during the Ethiopian refugee influx in the early 1970s. These problems resurfaced in the Great Lakes diaspora after 1994 with over 200 operational NGOs. However, the ironic consequence is that operational co-ordination can become more difficult as NGOs protect their 'turf', are frustrated by the prohibitions on delivering more integrated assistance packages and are compelled to identify and differentiate 'their' contribution in order to justify continued donor support (Zetter, 1995a; Harrell-Bond, 1986; Clay,

1989). To balance the picture, evidence from a number of refugee emergencies across the world suggests that NGOs, both before and after intergovernmental agencies 'take over' the programme, have developed co-ordinated and consensual ways of delivering assistance (Bennett, 1995a).

As the emergency phase gives way to longer-term 'care and maintenance', there is a shift in the provision of assistance from relief to development. The objectives are to decrease the refugee burden and re-establish the independence and autonomy of refugees. These objectives are, of course, very much in tune with the general ideology of NGOs. Consistent with these precepts, interventions in this stage involve different ways of working with refugees and emphasize community participation and empowerment, rebuilding sustainable communities and developing economic self-sufficiency. Mobilizing income-generating and skills development projects exemplifies the practical dimensions of enhancing the economic independence and the refugees' own survival strategies. Again, this is paralleled by 'softer' projects; for example, developing local capacity to take over the management and maintenance of water supply systems; programmes to facilitate the social and economic well-being of women, whose status and role is frequently decimated by the refugee exodus; developing leadership; and rebuilding community structures.

Nevertheless, the transformation from the emergency to the developmental phase (as NGOs prefer to describe it) is often difficult to achieve in practice – not just because host governments are resistant to programmes which facilitate the longer-term settlement of refugees. Despite the aspirations of NGOs, enhancing refugee autonomy entails disengagement and relinquishing control: the mechanisms for strengthening local capacity can be difficult to construct and the process may challenge the NGO's own sense of trust in its beneficiaries. Another, more readily identifiable difficulty is the legacy of the 'technical fix' approach which drives the programme design of the emergency phase. To put in place water supply or food distribution systems for large concentrations of encamped refugees demands sophisticated knowledge and experience. Consultation with refugee beneficiaries on the location of standpipes or the methods of weighing out food rations rarely takes place, since speed is imperative to save lives. But once the main infrastructure and delivery systems are in place, this pre-empts the subsequent mobilization of more community- or gender-sensitive methods of water or food delivery and management. These requirements, which are often integral to the precepts and objectives of NGOs, frequently look like bolt-on modifications.

If and when protracted exile gives way to repatriation, NGOs continue to be involved – most successfully, perhaps, in Mozambique. This entailed preparing for resettlement with cross-border interventions and so-called quick-impact projects (QIPs), in anticipation of the end of the war. Then, during and after repatriation, full-scale developmental programmes were mobilized to rehabilitate the devastated infrastructure and provide returnees with resources and equipment to re-establish themselves. As in Mozambique, so too in Rwanda many NGOs are now involved in reconstruction, capacity-building, development and reconciliation as key activities (Bebbington and Mitlin, 1996). Both in Mozambique (Egan, 1991; Bennett, 1995a) and in Rwanda (Africa Rights, 1994), this role has produced new and conflicting opportunities for NGOs; these are considered below.

Some of the successes and also the challenges and contradictory outcomes of NGO interventions have already been identified. In my own analysis of the Mozambican refugee relief programme in Malawi (Zetter, 1996a), other practical limitations to NGO projects were identified, especially in the developmental or 'care and maintenance' phase. Inevitably, a classic patron–client relationship existed between NGOs and the refugees. This increased refugee dependency, by inadequate identification of and response to local economic conditions and refugees' skills; unsatisfactory methods of recruitment; production, business plans and marketing strategies of limited sustainability; token participation and the imposition of external management ideologies; and lack of gender-sensitive and gender-aware policies. These findings, in particular the increased refugee dependency despite the avowed aims and objectives of NGOs, bear out research among other refugee populations (e.g. Getman, 1990; Kibreab, 1993; Mazur, 1987). Do the NGOs make a difference? In that less than 2 per cent of the refugee population in Malawi, for example, directly participated in the income-generating and skills development projects under review, it could be argued that the impacts were only marginal to the survival strategies of the 1.2 million refugees. On the other hand, given the levels of project budget, the opportunity cost of the investment and the humanitarian goodwill tapped from donors for such a limited return, these findings challenge the accountability and the claims made by NGOs.

The expansion in NGO activity and the increasingly competitive environment in which they operate has had two further effects. First, there is considerable sectoral specialization – for example, Oxfam's reputation and expertise lie primarily in water supply and public health, MSF in emergency medical provision and supplementary feeding programmes – matched by greatly improved professional competence. For the leading NGOs at least, it is no longer possible to claim, as in the past (Kent, 1990), that they lack experience and skills. Set against these achievements are the problems of programme co-ordination which have been noted above. In addition, NGOs' internal programme evaluations and published documents (e.g. UNHCR, 1989; Joint Evaluation, 1996; ICRC, 1995) demonstrate that, despite the extensive experience acquired in refugee assistance over the past three decades, the lack of institutional learning remains a critical shortcoming (Walkup, 1997; Edwards and Hulme, 1995). Limited preparedness limited assessments, poor intra-agency management and co-ordination between developmental and emergency functions and between the field operations in the South and the headquarters in the North, and limited human resources planning (especially for the recruitment of specialist staff and the reliance on less experienced staff) are the most frequently reported shortcomings.

The second outcome of the expansion of NGO activity is that, despite the proliferation of small NGOs both in the North and in host countries, a handful of long-established 'Northern-based' NGOs (NNGOs) dominate the agenda of the relief regime and operational responses (Zetter, 1996b). They have direct access to the formal and informal structures of intergovernmental and governmental organizations and donors. By networking among themselves they reinforce their power and control. These organizations are now big business with management structures and sophisticated organizational capability to match. Conversely, the NNGOs' avowed aims of partnership with Southern NGOs (Bebbington and Mitlin, 1996), strengthening local capacity and local institution-building, are not particularly evident in practice (Zetter, 1996b). The technical sophistication of NNGOs, their control over counterparts' budgets, the reporting requirements and accountability required of local partners are some of the mechanisms by which the scaling up of indigenous NGOs is constrained. The outcome, repeated in every refugee relief programme, is to crowd out local NGOs, which, from many perspectives, are better placed to render assistance to refugees (Kok, 1989).

The proliferation of NGOs suggests that they are fulfilling a crucial need as refugee numbers and assistance funds inexorably rise. However, this superficial picture conceals contradictions which go to the heart of the rationale of NGOs. To a considerable extent, the continued existence of NGOs has become increasingly dependent on the sustained flow of both refugees and international funds. Moreover, each refugee crisis seems to spawn a new wave of NGOs that are professionally inexperienced, often too small to make an effective or efficient contribution to the relief programme and, perhaps most worryingly, of sometimes questionable ethical intentions.

Another trend is evident in the role of NGOs. This is particularly associated with the 'complex emergencies' in the past decade, but emerged in earlier phases. NGOs were attractive to donors and intergovernmental agencies as operational partners because their humanitarian aims and precepts helped to reinforce the political neutrality (in theory) of such assistance. However, with this endorsement and their growing size, credibility and influence, they too embarked on a process of institutional change and redefinition. Because of their powerful position within the international relief system, the larger NGOs have extended their humanitarian response beyond the essential remedial function of providing material assistance, to include advocacy, human rights campaigning and conflict mediation on behalf of the forcibly displaced people they serve. In this extended role, their aim is to influence the political agenda of emergencies. But repeated experiences have exposed the dangers of assuming this role and NGOs have potentially compromised their implicit neutrality (Storey, 1997). One example of the problems this has created was in the Ethiopian famine in the mid-1980s, where famine relief appeared to be supporting the government programme of forcible resettlement (Clay, 1989). Cross-border operations while internal wars continued, for example in Somalia (Kirkby *et al.*, 1997), Afghanistan and Mozambique, raise questions of allegiance, even if the long-term objectives are peace, reconstruction and reconciliation (Oxfam, 1996).

Recent complex emergencies (such as the Great Lakes emergency of 1994–96) that appear to demand this more 'complex' mode of intervention exemplify the dangers of this extended strategy which combines humanitarian needs with more overt political intervention. The challenge for NGOs is to reconcile this new responsibility which they have accorded themselves with the fact that, of all the actors, they are best placed to understand the complex dynamics which lead to the crises (de Marrs, 1995), and to demonstrate an unambiguous humanitarian agenda. Appearing to condone the 'wrong side' in the case of Rwandan Hutu refugees in former Zaire, by providing large-scale assistance to those who committed genocide, the NGOs have received a difficult lesson. Of course, making the 'right' decision is virtually impossible in such turbulent and unpredictable situations. NGOs did much good. Did they do no harm? Ironically, by asserting their interest in the broader political agenda, the NGOs may have damaged both their reputation and trustworthiness as representatives of neutral humanitarian principles (de Waal, 1997).

These tendencies challenge the core principles and purpose of NGOs. Humanitarianism can no longer be justified only in terms of a self-fulfilling moral imperative which lies at the core of their rationale. NGOs are under increasing scrutiny and there is pressure to display clearer accountability to refugee beneficiaries as much as donors. This accountability has not been well articulated to date. The NGO community is now actively debating the significant tensions which their more explicit agenda has created. A code of conduct for NGOs working in emergencies now exists – the outcome of criticism of some NGOs in the Great Lakes emergency.

It is no accident that NGOs are also now engaged in a process of self-education about the complexity of humanitarian agendas and the contradictory outcomes of engagement in complex emergencies (Slim,

1997; Storey, 1997; Bryer and Cairns, 1997). Another part of this re-evaluation is concerned to better comprehend the dilemmas and the potential dangers of incorporation into highly politicized international interventions in refugee emergencies, which might further compromise their independence and neutrality.

As with the UNHCR, the evolution of the NGOs and their now dominant role in the refugee relief regime mirrors the evolution of the phenomenon of refugee flows in the last half century. While, from one perspective, this can be argued as the largely pragmatic adjustment to prevailing circumstances, the more penetrating institutional analysis outlined here identifies a classic process of interest mediation between the principal actors – UNHCR and the NGOs – and within the NGO community itself. Understanding the process of how institutional control is defined, competed for, sustained and legitimized sheds new light on why refugees' needs are not very effectively provided for, either by NGOs or by the intergovernmental agencies set up for that purpose.

HOST GOVERNMENTS AND THE IMPACT OF REFUGEES

There is, perhaps not surprisingly, rather less detailed research or operational evaluation of the role and interests of host governments than for the other two actors. As Richmond (1994) cogently argues, behind the humanitarian rhetoric the policy of many, if not all, governments today is not to afford welcome to asylum-seekers and refugees. There are material and practical reasons for this growing resistance which reflect the experience of the past few decades. The perception of refugees as a burden is well documented. One example which has recently received much attention is the severe and enduring environmental impacts of mass refugee movements in many African countries (UNHCR, 1996; Jacobsen, 1997). But there are also latent reasons for the new agenda of deterrence, control and restriction. There is now a more cynical and implicitly racist attitude in the developed countries of Western and Eastern Europe, North America and the Pacific rim, where, in different degrees, a world of refugees appears to threaten living standards, ethnic hegemony or even a country's independence (Richmond, 1994: Hocke, 1990; Macnamara, 1989).

There is a dichotomy between host governments in the North and countries experiencing mass influx of refugees in the developing world. Whereas Northern governments have the instruments and resources to limit refugee entry (e.g. Frelick and Kohnen, 1995; Joly, 1996), the countries of the developing world, which currently and in the future will continue to host the vast majority of the world's refugees, are denied these advantages. For example, the concept of quota refugees is one mechanism widely deployed by Western countries to demonstrate humanitarian credentials but to limit flows of asylum-seekers (e.g. Vietnamese refugees in the 1970s or Bosnians in the 1990s). Equally, whereas the developed countries have resources to ensure reasonable provision for those asylum-seekers who are admitted, in the developing world the numbers involved impose drastic pressures on already stretched economies and over-burdened social and physical infrastructure.

In the developing world, permeable borders and the economic, political and ethnic instability which can uproot millions in a short space of time render many of these states extremely vulnerable to the mass movement of refugees. Unfortunately for quite a number of countries across Africa and central America, the ebb and flow of refugees has made them both refugee hosts and refugee generators at different times. These factors further complicate how host governments articulate their interests.

Some common characteristics can be identified, although, as before, generalizations conceal contrasting and contradictory evidence. The fundamental interests which drive a host government are: protecting the integrity of the country; sustaining the political credibility of the government; and limiting the direct and indirect costs. In practical terms, three parameters define this set of interests: containment, control and burden-sharing.

The first objective is *containment*. The point has already been made that, for varied reasons, a government may not want to admit the existence of refugees. These factors include the wish to avoid international scrutiny of its own human rights record; the wish to avoid embarrassing neighbouring governments with the fact that refugees exemplify a loss of capacity to govern; or the desire to avoid the accusation that it may be supporting refugees in mounting insurrections against the government of the country from which they have fled or been exiled. The first and second examples illustrate the respective positions adopted by Malawi and Zimbabwe in response to Mozambican refugees in the mid-1980s; the third defines the position in the Great Lakes region surrounding the Rwanda crisis.

In the developed world, remote from most refugee crises, sophisticated instruments of regulation allow these countries a much greater degree of choice of how to operate self-interest and contain refugee flows. How and when asylum-seekers are accorded protection display overt political interests. Few Tamils or Kurds are accepted as asylum-seekers, although many would argue that their claims are justified, because it is not in the interests of European countries to recognize the instability in Sri Lanka or Turkey. On the other hand, Vietnamese refugees in the 1970s and, earlier, Hungarian refugees from 1956 were welcomed (but only in quotas) by the West. With their arrival, Western governments sought to reinforce a clear political message about the countries of the Eastern bloc and their potential allies. In the case of former Yugoslavia, European countries effectively enforced an agenda of containment within the framework of peacekeeping and humanitarian intervention.

For the countries of the South, as the uncontrolled influx of refugees accelerates, the process begins to threaten food security, the environment, the welfare infrastructure and the livelihoods of local host communities. At this stage, and then when full-scale intervention is mobilized, containment comes fully into play. Refugees flooding across a border tend to settle *en masse* and in many instances close to national borders – for reasons of solidarity, social cohesion, exhaustion after reaching safety, hope of speedy repatriation. But it is no accident that, in country after country, refugees remain permanently self-settled or forcibly encamped close to borders where they first settle, in locations which are often remote from government control and possibly sparsely settled.

Even where overcrowding makes it imperative to move refugees, new sites are designated which display similar characteristics. A conjuncture of interests – UNHCR, the NGOs and the host government – ensures this outcome. By consolidating these settlement processes and thereby containing the penetration of refugees into the country, host governments serve their interests. Since settlement is often in relatively remote parts of the country, the impact on more developed and intensively settled areas can be limited. Entry into the politically more sensitive urban economy can be more easily regulated. On the other hand, because these settlements are remote from infrastructure and services, the problems of providing assistance are that much more difficult.

The counterpart of physical containment is the aim to retain *institutional control* when large-scale international relief programmes are mobilized. The internationalization of refugee relief has potentially destructive effects on the capacity of national and local governments and agencies in the host country to organize and manage their own relief efforts. The process may go further in large-scale emergency programmes. Proliferation of NNGOs and intergovernmental organizations may create 'parallel' administrative structures which, in turn, may then undermine or incorporate the structure and authority of much of the governmental machinery (Bratton, 1989; Elliot, 1987; Zetter, 1995a). The effects of 'institutional destruction' (Morss, 1984) occurred in Sudan in the 1970s (Karadawi, 1983; Cromwell, 1988) and to a lesser extent in Pakistan in the 1980s (Baitenmann, 1990), for example. Not surprisingly, host governments seek to mitigate these challenges to their autonomy and integrity.

There are few examples where states have managed to mediate the domains of interest of these competing constituencies, retain some control and resist the development of parallel administration. Malawi kept close control of its programme in the late 1980s, by a process of exclusion and incorporation (Zetter, 1995a). NNGOs were mandated in very limited numbers, and allocated to specific areas to avoid duplication; all relief assistance was channelled through the main line ministries, which permitted further control and helped to ensure that the assistance met developmental objectives for local communities as well as for refugees. Of course, an autocratic regime and a country which had resisted external scrutiny facilitated these political and managerial interests. After a period of transition and competition for control between the main actors in the early 1990s, the programme reverted to type. First the UNHCR and then the NNGOs exerted increasing control of the expanding programme.

The case of Cyprus also demonstrates successful programme control. Deliberately the government chose not to create specialist or separate agencies, despite the scale of the crisis when over 200,000 displaced Greek Cypriots (about 40 per cent of the ethnic population) fled the Turkish invasion of the north. Additionally, the government's aim was to implement permanent solutions since the refugees (technically internally displaced persons, IDPs) were ethnically identical. A series of short-term action plans from 1974 to 1982 (Zetter, 1992) integrated the emergency needs of the refugees with longer-term developmental objectives for the country as whole. As in Malawi a decade later, all assistance from UNHCR and bilateral donors was channelled through line ministries. Similarly, only limited assistance was provided by external NGOs because, again, the government constrained their involvement.

Although, for obvious reasons, these unique conditions in Malawi and Cyprus could not be replicated elsewhere, both examples illustrate some of the salient processes by which the other governments might retain their autonomy and control of the programmes.

In general, the scale and speed of onset of refugee influxes constrain countries to an expedient, rather than a carefully structured, articulation of self-interest. In the Great Lakes emergency, only Tanzania, though hosting more than a million Rwandan refugees, retained some control, in partnership with UNHCR, over the delivery and co-ordination of the assistance programme. Acknowledged to have provided a substantial and competent input to the programme from its own resources (Joint Evaluation, 1996), at the same time it resisted longer-term assistance programmes which appeared to be prolonging the settlement of refugees.

The third parameter is *burden-sharing*. Many developing countries, when overwhelmed by refugees, have wrestled with the problem of how to define and, where possible, offset the burden that refugees represent. Some resource impacts are obvious. Refugees consume large volumes of local commodities: food, water and land. But there are less obvious impacts such as uncompensated expenditures from a host country's capital and recurrent budgets: the costs of maintaining infrastructure such as roads and water supply systems servicing refugee settlements, or additional staffing and administration (UNDP, 1987; Government of Malawi *et al.*, 1990). Similarly, in recent years the protracted impacts of refugees have been recognized. These are often experienced long after repatriation, such as the depletion of environmental resources of forest and woodland used for construction and domestic fuel (Jacobsen, 1997).

In other words, the argument put mainly by African countries was that, while the causes and consequences of refugee flows were a global problem, the burden of hosting the vast majority of the displaced fell unevenly on the world's poorer nations. Their economies and societies were the least able to cope with even their own domestic priorities and aspirations. Protracted exile of refugees and the failed experience with local settlement schemes intended as a long-term solution for refugees in exile in Tanzania and Zambia for example (Kibreab, 1989), reinforced these negative consequences.

From these propositions, articulated at the time of rapid growth in refugees in Africa in the 1970s, the concept of burden-sharing developed (Gorman, 1987, 1994; Cuenod, 1990) and was formally institutionalized by ICARA II (International Conference on Assistance to Refugees in Africa) in 1984. ICARA II explored the modalities of strengthening the economic and social infrastructure of host countries in order to increase their capacity to deal with large-scale influxes; this approach recognized that both refugees *and* hosts have developmental needs (Zetter, 1995b). This was followed by an ICVA/UNHCR initiative which advocated the provision and (mainly international) funding of refugee assistance within a long-term development framework (ICVA/UNHCR, 1985). Intergovernmental agencies, donors and NGOs attempted to mobilize the new thinking, and some 163 projects were identified. In practice, ambitious intentions to reshape the methodology and content of assistance programmes had little impact. Instead, as Cuenod (1990) contends, humanitarian assistance was redirected to the more limited objectives of enhancing the economic survival of refugees themselves – a pre-emptive strike by the developed country donors. In effect this left refugees with the worst of both worlds. Host countries, in general, were reluctant to pursue integrationist policies for refugees, while the donors were only prepared to fund self-sustaining assistance programmes, thereby reducing their financial commitment. These objectives have been reinforced in the post-Cold War world (Rogers and Copeland, 1993).

Burden-sharing engages wider debates about refugee impacts, assistance programmes and financial costs and gradually became reshaped into the concept of the relief-to-development continuum. Recognizing that many refugees remain in protracted exile, this concept attempted to develop practical steps to mitigate the burden by linking emergency programmes with longer-term development strategies for refugees *and* local host communities. Concentrating on the creation or enhancement of refugees' livelihood strategies, the developmental model emphasized process and policies appropriate to longer-term needs (Loescher, 1993; Adelman and Sorenson, 1994). By contrast, relief-driven emergency programmes tend to be reactive, concentrating on short-term palliative projects (Hussein, 1995).

NGOs were particularly enthusiastic in supporting burden-sharing and relief-to-development strategies. These concepts reflected many of the core precepts to which NGOs subscribed, such as participation and self-sufficiency. Equally, burden-sharing also justified and ensured a continuing role for NGOs in refugee assistance.

It is doubtful whether the host countries intended these outcomes. Neither is it likely that they intended (marginal) shifts of the burden from themselves to the refugees. Rather, the intention was to sustain and increase the flow of assistance at a time when UNHCR was under financial threat of cutbacks by its paymasters, and Northern donors were beginning to tire of the financial costs of refugees in the developing world. In retrospect, it would seem that the host countries were finessed by both the donors and the NGOs. From the point of view of the refugees, their experience, as discussed earlier, was continued co-option within projects which did little to enhance their autonomy or self-sufficiency (Zetter, 1996a). Their independent survival strategies continued as before.

The Malawi programme is one example where some attempts were made to implement these new methods. As we have seen above, economic self-sufficiency, enhancing refugees' survival strategies and sustainability were characteristic elements of this new approach. In practice refugees survived, as in the past, on their own skills, resources and adaptability, and on judicious use of assistance to satisfy their own priorities and needs.

More recently, as the complex emergencies of former Yugoslavia and Rwanda illustrate, these approaches are both conceptually limited and technically impractical. The turbulence of the crises, the speed and above all the enormous scale of exodus (especially from Rwanda) initially overwhelmed the international humanitarian agencies; emergency relief was the imperative and would have pre-empted a developmental programme even if this had been conceivable. But more significantly, the structural complexity of the crises made the developmental approach fraught with problems. As the ethnic dividing lines of former Yugoslavia became permanent, the relief operation shifted into developmental gear with reconstruction-led programmes in Croatia and Bosnia-Herzegovina. In the Rwandan crisis, on the other hand, the complexity of conditions – the huge exodus, mass displacement and government upheaval in Rwanda, the reluctance of Tanzania to countenance developmental relief, the collapse of former Zaire, the unforeseen repatriation and diaspora of the refugees – rendered a developmental approach both politically and operationally a formidable challenge.

By contrast, a rather different approach emerged in response to the mass uprooting in Nicaragua, El Salvador and Guatemala in the 1980s. Here, the International Conference on Refugees, Displaced and Repatriates of Central America (CIREFCA) helped to provide 'an international forum for analysing, discussing and looking for solutions to the problems of forced migration' (Burge, 1995, p. 150; UNHCR, 1995c). Accepting the existence of mass uprooting, but neutralizing the need for recipients to 'take sides', provided the opportunity for positive action to resolve the regional crisis; since each country was both a generator and recipient of refugees, their reciprocal interests were best served by this diplomacy!

These contrasting experiences illustrate how difficult it is to anticipate major new processes and types of refugee emergency. Equally, they confirm the challenge to learn and apply the lessons from earlier crises to a new era of mass exodus.

Conclusions: the refugees' interests

Where do refugees fit into these debates and changing models of humanitarian assistance? How are their interests served by the evolving international agenda and framework? These questions have been implicitly answered in this chapter, and other chapters in this book deal much more fully with refugees, their responses, needs, ambitions and resources. But a footnote to this chapter is relevant to set these questions within the context of an international perspective.

It is the problematic characteristics of forced migration for the international community which, as we have seen, drive the responses of the various actors in the refugee assistance regime and determine how their interests are deployed. This had been evident even before the foundations of the current regime were laid down in 1951. Two aspects, only, are considered here: dependency, and containment and restrictionism.

Dependency

First, despite the apparently positive humanitarian objectives set out in the Convention and enacted by UNHCR and the assistance agencies, a perception remains that refugees are a problematic category of people constituting a burden of dependency on the international community. On the face of it, refugee survival and dependency seem to go hand in hand. Thus relief aid and assistance are the counterpart to humanitarian needs presented in their most basic form. It is, perhaps, almost counter-intuitive to question the prevailing image, promoted by the media, of hundreds of thousands of encamped, vulnerable refugees. Most refugees are the unwitting victims of root causes of exodus over which they have had little or any direct control. Or they are the persecuted survivors who challenged the suppression and abuse of human rights. In either case, the concept of sanctuary coupled with the loss of familiar economic and social support systems and individual autonomy combine to construct a powerful image of dependency and the need for assistance.

To what extent, though, are refugees conceived or labelled in this image by the way in which the scope, form and organization of the international humanitarian relief regime has been institutionalized? (Zetter, 1988, 1991). A contrasting view questions the extent to which refugees are indeed a burden. While this may seem an academic question, given the extremities of violence, persecution and forced mass exodus in this century, the evidence is not always clear-cut and presents salutary lessons to the humanitarian providers.

Of course, food and medical aid and the supply of potable water are undeniable emergency needs. As in previous refugee crises, so too in the Great Lakes emergency in 1994–6, these resources, delivered with considerable professional competence, saved hundreds of thousands, if not millions, of lives. The fundamental question, to which the humanitarian regime has not yet been able to provide the answer, remains. How to render essential assistance without incorporating refugees as dependent beneficiaries? If the challenge was merely operational, to design different forms of aid delivery, this would be difficult enough. However, the problem is more profound. The interests of all the actors (except refugees) are best served by containing and controlling refugees – political, diplomatic, logistical, security, media profile – in short, by sustaining dependency. The relief regime's own survival and institutional maintenance depends on the image of dependent clients.

If, however, the 'failure' of institutionalized aid delivery is considered a problem of designing more appropriate international assistance programmes, then agencies should more fully investigate the paradoxical yet clear evidence that many refugees survive unaided. Formally provided assistance reaches only a proportion of enumerated refugees, even in situations of mass influx. Of Mozambican refugees, only 40 per cent in Malawi and 50 per cent in Zimbabwe were encamped and therefore received assistance (Zetter, 1996a; Government of Malawi et al., 1990). These figures are high in comparison to estimates of 20 per cent of Eritreans in Sudan in the early and mid-1980s (Kok, 1989), and only 5 per cent of refugees in Slovenia and less than 50 per cent in Croatia in the diaspora following the break-up of former Yugoslavia (Harrell-Bond, 1993). Even in these cases, those who were recipients did not survive on formal assistance alone. The main point is that substantial numbers of refugees survive without dependence on *any* formally constituted assistance programmes.

How this occurs inevitably varies from emergency to emergency, but there is sufficient evidence to exemplify some of the lessons to be learned by the international relief providers. Several factors are crucial. Refugees' own survival strategies, their resourcefulness both as independent survivors and in deploying assistance, where relevant, to match their needs and priorities, are key (e.g. Chapter 4; Kibreab, 1993). Associated informal support mechanisms may also be significant. The scope of, and access, to opportunities available within the local and regional economy are other significant factors (Ager *et al.*, 1995; Kok, 1989; Wilson *et al.*, 1989; Wilson, 1992). As Robinson's 1993 study of the integration of Ugandan Asians in Britain after their exile in 1972 demonstrates, these factors relate as much to a developed country situation as to conditions of mass influx in the developing world.

The challenge of recasting refugees in a non-dependent image is not only one of redefining the interests of providers and reconstructing an image of refugees. It is also, as I have suggested, contingent on the form and objectives of the relief programmes and perceiving refugees, proactively, as a resource. Despite the prevailing attitude of resistance in the developed world, refugees are demonstrably a positive economic asset, even where social and economic exclusion are the prevailing attitudes of the host community. Robinson's study is one of many to illustrate this point.

Perhaps the most sophisticated example of how refugees have been explicitly deployed as a developmental resource is the case of Cyprus cited earlier. Here, relief and development programmes were integrated after the destruction of the island's economy in the 1974 invasion. The very large number of refugees constituted both a resource for the rebuilding of the economy – supplying labour for new industries and massive housing and infrastructure projects as the leading sectors – and the direct beneficiaries of the development projects, since the programmes provided virtually every refugee family with permanent housing within fifteen years (Zetter, 1992).

Containment and restrictionism

Increasing regulation of international migration has been one of the defining features of this century. It has been one of the tools by which nation-states have sought to define and protect their ethnic identity and economic capacity. Uncontrolled migration appears to threaten these attributes.

Refugees are perceived as an especially problematic and threatening category of migrant. For the host countries immediately impacted, there are severe resource pressures, tension in relationships with neighbouring exiling states, and perhaps internal destabilization. Refugees often arrive in large and uncontrollable numbers, usually spontaneously and with limited support and survival systems. For the international community more generally, the threat of regional instability and broader concerns about human rights are significant, among other factors. For these reasons, containment of refugees is the major objective of all the stakeholders, except the refugees. Although international humanitarian assistance is synonymous with the evolution of the refugee regime during this century, it is, in many respects, a mechanism which conceals, not very adequately, the broader objective of containment.

In this context, it is indeed ironic that the relief-to-development debate has been taken full circle by the international community. No longer is it conceived in terms of burden-sharing or responding in an appropriate and practical way to the humanitarian needs of refugees in protracted exile. Now, in a blurring of the links between relief and development (Macrae, 1997), the concept supplies the rationale of aid conditionality to remove the commonly assumed root causes of refugee flows, such as human rights abuse, the denial of political and cultural plurality and the maldistribution of development itself (see, for example, World Bank, 1997, pp. 138–9).

As the long-term 'solution' to tackling the root causes of refugee flows, this latest stage in the evolution of the international refugee regime has much to commend it. However, the strategy of creating a world of stable governments which tolerate pluralistic multiethnic and multicultural societies and where there is no abuse of human rights seems a distant aspiration. There will be many more refugee crises before this ideal is achieved.

Meanwhile, in different degrees related to the capacity of individual countries to control border movements, the global machinery of deterrence, restrictionism and containment has been firmly put in place during the past decade. Thus, at the end of a century which has seen the forced exodus of hundreds of millions of refugees and the institutionalization of a powerful international label, the humanitarianism which created the label is still a compromised concept. The label itself remains problematic.

Notes

1   The Statute of the Office of the UNHCR was annexed to Resolution 428 (V) adopted by the UN General Assembly on 14 December 1950.
2   Global Humanitarian Emergencies 1995, United States Mission to UN, January 1996, cited in Randel and German (1996, p. 236).
3   See Ferris (1993, ch. 3) and Bennett (1995a) for further discussion of the role of NGOs and refugee assistance.

References

Adelman, H. and Sorenson, J. (eds) (1994) *African Refugees: Development Aid and Repatriation*. Boulder, CO: Westview Press.

Africa Rights (1994) Humanitarianism unbound? Current dilemmas facing multi-mandate relief operations in political emergencies. Africa Rights Discussion Paper No. 5, November 1994, London: Africa Rights.

Ager, A., Ager, W. and Long, L. (1995) The differential experience of Mozambican refugee men and women. *Journal of Refugee Studies*, 8 (3), 265–87.

Allen, T. and Morsink, H. (eds) (1994) *When Refugees Go Home: African Experiences*. London: James Currey in association with UNRISD.

Baitenmann, H. (1990) NGOs and the Afghan war: the politicization of aid. *Third World Quarterly*, 12 (1), 62–85.

Bebbington, A. and Mitlin, D. (1996) NGO capacity and effectiveness: a review of themes and NGO-related research recently funded by ESCOR. London ODI, May.

Bennett, J. (ed.) (1995a) *Meeting Needs: NGOs and Co-ordination in Practice*. London: Earthscan.

Bennett, J. (1995b) Introduction: recent trends in relief aid: structural crisis and the quest for a new consensus. In J. Bennett (ed.), *Meeting Needs: NGOs and Co-ordination in Practice*, pp. xi–xx. London: Earthscan.

Bratton, M. (1989) The politics of government–NGO relations in Africa. *World Development*, 17 (4), 569–87.

Bryer, D. and Cairns, E. (1997) For better? For worse? Humanitarian aid in conflict. *Development in Practice*, 7 (4), 363–74.

Burge, A. (1995) Central America: NGO co-ordination in El Salvador and Guatemala 1980–94. In J. Bennett (ed.), *Meeting Needs: NGOs and Co-ordination in Practice*, Chapter 7. London: Earthscan.

Clay, J. (1989) Ethiopian famine and the relief agencies. In G. Loescher and B. Nicholls (eds), *The Moral Nation: Humanitarianism and US Foreign Policy Today*. Notre Dame, IN: Notre Dame Press.

Collinson, S. (1994) *Europe and International Migration*. London: Pinter for the Royal Institute for International Affairs.

Cromwell, G. (1988) Notes on the role of expatriate administrators in agency assisted refugee programmes. *Journal of Refugee Studies*, 1 (3/4), 297–307.

Cuenod, J. (1990) Refugees: development or relief. In G. Loescher and L. Monahan (eds), *Refugees and International Relations*, pp. 219–54. Oxford: Clarendon Press.

Cunliffe, S.A. and Pugh, M. (1997) The politicisation of UNHCR in the former Yugoslavia. *Journal of Refugee Studies*, 10 (2), 134–53.

de Marrs, W. (1995) Waiting for early warning: humanitarian action after the Cold War. *Journal of Refugee Studies*, 8 (4), 390–410.

de Waal, A. (1997) *Famine Crises: Politics and the Disaster Relief Industry in Africa*. London: James Currey.

Deng, F.M. (1995) The international protection of the internally displaced. *International Journal of Refugee Law*, 7 (special issue), 74–86.

Edwards, E. and Hulme, D. (eds) (1995) *Non-Governmental Organisations: Performance and Accountability – Beyond the Magic Bullet*. London: Earthscan/Save the Children Fund.

Egan, E. (1991) Relief and rehabilitation projects in Mozambique: institutional capacity and NGO executive strategies. *Development in Practice*, 1 (3), 297–307.

Elliot, C. (1987) Some aspects of the relations between North and South in the NGO sector. *World Development*, 15 (Supplement), 57–68.

Ferris, E.G. (1993) *Beyond Borders: Refugees, Migrants and Human Rights in the Post-Cold War Era*. Geneva: WCC Publications.

Frelick, B. and Kohnen, B. (1995) Filling the gap: temporary protected status. *Journal of Refugee Studies*, 8 (4), 339–64.

Getman, T.R. (1997) Relief agendas and the refugee's welfare: the Horn of Africa. *International Journal of Refugee Law*, 2 (special issue), 2, 107–17.

Goodwin-Gill, G. (1997) The United Nations reform and the future of refugee protection. Open e-mail, 4 June.

Gorman, R.F. (1987) *Coping with Africa's Refugee Burden: A Time for Solutions*. Dordrecht: Martinus Nijhoff.

Gorman, R.F. (1994) Refugee aid and development in Africa: research and policy needs from the local perspective. In H. Adelman and J. Sorenson (eds), *African Refugees: Development Aid and Repatriation*, pp. 227–44. Boulder, CO: Westview Press.

Government of Malawi/World Bank/UNDP/UNHCR (1990) Report to the Consultative Group on Malawi on the Impact of Refugees on the Government Expenditure Programme, Government of Malawi, Lilongwe, April (unpublished).

Hathaway, J.C. (1991a) Reconceiving refugee law as human rights protection. *Journal of Refugee Studies*, 4 (2), 113–31.

Hathaway, J.C. (1991b) *The Law of Refugee Status*. Toronto: Butterworths.

Harrell-Bond, B.E. (1986) *Imposing Aid: Emergency Assistance to Refugees*. Oxford: Oxford University Press.

Harrell-Bond, B.E. (1993) Creating marginalised, dependent minorities: relief programmes for refugees in Europe. *The Courier*, 140 (July–August), 68–71.

Harvey, C. (1997) Restructuring asylum: recent trends in United Kingdom asylum law and policy. *International Journal of Refugee Law*, 9 (1), 60–73.

Hocke, J.-P. (1990) Beyond humanitarianism: the need for political will to solve today's refugee problem. In G. Loescher and L. Monahan (eds), *Refugees and International Relations*, pp. 37–48. Oxford: Clarendon Press.

Hussein, K. (1995) The nutritional crisis among Mozambican refugees in Malawi: an analysis of the response of the international agencies. *Journal of Refugee Studies*, 8 (1), 26–48.

ICRC (International Committee of the Red Cross) (1995) Strengthening the co-ordination of humanitarian assistance. ICRC Statement at the UN General Assembly, 50th Session, Plenary Meeting, Item 20, 29 November, New York.

ICVA/UNHCR (1985) Workshop on developmental approaches to refugee situations, Puidoux, 1–4 December 1985. Geneva: ICVA/ UNHCR.

Jacobsen, K. (1997) Refugees' environmental impact: the effect of pattern of settlement. *Journal of Refugee Studies*, 10 (1), 19–36.

Joint Evaluation of Emergency Assistance to Rwanda (1996) *The International Response to Conflict and Genocide: Lessons from the Rwanda Experience*, vol. 3. Copenhagen: Humanitarian Aid and Effects.

Joly, D. (1996) *Haven or Hell: Asylum Policy in Europe*. London: Macmillan.

Karadawi, A. (1983) Constraints on assistance to refugees: some observations from the Sudan. *World Development*, 11 (6), 537–47.

Kent, R. (1990) Emergency aid: politics and priorities. In G. Loescher and L. Monahan (eds), *Refugees and International Relations*, pp. 63–84. Oxford: Clarendon Press.

Kibreab, G. (1989) Local settlements in Africa: a misconceived option? *Journal of Refugee Studies*, 2 (4), 468–90.

Kibreab, G. (1993) The myth of dependency among camp refugees in Somalia. *Journal of Refugee Studies*, 4 (6), 321–49.

Kirkby, J., Kleist, T., Frerks, G., Flikkema, W. and O'Keefe, P. (1997) UNHCR's cross border operations in Somalia: the value of quick impact projects for refugee resettlement. *Journal of Refugee Studies*, 10 (2), 181–98.

Kok, W. (1989) Self-settled refugees and the socio-economic impact of their presence on Kassala, eastern Sudan. *Journal of Refugee Studies*, 2 (4), 419–40.

Larkin, M.A., Cuny, F. and Stein, B.N. (eds) (1991) *Repatriation under Conflict in Central America*. Washington, DC: CIPRA and Intertec Institute.

Loescher, G. (1993) *Beyond Charity: International Co-operation and the Global Refugee Crisis*. New York: Oxford University Press.

Loescher, G. and Monahan, L. (eds) (1990) *Refugees and International Relations*. Oxford: Clarendon Press.

Macrae, J. (1997) Aiding an unstable world: some thoughts on relief and development assistance after the Cold War. Unpublished paper at an Oxfam Seminar on Conflict, Oxford, January.

Macrae, J. and Zwi, A. (eds) (1994) *War and Hunger: Rethinking International Responses to Complex Emergencies*. London: Zed Books in association with Save the Children Fund.

Macnamara, D. (1989) The origins and effects of 'humane deterrence' policies in South-east Asia. In G. Loescher and L. Monahan (eds), *Refugees and International Relations*, pp. 123–34. Oxford: Clarendon Press.

Mazur, R.E. (1987) Linking popular initiatives and aid agencies: the case of refugees. *Development and Change*, 18, 437–61.

Morss, E. (1984) Institutional destruction resulting from donor and project proliferation in sub-Saharan African countries. *World Development*, 12 (4), 465–70.

Mortimer, E. (1997) The treatment of refugees and asylum seekers: an essay on a Ditchley Foundation conference held at Ditchley Park, Oxfordshire, UK, 27–29 September 1996. *Journal of Refugee Studies*, 10 (2), 199–207.

OECD (1993) *Human Rights, Refugees, Migrants and Development: Directory of NGOs in OECD Countries*. Paris: OECD.

Oxfam (1996) *Development in States of War*. Oxford: Oxfam.

Randel, J. and German, T. (eds) (1996) *The Reality of Aid 1996: An Independent Review of International Aid*. London: Earthscan ICVA.

Richmond, A.H. (1994) *Global Apartheid: Refugees Racism and the New World Order*. Toronto: Oxford University Press.

Robinson, V. (1993) Marching into the middle classes? The long term resettlement of East African Asians in the UK. *Journal of Refugee Studies*, 6 (3), 230–47.

Rogers, R. and Copeland, E. (1993) Forced migration: policy issue in the post-Cold War world. Fletcher School of Law and Diplomacy, Tufts University.

Rogge, R. (1991) Repatriation of refugees: a not so simple option. UNRISD Symposium Papers. Geneva: UNRISD.

Slim, H. (1997) Doing the right thing: relief agencies, moral dilemmas and moral responsibility in political emergencies and war. *Studies on Emergencies and Disaster Relief*, Report No. 6. Uppsala: Nordic Africa Institute/SIDA.

Stepputat, F. (1994) Repatriation and the politics of space: the case of the Mayan diaspora and return movements. *Journal of Refugee Studies*, 7 (2/3), 175–85.

Storey, A. (1997) Non-neutral humanitarianism: NGOs and the Rwanda crisis. *Development in Practice*, 7 (4), 384–94.

Thorburn, J. (1995) Transcending boundaries: temporary protection and burden sharing in Europe. *International Journal of Refugee Law*, 7 (3), 459–81.

UNDP (1987) *Report on a Programming Mission for Longterm Assistance to Displaced Persons in Malawi Oct/Nov 1987*. New York: UNDP.

UNHCR (1989) *Lessons Learned Survey: Mozambican Refugee Emergency*. UNHCR TSS Mission Report 89/39. Geneva: UNHCR.

UNHCR (1994) NGOs and the UNHCR. *Refugees*, 97 (3). Geneva: UNHCR.

UNHCR (1995a) Refugees: the high cost. *Refugees*, 102 (4). Geneva: UNHCR.

UNHCR (1995b) *UNHCR and NGOs: Directory of Non-governmental Organisations*. Geneva: UNHCR.

UNHCR (1995c) The human side of CIREFCA. *Refugees*, 99 (1), 15–21. Geneva: UNHCR.

UNHCR (1995d) *The State of the World's Refugees: In Search of Solutions*. New York: Oxford University Press.

UNHCR (1996) *Environmental Guidelines*. Geneva: UNHCR.

UNHCR (1997a) Rebuilding a war-torn society: a review of the UNHCR reintegration programme for Mozambican returnees, UNHCR, 1996. *Refugee Survey Quarterly*, 16 (2), 24–72.

UNHCR (1997b) *The State of the World's Refugees: A Humanitarian Agenda*. Oxford: Oxford University Press.

UNHCR (1997c) UNHCR at a glance. *Refugees*, 109 (3). Geneva: UNHCR.

UNRISD (1995) *States of Disarray: The Social Effects of Globalisation*. London: UNRISD/Banton.

US Committee for Refugees (USCR) (1996) *World Refugee Survey*. Washington, DC: USCR.

Vincent, R.J. (1989) Political and economic refugees: problems of asylum and resettlement. Report of the Ditchley Conference, Ditchley Park, Oxfordshire, 13–15 October 1989. *Journal of Refugee Studies*, 2 (4), 504–12.

Walkup, M. (1997) Policy dysfunction in humanitarian organisations: the role of coping strategies, institutions and organisational culture. *Journal of Refugee Studies*, 10 (1), 37–60.

Warner, D. (1994) Voluntary repatriation and the meaning of return home: a critique of liberal mathematics. *Journal of Refugee Studies*, 7 (2/3), 160–74.

Wilson, K. B. (1992) Enhancing refugees' own food acquisition strategies. *Journal of Refugee Studies*, 5 (3/4), 226–56.

Wilson, K.B., Cammack, D.R. and Shumba, F. (1989) *Mozambicans in Malawi: A Study of Aid, Livelihood and Development*. Oxford: Refugee Studies Programme; Rome: World Food Programme.

World Bank (1997) *World Development Report: The State in a Changing World*. Oxford: Oxford University Press.

Zetter, R. (1988) Refugees: a label and an agenda. Editorial introduction to the first issue of the *Journal of Refugee Studies*. *Journal of Refugee Studies*, 1 (1), 1–6.

Zetter, R. (1991) Labelling refugees: forming and transforming a bureaucratic identity. *Journal of Refugee Studies*, 4 (1), 39–62.

Zetter, R. (1992) Refugees and forced migrants as development resources: the Greek-Cypriot refugees from 1974. *Cyprus Review*, 4 (1), 7–39.

Zetter, R. (1995a) Incorporation and exclusion: the life cycle of Malawi's refugee assistance programme. *World Development*, 23 (10), 1653–67.

Zetter, R. (1995b) Shelter provision and settlement policies for refugees. *Studies on Emergencies and Disaster Relief*, Report No. 2. Uppsala: Nordic Africa Institute/SIDA.

Zetter, R. (1996a) Refugee survival and NGO project assistance: Mozambican refugees in Malawi. *Community Development Journal*, 31 (3), 214–29.

Zetter, R. (1996b) Indigenous NGOs and refugee assistance: some lessons from Malawi and Zimbabwe. *Development in Practice*, 6 (1), 37–49.

Zolberg, A., Suhrke, A. and Aguayo, S. (1989) *Escape from Violence: Conflict and the Refugee Crisis in the Developing World*. New York: Oxford University Press.

4

Modernity, globalization, refugees and displacement

Howard Adelman

Introduction

The experience of refugees can be understood only within the context of institutions and norms created to deal with the issue of forced migration. This chapter is intended to situate the refugee experience within the context of modernization and globalization, particularly the transformations wrought since World War II. The thesis is simple. Refugees are the products of modernity. Their plight became acute when the processes of modernity became globalized, when the political system of nation-states first became extended over the whole globe and efforts were made to sort the varied nations of the world into political states. When this nationalist rationalization itself seemed to threaten the rule of reason, a significant shift took place. This occurred in the post-World War II period when normative globalization was instituted. Instead of trying to make nations and states congruent, the stability of states and borders was to be maintained. Loyalty to the state would be inculcated through the rights and privileges accorded citizens. When states failed to provide such protection, the persecuted subjects who fled those states would be protected by states that recognized the rights of individuals; those refugees would be protected as if they were citizens, either by the states which provided refuge or by the international system responsible for the implementation of those universal norms. Economic globalization began to undermine this refugee regime in turn as the instruments of modernity proved inadequate in coping with the refugee crisis. A third refugee regime is emerging which goes back to the basic principles of modernity, stressing individual rationality, self-reliance and self-determination in resolving the plight of refugees, once again resorting to placing the primary stress on the nation-state (cf. Westin's discussion of Chapter 2) as the instrument of modernity with which to deal with a refugee crisis.

Modernity

The essence of modernity is the religion of rationality.[1] The religion of reason labels any other form of religious faith as superstition and makes it incumbent on all adherents to this rational religion of the enlightenment to attempt to transform the world into one which mirrors rational thought. Rationality is defined as reflective thought which conforms to the actual operation of the world. The measure of the rational is the utility of objects, and the utility of thought in comprehending and mastering the world. To ensure that the dual sovereignty of reason and evidence reign, critique is applied to prevent irrationality from corrupting the modern Western faith in evidential rationality.

What are the enemies of the religion of reason? There are three. The tissue of superstitions, prejudices and errors shared by the masses is the first. For example, if most people believe, at least deep down, that our skin colour or physical characteristics on the outside reflect inner character differences or intellectual capacities, in spite of the enlightenment attack on such false beliefs for over two hundred years, then such racial convictions must be strenuously attacked by the religion of reason. Racism has no place in the rational enlightenment. Nor do any other set of beliefs which deny that reason ultimately unites us all. The religion of reason recognizes that there are divisions among people, but that whatever divides us, we are united in being rational.

Second, the reason for any false consciousness among the masses (the elevation of any other factor above reason) is attributed to an élite, an evil élite, a priesthood which has led the masses astray in order to gain power and control for itself. For Karl Marx, traditional religion was the opiate of the masses. But the heirs of Marx became a priesthood of a collectivist materialist religion in the name of the avant-garde of the Communist Party, which labelled enemies by a different externality: their ownership of property rather than the colour of their skin. Or, in the cruel religion of Leninism, it was simply by their opposition to the Bolshevik priesthood then in charge.[2] These ideologues of communism were revealed to be far more evil than the priesthood of the traditional religious establishment ever managed to be. They constructed a mental ideological order that bore little resemblance to the rational order of the world and produced the most dysfunctional system in the worship of functionality. The house of cards they constructed collapsed in on itself. In contrast, atavistic and/or corrupt pre-enlightenment dictatorial leaders who remain in power are overwhelmingly remnants of premodern thought rather than exemplifications of the religion of modernity gone mad. With the downfall of the most irrational religion among the panoply of religious rationality, with the end of faith in the communist ideology, faith in any avant-garde priesthood seems to have suffered a severe, if not fatal blow.

The third enemy of the rational enlightenment is despotism. When a ruler constituted himself as an authority over all others, he was guilty not only of usurping the rights of those who were ruled, but of offending against the enlightenment itself. For the premise of the enlightenment is that each individual, and only the individual, has within him- or herself the power to think and to make rules governing the collectivity and, therefore, to delegate the power for making such rules to a representative. No one has the right to usurp that power.

Thus, individual rights and critical rationality form the bedrock of modernity to resist the enemy of mass gullibility. For mass superstition is not an inherent feature of individual human beings, but is attributed to an élite of 'con artists' who become the ideologues of an intellectual 'pyramid scam' to rob the people of their ability to think for themselves. When this happens, the political realm is left open for tyrants to exploit the people and grind them down physically as well as intellectually.

The vehicle of modernity for transforming premodern superstitious realms into a rational order of individual freedom has been the modern nation-state. The state is perceived to be the instrument for actualizing the ethical ideals of modernity, an instrument whereby a collectivity of individual wills can guarantee each individual's freedom of conscience and thought at the same time as each individual can possess rights and freedoms only if he or she is a member of a state. Paradoxically, the supreme authority for protecting those rights is vested in the state, since the only way an individual can possess freedom in the modern world is if he or she is a member of a state.[3]

Within the protective cover of the state, the individual is free to pursue his or her desires, which in their most abstract form are expressed by the desire to extend the self. If negative freedom is defined by rights, positive freedom is defined by interests. If individual rights are the bedrock norms of the individual in the nation-state, possessive individualism is the most positive expression of that freedom. But possessive individualism leads to competitiveness. And the states need passions which bind in addition to those which encourage individualism and competition. The cohesiveness of the aggregate of individual members of the state depends on a sentimental identification of each member with one another in some form of nationalism or another. The character of the nation depends on an irrational foundation of sentiment and not reason. Individuals are bound to other individuals in a community through membership in the same nation. Thus, the political realm has two radically different dimensions, an affective one of communitarian feeling and a rational one of individual membership. 'The modern era began with the creation of separate, independent sovereign states, each of them organized around a particular nation, with its own language and culture, maintaining a government that was legitimated as expressing the national will, or national interests'

(Toulmin, 1990, p. 7). The individual private realm also has two dimensions: the pursuit of rational self-interest in the civil society quite separate from the state, and the dependence on the state to protect the rights of the individual, a state which controls entry into membership.[4]

Therefore, modernity is, politically, a doubly dichotomous conception, consisting of both individuals and collectivities, individuals with both interests and rights, and collectivities which bind people together through sentimental national attachments while controlling membership and ensuring rights to individuals through the state as the expression of rational instrumentality. Modernity is also a diachronic concept, defining a period in history differing from all previous periods in very optimistic terms. Previous periods not governed by modernistic premises were, and contemporary geographical areas still living in a premodern world are, infected with dark superstitions and irrational beliefs, without the freedom, rationality and civilization characteristic of our purportedly tolerant, enlightened age which respects the integrity and dignity of the individual and the ability of scientific rationality and technical progress to thrust us out of a dark and impoverished system.

The effect of modernity was to create a rational faith in a cosmopolitan world in which rich inherited traditions were equated with superstition, where well-grounded moral precepts were viewed as restrictions of the rights of free thought and behaviour, where spiritual sensibility and the faith in another who has absolute authority over oneself were seen as the ultimate surrender of the right to self-determination (Connolly, 1993). Self-certainty or trust in oneself, proceeding with systematic rationality to deal with issues, and beginning with a clean slate free of traditions, was the foundation of a rational order (Toulmin, 1990, p. 179). The only criteria for action can be those one has fashioned by oneself and legislated for oneself.[5] Into this cosmopolitan culture of universalism, subjective consumerism combined with objective bureaucratic rationality move the world towards a global economic order. Globalization is the synchronic completion of the diachronic concept of modernity (Featherstone, 1990).

Globalization

Globalization means many things. I shall divide it here into three phases: physical globalization, in which the whole earth is treated as a single entity (McNeill, 1992); normative globalization, in which the principles of modernity become universal as norms – though not as practices – around the world; and economic globalization, in which abstract principles are united with practical production and distribution processes of goods and services.

On the natural end of the spectrum of geographical globalization, the globe is considered as a single environment. Global warming affects all life on the earth. The perturbations produced by a two- to four-degree rise in temperature over the next few decades will increase the amount of extreme weather that will afflict us all, not only those living in vulnerable agricultural zones. Physical globalization also refers to the radical transformation in the ease of travel from one part of the globe to another.[6] If there are droughts in northern Kenya, the movements of people in the area to escape drought and gain access to food will have repercussions in as remote a location as Canada, as some of those affected by the local dislocations seek new lives in a more stable environment. But the most critical aspect of physical globalization for our purposes is the division of the whole world into one political system of nation-states.

Normative globalization entails the celebration of the individual and the adoption of the principles of individual rights and rational standards as universal norms. Utility and functionality become the measures of that rationality at war with superstition, priestly ideological élites and despots. Freedom of conscience and thought of individuals become the foundations for a self-legislating political order (Held, 1995; Krasner, 1983). International institutions as well as nation-states assume responsibility for monitoring and enforcing those norms (Brown, 1992; Diehl, 1997).

Most commonly, however, globalization refers to the current dramatic changes in the world economy (Mittleman, 1996). Globalization is characterized by the total abstraction of capital in the form of instantly transferable 'money' through electronic means anywhere around the world, so that investment capital can shift readily and rapidly to whichever location will show the best return on investment. The rationality of the market is opposed to any artificial boundaries of currency controls, tariffs, duties, etc. which impede the flow of capital, services or goods around the world. The world of global capital is totally divorced from both nature and history, where value depends primarily on the faith in the global system itself.

Economic globalization is based on a consumer culture in which the quest for consumer goods by all humans around the world – not simply the means to feed, clothe and house oneself in a secure way – becomes the driving force of the economy. The pure abstraction of capital (divorced from both nature and history) conjoined by subjective desire (focused on consumer goods for the individual) is seen to be best realized in a system in which the market becomes the arbiter of rationality. Instead of élite planners, the market, the collectivity of individual decisions around the world, is left to redistribute production resources so that manufacturing can shift rapidly to low-wage areas, and goods are best marketed globally as standard products. In such a system, governments increasingly transform themselves into 'trade boosters' for locally based enterprises and gradually reduce their role as guarantors of the well-being of the commonwealth; the welfare state slips into decline as a distortion of the market economy and an impediment on the ability of one state to compete with another.

The priesthood for global economic rationality is made up of neo-liberal ideologues. The fundamentals of the faith require that all regions and nations undergo massive restructuring and adjustment to get rid of the burden of bloated state bureaucracies and health, education and welfare establishments that act as a crippling weight on the flexibility and responsiveness of the entrepreneurial capacities of individuals and firms. To respond to the challenge of globalization, developed states have pursued strategies involving the reduction of state debts, the downsizing of the workforce in both government and large firms, the expansion of trade through reduced tariffs, and the creation of larger, more encompassing free trade zones, reduced production costs using techno-logical and production innovation such as post-Fordist manufacturing and just-in-time delivery systems, and reductions in the costs of the state allocated to the productive sector. Rational economic efficiency has become the mantra, even as widespread social pain may be its cost in the utilitarian faith that short-term pain is necessary to achieve long-term gain and, hence, happiness for the greatest number.

Globalization also has an affective side. When the political nation-state system spread over the whole globe, affects were attached to nations. When the global system became a normative system of universal values upholding the rights of individuals, our compassion went out to the needs of those individuals who were deprived. And when economic globalization became the dominant force of our time, that compassion for others was fused with pride in our own nation and demands that it do something for those who were suffering. For in addition to the globalization of instrumental rationality in the neo-liberal ideal of the market, there is also a globalization of sentiment and symbols facilitated by global television. Ironically, though the world of radio made information available globally, its primary affective impact was to arouse panic; radio proved to be the best instrument to heighten irrational fears and divide people and became the ideal instrument for dictators to stoke hatred and enmity, whether used by the Nazi propaganda machine or Radio Mille Collines in Rwanda to arouse genocidal passions among the Hutus against the Tutsis. Television, on the other hand, is a medium for fostering sentimental global unity. Watching scenes of starving children in Africa evokes pity and compassion. Political action is soon dictated by the politics of sentiment as viewers watching the plight of helpless refugees demand action by their governments to intervene to provide protection for those refugees.

If the trademarks of physical globalization are the nation and the state, if the trademarks of normative globalization are abstract individual rights and self-determination, the trademarks of economic globalization are both universal greed and, paradoxically, a demand to take action based on compassion for others.

Refugees, displacement, modernity and the separation of peoples

Where do refugees fit in terms of both modernity and globalization?[7] They are the most symbolic exemplification of the rallying cry of modernity, for refugees are viewed as the products of the dark, irrational forces of premodernity, while their salvation is the epitome of what modernity stands for in its most virtuous guise. At the same time, whereas all ages have witnessed people forced to move from their homes, refugees are a creation of the modern world. They are not just forced migrants but are part and parcel of the development of the nation-state (Zolberg *et al.*, 1986).

The term 'refugee' was first applied to the Huguenots, French Protestants who fled religious persecution in France at the end of the sixteenth and the beginning of the seventeenth century – at the dawn of modernity.[8] The modern concept of a refugee is inseparable from the conceptions of Protestantism and its revolt against what it believed to be medieval superstition. Protestantism stood for individual conscience as a determinant of faith and religious practice. It was also a revolt against a medieval sacramental system in which a divine being doled out rewards and punishments based on human deeds; do what you are told and do penance for your failures as determined by ecclesiastical authority. Protestantism was the break with the need for an intermediary between humans and God within Christianity. Against hierarchical authority stood a communion in which each person was his own priest. Within the earthly realm, individual choice and human reason ruled. Only in the sacred realm were humans required to surrender themselves to divine will. Individual salvation in the eternal world was the agent of divine grace, provided, of course, that the individual surrendered him- or herself to the force of that grace. But the corollary was that salvation in the earthly realm depended on human effort alone. Protestantism is identified with the celebration of the individual and the freedom of that individual, with instrumental rationality being the way to deal with the affairs of this world. Modernity is but the universalization of this Protestant ideology while bracketing the theology of salvation in the next world.

In France in the latter part of the sixteenth and the beginning of the seventeenth centuries, many in the intellectual classes as well as the middle class and the aristocracy became Protestants. Religious war broke out between the Catholics and Protestants of France. The fight was over power and the divine right of royal succession. But it was most emblematically about tolerance. The Edict of Nantes, issued by Henry

IV just before the end of the sixteenth century, promised the Protestants complete religious freedom. But the seventeenth century witnessed both the growth in power and strength of the Protestants and their increased persecution at the hands of the absolute monarch, culminating in 1685 with the revocation of the Edict of Nantes. Up to a million refugees – the Huguenots – fled to England, Germany, the Netherlands, and the British colonies in America.

The Huguenots were archetypically refugees of modernity, not only because they stood for the values of modernity – individualism, tolerance for different beliefs, and the rule of reason, at least in this world – but also because they were products of a state apparatus used to drive out anyone who did not conform to a homogeneous identity of the nation (in this case, in terms of religion) and the whims of a despot. Those who engaged in persecution were defenders of an authoritarian system inherited from the medieval world determined to crush individual freedom and the rights of freedom of conscience and belief. It would not be until 1787, just before the French Revolution and the overthrow of the absolute monarchy of Louis XVI, that Protestant marriages were legally recognized in France.

Refugees have come to characterize the twentieth century because it was only in the twentieth century that the total globe was colonized and set on a course of being divided into self-governing nation-states. The nation-state epitomized the contradictions of modernity. On the one hand, each nation-state consolidated itself around a sentimental communal and sometimes atavistic sense of a homogeneous nation. At the same time, the state was the vehicle of universal citizenship and, in idealist liberal belief, the upholder and defender of individual rights. The result was that people were pushed out of one territory because of the rise of one form of virulent homogeneous ideology or another, resulting in persecution. The rational instruments of a modern state bureaucratic system rose up to prevent individuals entering the territory of a state of which they were not members. Those not tolerated by a nation-state had fewer and fewer 'free' territories to which to flee, and, by the twentieth century, none at all as the whole globe became divided among nation-states in the first phase of physical globalization (Marrus, 1985).

Thus, the twentieth century became the century of refugees, not because it was extraordinary in forcing people to flee, but because of the division of the globe into nation-states in which states were assigned the role of protectors of rights, but also that of exclusive protectors of their own citizens, including the role of gatekeeper to determine who could become new citizens. When the globe was totally divided into states, those fleeing persecution in one state had nowhere to go but to another state, and required the permission of the other state to enter it.

Three phases emerged in dealing with the issue of refugees in the twentieth century, revealing different modes of coping with the contradictions within the nation-state. Between the World Wars I and II, refugees were dealt with not by challenging the right to set up homogeneous national regimes, but by acceding to those forces as refugees were people expelled by one country to cleanse that country of an alien nationality. Population exchange and, to some degree, border adjustments became the major model for dealing with a refugee population, a situation barely changed since the Protestant countries took in the Huguenots who fled France in the seventeenth and eighteenth centuries. Thus, the Greek–Turkish population exchanges in 1922–3 were attempts to solve the refugee crisis produced by the formation of nation-states out of the disintegration of the Ottoman Empire by shifting people to different political jurisdictions so that they could be integral elements in the national self-definition.[9] The state would look after their rights and allow their expression as individuals. Membership in a purportedly homogeneous nation would look after their sentimental attachments.

The modern system of dealing with the refugee problem by sorting everyone out into nation-states did not work for those who lacked a territorial base to which they could return. The system (which, in effect, endorsed the right of nation-states to exclude those attempting to enter their states as they fled persecution) came to haunt the countries of the West after World War II. The genocide of 6 million Jews may have been the direct responsibility of the Nazis, but the death of 6 million exemplified the moral failure of Western countries which had prevented all but a token number of Jews from obtaining sanctuary (Abella and Troper, 1982; Wasserstein, 1979; Wyman, 1968, 1985).

In the immediate few years after the end of World War II, the interwar period definition of a refugee as a product of population exchanges persisted, and population redistribution and exchange continued at first as the method of handling the refugee problem. Population exchange took place on a massive scale between the new states of India and Pakistan in 1948. The prewar method of dealing with refugees was signified by the debate in the UN after the war over whether the Jews of Europe were displaced persons or refugees. If displaced persons, they would have to be returned to their countries of origin. If refugees, they would be entitled to resettlement in other countries and territories. Lest that other territory be Palestine, the UK and the Arab states opposed designating the remnant of Jews in the refugee camps of Europe as refugees.[10] But the majority of states then in the UN thought otherwise, and voted to designate the Jews as refugees. The vast majority of Jewish refugees sought resettlement in locations other than the countries from which they had fled. When most countries would not take them in or took in only token numbers, most of the Jewish refugees opted to go to Palestine.

In Palestine, one of the last efforts of nationalities – Palestinians and Jews – attempting to sort themselves out territorially and politically took place from the 1940s until the 1990s, and is still continuing (Adelman, 1983, 1986, 1994a, 1995, 1997; Abu-Lughod, 1988). In this remnant of a prewar method of dealing with refugees, the United Nations Relief and Works Agency for Palestine Refugees in the Near East (UNRWA) (Adelman, 1992) was created in 1950, not to provide legal protection for individuals suffering from persecution, but to integrate economically the Arab refugees from those portions of Palestine which were now controlled by the Jewish Zionists into the surrounding Arab states into which they had fled (Adelman, 1988), just as the Jewish Palestine refugees forced to flee from the Arab-controlled sector had fled and were absorbed into the new state of Israel. But the old system did not seem to work any longer, as the Palestinians and Arabs in general resisted the solution because they identified the Jews not as a local rival nation, but as the remnant of colonialism which needed to be pushed back to Europe from which the Zionist Jews originally came. This ignored, of course, the fact that the dynamic of ethnic sorting had created an Israel in which, until the arrival of the Jews from the former USSR in the 1990s, the majority of Jews in Israel were Jews from Arab lands who fled from fear of persecution following the creation of Israel. By the time the Middle East peace process caught up with partition and the dividing of a territory between competing national groups unable to coexist politically in the same state, UNRWA had become the largest international organization in the world with over 20,000 employees. UNRWA had evolved into the education and, in part, health and welfare ministry of the Palestinian people, and a guaranteed conduit of assistance to Palestinians from wealthy donor countries.

After the late 1940s, the exchange of populations as a method of dealing with refugees had seemed to be part of the ancient past until revived in the 1990s. The pre-World War II methods of dealing with conflicts by sorting out nationalities and adjusting borders re-emerged in the Balkans. As Yugoslavia disintegrated, genocidal warfare and a redistribution of population took place among the former republics of Yugoslavia and within those republics. The hellish warfare in the territory, and then the genocide of a million Tutsi in Rwanda in 1994 (Prunier, 1995; Adelman with Suhrke, 1996), seemed to augur a return to an earlier and even weaker system for settling intrastate conflicts and dealing with the plight of refugees. Yugoslavia and Rwanda were not the only regions to fall back on ethnic cleansing as a method for dealing with refugees. In the war over the predominantly Armenian enclave of Nagorno-Karabakh in Azerbaijan, 400,000 Armenian refugees were forced to flee from the remainder of Azerbaijan, while 700,000 Azeris and Kurds fled Armenia, Nagorno-Karabakh and the areas of Azerbaijan captured by the Armenian separatists by the time the ceasefire was signed in December 1994 (Rieff, 1997).

The state, international norms and a new refugee regime

Modernity divided the world into nation-states and relied on states to defend the members of their nation and the rights of their individual members. Refugees proved to be the Achilles' heel of the system. For if one group of nation-states did not provide protection for its own people and instead persecuted them, and if other states would not take them in under the argument that they were responsible only for defending the rights of their own citizens and those who shared the dominant nationality, then individuals were left bereft and unprotected by the system. And with the division of the whole globe into nation-states, there was nowhere to go for these refugees. Further, there were too many nations, possibly 5000. An international system was hard enough to develop on the basis of 150 or even 200 states. This was particularly true when decolonialization built up a full head of steam, and the new states, particularly in Africa, often consisted of many different nationalities (Adelman and Sorenson, 1994).

After World War II, a new international system emerged which depended for its security not on population exchanges and border adjustments, but on the sanctity of borders and a new international system for people who were forced to flee regimes which failed to provide for their protection. The development of the system was helped by the widespread belief that war and conflicts were primarily products of unrestrained irrational nationalism or international collectivist totalitarian ideology.

Two systems developed: an obligatory and a voluntary one. The obligatory system for dealing with refugees focused on the rights of individuals, on a universal system of law, and the protection of those who had a well-founded fear of persecution. The shift from the stress on the nation to the individual was epitomized by the creation of the international regime for defining and dealing with refugees (see Chapter 3). The international refugee convention was passed during the immediate post-World War II period in 1950 to define a refugee as an *individual* whose rights had been breached, because the person had developed a well-founded fear of persecution on one of the presumably atavistic grounds of collective homogenization – such as religious or political beliefs or race. UNHCR was created as the international agency responsible for the protection of these refugees. At first, the definition applied only to refugees produced in Europe, but as the concept of the nation-state was globalized with postwar decolonization, so too was the individualistic concept of the refugee, and the 1967 Protocol was passed in which the Convention definition of a refugee became universal.

The universalization of the refugee regime replaced the pre-World War II system of national sorting and boundary adjustments. But its jurisdiction stopped at the border of any nation-state. Though it was a regime focused on individuals, rights and persecution, the regime applied to individuals only if they were not within the borders of their home states. The concept of 'refugee' applied to those persons who had crossed a border and were no longer within the jurisdiction of the nation-state in which the individuals allegedly suffered the persecution. Those who were forced to flee but did not cross a border were now termed 'displaced' and were differentiated from refugees. Displacement no longer meant a person outside the borders of his or her home state who could be and ought to be sent home, but a person displaced *within* a home state outside the protection of the international refugee regime. If the concept of the 'nation' had been the key to the refugee regime in the pre-World War II period, the state – source of sovereignty and site of sanctuary – became central to the postwar refugee regime.

Alongside this system, which became obligatory for any nation-state that signed the Convention, a voluntary system emerged for dealing with large masses of refugees who fled for various reasons, but where alleged individual persecution was not the central issue. Refugees from Hungary in 1956 (Adelman, 1991, 1994b), from Czechoslovakia in 1968, from Uganda in 1972, from Chile in 1973, were in flight from regimes which were generally oppressive, whether or not the individuals who had fled had been targeted for persecution. This was true of many Central Americans and Indochinese who fled their countries in the 1970s and 1980s. These refugees were resettled as humanitarian refugees rather than as Convention refugees by a voluntary system of resettlement into countries of asylum. Those countries were not obliged to take in the refugees, but their humanitarianism combined with their self-interest in admitting immigrants with skills and talents (particularly when this intake complemented their ideological opposition to the regimes from which the refugees fled) meant that many refugees could be accommodated.

Why did this regime begin to founder during the 1980s? There were too many people: the population of the world had expanded from 1 billion at the beginning of the century and was approaching 6 billion by the end. There were too many wars, primarily intrastate wars. Refugees from the Iran–Iraq war, refugees from the overthrow of the Shah in Iran, the civil war in Sri Lanka and the civil war in Lebanon, the 5 million refugees from the horrific Afghan war, refugees from the persecutions in Myanmar, and from the many wars in Africa (from Mozambique and Angola, from the even more vicious successor to Idi Amin, from wars in Liberia and Sudan, in Somalia and Ethiopia, from the war between the Islamic fundamentalists and those who resisted a religious takeover in Algeria) – refugees from wars all over the world began to flood Western states.

In the pre-World War II refugee regime, the nation-state was the instrument for solving the problem of refugees by focusing on nationality and moving populations and borders to align nationalities with states. In the postwar refugee regime, the focus became the state rather than the nation. Borders remained sacrosanct, and refugees were recognized as having rights to the protection of some state. The permanent resolution of the refugee problem required either return to the state from which the refugee had fled, settlement in the country of first asylum, or resettlement abroad. Those refugees who reached the border or airport of a state that had signed the Convention could claim refugee status as a matter of right.

This mushrooming of the refugee population seeking security occurred in conjunction with three other developments: (1) the ease of access to transportation that occurred with globalization; (2) the legalization of the Convention protection within the domestic codes of developed states; and (3) economic crises in developed states, at the same time as globalization and automation reduced the need for unskilled labour. The primary challenge came with the rise of the numbers of refugees claiming asylum as Convention refugees. In signing the refugee convention, a nation-state had surrendered absolute control over the most sensitive and central aspect of its sovereignty, the right of the nation-state to determine who could and who could not become members. At the beginning of the 1980s, even though many countries had signed the Geneva Convention on refugees, Convention refugees were a very tiny part of the international refugee regime. That is, there were very few refugees who landed in a Western developed country and demanded the right to stay and be protected by that country because they were a refugee. The surrender of absolute sovereignty had been slight and only token. Increased intrastate conflicts, modern global communications and transportation, and the internationalization of a rights regime within the domestic law of developed states combined to force changes in the system. For example, at the beginning of the 1980s, less than 300 persons arrived in Canada each year to claim refugee status. By the end of the 1980s that number had increased one hundredfold. What was envisioned to be a tiny surrender of sovereignty was beginning to be seen as an ominous one as each year the equivalent of perhaps 0.1 per cent of the population of a country arrived at the doorstep (or, more frequently, at an international airport) to claim refugee status. Over a ten-year period, 1 per cent of a population would claim refugee status and membership by right so long as they could establish that they were Convention refugees.

Further, once those refugees had arrived in the country, the very rights regime that expressed the essence of modernity was extended to ensure that those refugees had the same rights as did a citizen. In the landmark *Singh* case in Canada,[11] the existing regime established to adjudicate refugee claims at the beginning of the 1980s was deemed illegal because it did not allow the credibility of the refugee to be assessed by allowing the refugee to appear before the tribunal hearing the claim. A new system was put in place which enhanced the ability of refugees to make successful claims.

The numbers increased dramatically. The rights to hearings, to counsel, to welfare – it varied by jurisdiction – also increased to provide those in a country with many of the same rights and protections as citizens of the country. Those who believed that they were defending the sacrosanct character of borders and the right of states to choose their own members counter-attacked, impelled by chronic high levels of unemployment as the need for raw labour in manufacturing shifted to low-cost Third World regimes, and a backlash to immigration grew in response to rising chronic unemployment and the availability of only lower-wage service jobs (see Westin's analysis in Chapter 2). A host of measures were introduced to prevent refugee claimants as well as other illegal migrants from getting through the portals of a country in the first place. Visa requirements were extended to apply to those arriving from many new countries from which visas had never previously been required. Severe and effective carrier sanctions were introduced against airlines for transporting passengers who lacked the proper documentation permitting entry into the country. As the tide of globalization began to appear to overwhelm the sanctity of the modern nation-state, using its most central precepts of rights to widen the portals, dikes were thrown up to resist the forces of globalization that seemed to bring more and more refugees to claim the protection of developed countries.

At the same time, globalization, which is the culmination of the enlightenment religion in our contemporary period, released forces which have contributed to the increased production of refugees as well as the increased reluctance of developed states to allow them to enter their territory (Wiener, 1995; Cornelius *et al.*, 1994). Take the case of refugee warriors. Refugee warriors are the products of long-term conflicts; their status remains unresolved because the original conflict was not solved and no permanent resolution has been found to the refugee crisis. Though the universal refugee regime is supposed to ensure that no refugee is left without the protection of a state to which he or she can belong, the reality is that permanent solutions have not been found for many refugees. The Palestinians were the best-known case of refugee warriors, but they were also the only post-World War II refugees legally omitted from the protection of the refugee convention; the interwar solution was intended to be applied to them to solve their problem, but it never became operational until the 1990s.

The Tutsi refugees who fled the revolution and overthrow of the monarchy, and the establishment of a Hutu regime in 1959–62 in Rwanda, were another – if less well-known – example of 'refugee warriors'. When they were not permitted to return to Rwanda, and when the countries immediately surrounding Rwanda to which they had first fled, such as Uganda and Zaire, denied them the right to become equal citizens, the refugees took up arms – allegedly with the tacit support of the existing regime in which they lived – and led an invasion against the dictatorial regime in their home country, Rwanda. This was not in the name of Tutsi return, but in the name of universal justice and opposition to corruption and cronyism (Adelman, 1996a).

Ironically, they were assisted in their cause by other forces of globalization – for, with the end of the Cold War, the protection of human rights, and pressures to institute democracy and good governance, became goals of countries providing aid. Imposing these as conditions of aid, along with other forms of diplomatic pressure, weakened the totalistic power of the regime on its citizens and the media of communication within the country. Further, an even earlier technique intrinsic to globalization had been imposed on countries such as Rwanda: structural adjustment. As the price of core exports and raw materials had fallen in the 1980s – in the case of Rwanda, the price of tin and then its key cash crop, coffee – the balance of payments of the regime was totally thrown out of alignment, and the IMF and World Bank imposed conditions of credit requiring Rwanda to cut its domestic programmes and civil service to cope.

Suddenly, dictatorial regimes, whether benign or ruthless, whether relatively honest or thoroughly corrupt, or weak democracies dominated by a single ethnic group in a multiethnic society and weakened from within by imposed political and economic reforms, were faced with civil war and the need to increase political and economic controls to muster the resources to put down the rebels. Such efforts, of course, only exacerbated the problems. With variations, these problems have been encountered in Afghanistan (with 5 million refugees), Sri Lanka, Sierra Leone, Rwanda and, most recently, Zaire/Congo. As refugee warriors often serve as catalysts of war, their numbers are joined by hundreds of thousands and millions of internally displaced people forced to flee their homes – or refugee camps – to escape the fighting.

As fractures began to emerge in the normative international system for dealing with refugees, as a resurgence in ethnic cleansing and the separation of peoples occurred, the solution to the refugee crisis began to refocus on the sources for their production and the need to ensure that citizens could return to and live in their home states without fear of violence and persecution. And these initiatives were instigated not by the international normative regime, but in spite of it. The era of regional solutions had begun.[12]

Global problems and regional solutions

Fears of an atavistic return to an earlier era, though certainly founded in some of the events just cited, have been offset by many other events that are once again in the process of transforming the international refugee regime, for the third time in the twentieth century. If in the three or four decades after World War II globalization seemed to be the fulfilment of modernity, by the 1990s the nation-state as the primary political vehicle for instituting modernity seemed also to have become the prime victim of globalization. Countries had less and less autonomous control over their production, trade, fiscal and monetary controls, and, most critically of all, the absolute right to select which individuals could become members of the polity. It appeared that the rationality of modernity would have to sacrifice its primary reliance on the nation-state. The postwar regime of dealing with refugees as individuals with legal rights or as mass movements to be dealt with as humanitarian charity cases to await repatriation in refugee camps or for resettlement in new countries had replaced the pre- and immediate post-World War II period of shifting borders and transfers of population. The first system tried to align nationalities and political units at the local level. The second system attempted to develop a global political and humanitarian regime. But the full-blown emergence of globalization undermined the normative regime. Access to refugee determination systems within states was limited. Voluntary resettlement was reduced. The access of refugees from the Third World to the sanctuary of states in the First World was increasingly restricted.

One of the first regional co-ordinated plans indicating the shift was the Comprehensive Plan of Action (CAP) developed in June 1989 to reverse the flight of Indochinese and their quest for asylum. The 'Boat People' movement, which had begun in the latter part of the 1970s, had been one of the largest and most successful voluntary efforts of countries to resettle refugees in First World states. But the reasons for flight seem to have declined as Vietnam followed the pattern of China in maintaining Communist control but developing a market economy. Further, visitors reported that returnees were no longer being sent to labour camps or even discriminated against when they returned. Yet the flights from Vietnam began to increase again in the late 1980s, and Hong Kong, as the prime example, could no longer find countries willing to resettle the long-stayers let alone the new arrivals. As a substitute for forced repatriation, the new plan instituted a refugee determination system, a very restrictive one, for processing refugee claimants as Convention refugees. At the same time, a system of orderly immigration was instituted, primarily to facilitate family reunification. The combination of (1) a Convention refugee adjudication system restricting access for resettlement, (2) the orderly departure programme, and (3) the removal of the threat of persecution of returnees led to a dramatic decline in departures and the end of the Vietnamese 'refugee' problem.

The peace plan for Kampuchea led to a significant emptying of the refugee camps along the Thai border of Kampuchea. In Central America, the regional peace process in the various countries, combined with the reintegration of guerrillas, displaced persons and refugees, worked to reduce dramatically the refugee problem in Central America. A Regional Conference on Migration was held in Puebla, Mexico, in 1996 to take up issues such as return and reintegration as well as the concern of the developed world with trafficking in migrants. Very recently, in Gaborone in Botswana, the countries of former British Africa, excluding Nigeria but including Mozambique, dealt with the issues of human rights, democracy and good governance. Virtually all these countries, which had been mainly dictatorships, white racist regimes, or satraps of such a regime, were now electoral democracies. In some cases, the changes were more apparent than real – Jerry Rawlings transforming himself from a military ruler to an elected head of state – and Daniel arap Moi, though remaining the president of a nominal electoral democracy in Kenya, seemed to be leading his country downwards if the decline in democratic measures is any indication. Nevertheless, even in Africa, the moves to democracy and good governance have gone some way to reduce the causes and circumstances giving rise to refugee flows.

At the same time as these initiatives were taking place in the developing areas of the world, parallel co-operation initiatives were under way in the developed world. This was most marked in Europe, both to create barriers to entry and to attempt to deal with the issue of refugees offshore (Widgren, 1993, 1994; Collinson, 1994; Baldwin-Edwards and Schain, 1994; Claude-Valentin, 1995; see also Chapter 2). The move to restrictionism actually began in the 1970s, but it initially targeted labour migration. By the later part of the 1980s, the focus was on irregular migration and asylum-seekers. The Intergovernmental Consultations on Asylum, Refugee and Migration Policies in Europe, North America and Australia provides an informal forum for co-ordinating refugee policy among all the developed states.

A third international refugee regime was emerging. Economic globalization, which seemed to reduce the degree of autonomy and self-control of any local state, also increased the degree to which a country was responsible for its own survival and success. Local control declined, but local responsibility increased. This was as true in the field of refugees as in the economic realm. If the second phase of the international refugee regime was characterized in Third World countries by an ineffective and self-defeating ideology of import substitution and exporting the peoples of a country as immigrants and refugees, the third phase can be characterized by a focus on economic exports and ensuring that a country's own people can stay or return home. This third wave in the development of the method of dealing with refugees became noticeable in the 1990s. In this phase, globalization, as the culmination of modernity which weakened the nation-state economically, also strengthened the reliance of nation-states on the initiative and enterprise of its own citizens. In the refugee realm, it meant much greater reliance on the initiatives of refugees and their home and host countries to resolve the refugee issue, and less reliance on the initiatives and organizing capacity of the international system. It also meant a direct conflict with the nation-state and the abstract conception of the rights of individuals which so characterized the second phase of modernity when applied to the refugee regime which came to fulfilment in the post-World War II period.

Increased efforts were initiated to settle problems in the regions in which the refugees were produced, including the willingness at times to engage in humanitarian intervention to deal at least with the humanitarian problems of the refugees, if not the military/political/legal problems which gave rise to the refugees in the first place. Most symbolically of all, UNHCR was slowly transformed from an agency dealing with the protection of refugees into one that took as its prime mandate the needs of refugees *and* displaced persons within the borders of their own state. In the 1990s, UNHCR evolved into the largest relief agency organized to serve refugees and displaced persons (see Chapter 3). As Tom Weiss and Amir Pasic argue, though for very different reasons, UNHCR has developed into the foremost single humanitarian agency for setting priorities, raising and distributing resources, and co-ordinating emergency inputs in complex emergencies (Weiss and Pasic, 1997) obviating the need to distinguish between refugees, internally displaced persons, returnees and war victims.

If refugee rights cannot be adequately protected by an international system of law operating through nation-states, and if the system of maintaining refugees in permanent camps as welfare dependants in a complementary system of needs also meets resistance from a world of nation-states unwilling to pay for such services, how can an expanded mandate be handled by the same agency? And what happens to refugee protection as distinct from refugee welfare? The globalization of the media and the politics of sentiment take over to arouse the will of the populace to pressure their governments to intervene actively on behalf of all these casualties of violent conflict (Adelman, 1996b), but the intervention turns into a money machine for international welfare. The international system becomes even more impotent in resolving the source of the violence and the causes of refugee production. An international system of refugee protection built on rights complemented by an international welfare system dealing with refugee needs is replaced by a more global welfare system, but locally based initiatives deal with root causes. The refugees and local regimes take the problem into their own hands, complemented by actions 'forced' on governments by a populace aroused as satellite communications allow the daily portrayal on their television screens of the plight of desperate refugees. If the second phase in the development of an international refugee regime foundered on the fundamental contradiction between the philosophical premises of modernity dependent on a Western nation-state system for its realization when applied to refugees, and the effects on refugees of globalization as the culmination of the development of modernity, a new regime had to develop which was built on local state action and regional initiatives.

If the measure of the rational for modernity is the utility of objects and thought in comprehending and mastering the world, then the utility of international agencies and resettlement states as the prime instruments for dealing with refugees can no longer be supported. The ultimate dual sovereignty of reason and evidence have determined that an international institutional system cannot solve the refugee crisis, either by forming states for every nation, or by acting as the prime protector of individuals. Four arguments – empirical, instrumental, legal and moral – support this contention that a global refugee regime based on local responsibility and regional initiatives is emerging to bypass the dependence on developed nation-states and international institutions, while the international system evolves as an interim welfare 'stop-gap' for those who are victims of these violent conflicts, whether they be refugees, displaced persons or returnees.

The empirical argument is based on the pattern of refugee flows (see Figure 4.1). Refugee numbers reached a world peak in 1990 with the demise of the Cold War, as the crumbling of the Soviet empire generally ended the need of the citizens of those territories to flee persecution by the state. The number of refugees in the Middle East had begun to decline in the same period.

The number of refugees from South and Central America had begun to diminish just a few years before, as the civil wars in those areas began to be replaced by legal regimes which recognized and took cognizance of the political legitimacy of both sides and as more and more dictators in Latin America were replaced by democratic regimes. The rise of the Asian tigers corresponded with a sharp decline in refugees produced in Asia, though serious trouble spots remained – Sri Lanka and Myanmar are examples. The one region in which the number of refugees continued to increase was Africa, but even in Africa the latter part of the 1990s has witnessed a number of refugee returns, the most dramatic being the return of the Hutu refugees to Rwanda. It is the African examples that I will use to make my main instrumental, legal and moral arguments that a new refugee regime is emerging.

The international regime was unable to resolve the plight of the Tutsis from Rwanda over a thirty-year period, either by ensuring they could return or by ensuring they could gain equality of citizenship in the countries of settlement surrounding Rwanda. They went to war to solve the problem on their own. In the Rwandan civil war, over 2 million Hutu

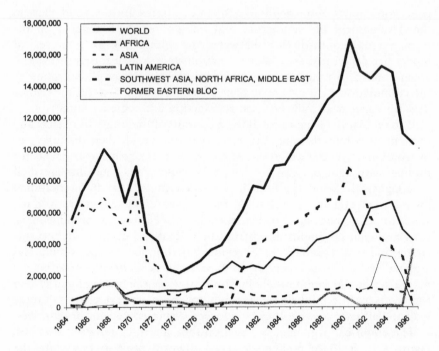

Figure 4.1 Refugee numbers 1964–96
Source: Prepared by Dr Susanne Schmeidl (*International Forced Migration: Exploring a Refugee Early Warning Model*. Westport, CT: Praeger, forthcoming)

refugees fled the loss of the civil war by the Rwanda Patriotic Army (RPA) against the invasion led by the Rwanda Patriotic Front (RPF). The refugees were mainly located in Zaire and Tanzania, with a small number in Burundi. Until the summer of 1996, very few of the refugees returned in a programme of voluntary repatriation organized by UNHCR and supported by the international community. Though the new Rwandan regime espoused a policy of welcoming back the refugees and returning to them their houses and lands (even if the houses and lands had been seized since by others), few took up the offer. The major reason presented by international agencies for the failure of return was the non-functioning of the justice system and the fear among the refugees that they would be subjected to vigilante justice and imprisoned if they returned. By and large, led by the voices of Amnesty International, the legitimacy of this fear was reinforced.

But the main force keeping the refugees in camps was the control of the camps by the Interahamwe and the ex-FAR (Forces Armées Rwandaises) soldiers of the former Rwandan regime. Some countries and agencies called for an interventionist force to free the refugees from such control, but nothing happened, even when militants used the camps as a base to engage in ethnic cleansing in the host country, attacking and driving out populations of Tutsis who had been resident in Zaire for two hundred years. This population, along with other discontented Zaireans, rebelled against both the militants in the camps and the Zairean government. The result was that the camps were attacked and refugees were cut off from humanitarian food and health services as well as housing as they fled their camps.

Globalized sentiment was aroused, stimulated by television clips of the desperate state of the refugees broadcast around the world. An aroused international community planned to intervene, but torn between the politics of the USA – always wary of any intervention since the Somalia fiasco (Hirsch and Oakley, 1995; Weiss, 1995, 1996) – and the partisan politics of France which supported Zaire, the best the Canadian-led interventionist force could contemplate was a humanitarian expedition to supply food and health services to the refugees. But this would have meant interposing an international force within a civil war context. It would also probably have led to increased pressures for a ceasefire and allowed the militants in the camps to reconsolidate their control over the refugees. Faced with this possibility, the threat of international intervention acted as a catalyst to speed up the attack of the rebels against the militants. Their success freed the bulk of the refugees from militant control, allowing most to march home. Given the example in Zaire, the Tanzanian government in a parallel initiative freed the refugees from their militant controllers, and the refugees went home.

The instrument for repatriation was not the international humanitarian community, but local communities which followed the principle that only a local state could be the protector of its citizens. Refugees left in camps threatened the stability of the region and provided opportunities for militants to exploit international humanitarian aid and local refugee populations. The danger of modernity is that it places individual freedom and rights on an abstract pedestal, and forgets that they are exercised within a historical context and by governments to which the individuals belong. The key to a solution is facilitating refugees and local states to assume the responsibility for re-establishing refugees as responsible citizens in their own communities. The globalization of sentiment can help only if it is secondary to this process, and the local collectivity retains primary responsibility for dealing with refugees.

If the instrument for solving the refugee crisis shifts back from international agencies and abstract principles to local actions and concrete pragmatic solutions, what are the implications for international refugee law and the moral regime of humanitarianism that has emerged? The legal regime developed will remain in place for those who have the means to access it, but it will remain a very expensive solution to handle from 1 to 2 per cent of the global refugee population (broadly equivalent to the total cost of assistance for the rest of the world's refugees combined). The abstract universal principle that every individual should have his or her rights protected by a state, and if persecuted by one state, the right to demand the protection of the state in which the individual found asylum from that persecution, will be maintained. It will, however, be a principle used by very few. Pressures will increasingly be brought to bear on states to ensure that they assume proper responsibility for the rights of their own members, including the right to return and live free from fear of persecution.

What happens to the morality of pure humanitarianism? Humanitarian agencies are slowly coming to recognize that they cannot remain pure. Their hands must get dirty as choices must be made among lesser evils, rather than in quest of the ultimate good. Even the dedication to pure humanitarian assistance alone may – rather than resolve the problem – perpetuate the plight of refugees and forestall solutions.

Notes

1   See Rengger (1995) for a contemporary discussion of the dialectic tension in the conception of modernity between descriptive and prescriptive rationality. Modernity is, as Hegel said (1977, p. 536), both 'the certainty of self-conscious Reason that it is all truth' and the establishment of the knowledge based on that subjective conviction that the actual world is rational.

2   See Pipes (1996) for documentation on Lenin as a pathological killer and the instigator of the Red Terror in 1918 to destroy both real and imagined opponents of the Bolsheviks. Unlike most revolutionaries, Lenin admired the terror unleashed by the French Revolution and believed such terror reinvigorated a country.

3   As Marx (1963) described it, the abstraction of the *state* was not born until the modern world was articulated in German idealism because the abstraction of private life was not created until modern times.

4   Lefebvre's (1995) Eleventh Prelude provides a parallel discussion of Marx's and Baudelaire's understanding of this dichotomy.

5   '[T]he only source of normativity that presents itself is the principle of subjectivity from which the very time-consciousness of modernity arose. This philosophy of reflection, which issues from the basic fact of self-consciousness, conceptualizes this principle ... the rationality of the understanding, which modernity knows as its possession and recognizes as its only source of obligation, has to be expanded into reason, following in the tracks of the dialectic of the enlightenment' (Habermas, 1995, pp. 41–2).

6   This is not only a matter of improvements in the technology of transportation and communication (Zacher and Sutton, 1996). Global rules and regimes need to be created (Bushrui *et al.*, 1993). Culture is also involved.

7   See Richmond (1994) for a much more pessimistic account in which refugees are but symptoms of the growing divide between the rich and the poor on a global scale.

8   The *Oxford English Dictionary* identifies 'refugee', from the French *refugie*, as 'one who, owing to religious persecution or political troubles seeks refuge in a foreign country; orig. Applied to the French Huguenots who came to England after the revocation of the Edict of Nantes in 1685' (Oxford University Press, 1971).

9   The ideals of Greek national independence rooted in European modernist thought were conveyed to Greeks through the Fichte of Greek thought, Adamantios Korais (Chaconas, 1942). The struggle for Greek independence culminated in the population transfers of the 1920s (Dakin, 1972; Pentsopoulos, 1962).

10   The Arabs fought to make the objective of the International Refugee Organization (IRO) dealing with the Jews, repatriation and *not* resettlement. To prevent resettlement in Palestine, they tried to introduce conditions to resettlement, namely the consent of neighbouring countries and of the indigenous population. They also wanted the IRO to have exclusive authority to settle European refugees, largely through repatriation. They suggested that all private organizations working for resettlement transfer their assets to the IRO for that purpose. In the IRO constitution, a distinction was made between refugees – pre- or postwar victims of Nazi or fascist regimes or of racial, religious or political persecution – and displaced persons (DPs) who were displaced in the course of, or after, World War II. As far as the DPs were concerned, the IRO was 'to encourage and assist in every possible way the early return to their countries of origin'. (For a more detailed account of the Arab efforts to keep the Jews from moving to Palestine via the debates over the IRO constitution and in the United Nations, see Robinson, 1947.) If Jews were classified as DPs, that classification would direct the IRO to arrange for their repatriation. If Jews were classified as refugees, then Palestine was the obvious place for them to be resettled, given the terms of the Mandate and the limitation of other options. As the Report of the High Commissioner for Refugees submitted to the Twenty-First Ordinary Session of the League of Nations Assembly had noted, 'Palestine alone has made a contribution of any size' in reference to large-scale or group settlement of Jews (Records of the Twenty-First Ordinary Session of the League of Nations, p. 232). The Arab countries, led by Egypt,

attempted to set repatriation as the goal of the IRO for *all* persons, whether refugees or DPs. Mr Kamel, the delegate of Egypt, proposed amending paragraph 2 of the Preamble of the Draft Constitution of IRO to require serious reasons to justify resettlement (21st meeting of the Third Committee of the United Nations General Assembly of the United Nations on 12 November 1946). Though defeated, on 19 November 1946 Kamel tried again unsuccessfully by proposing the deletion of the phrase 'concerning displaced persons' from Annex I, section IB. Passing the amendment would have meant that repatriation was advisable for both refugees and displaced persons. These attempts to dry up the source of Jewish immigration to Palestine were not restricted to the Arab countries. The UK played a leading role. The British delegate, supported by the Lebanese delegate, opposed the provision (which passed) defining German and Austrian residents of Jewish origin as 'refugees'. The opposition argued on what could be said to be a very high moral principle: the ostensible high ground that this was merely a backhanded attempt to clear Europe of its Jews, in other words to accomplish Hitler's goal of making the German-speaking parts of Europe *Judenrein*. Though the British acknowledged the difficulty Jews would have in living in places where they had been so persecuted, they admitted their real motives when they declared their 'fear that the new provision might well involve the new IRO in schemes for Jewish immigration into Palestine, a matter which is being separately dealt with by bodies specially concerned with that problem' (E/REF/87, 30 May 1946). It was clear to all that all these legal manoeuvres were aimed specifically at stopping Jewish migration to Palestine. The clearest indication of support for the Jewish refugees going to Palestine emerged in the Committee on Finances of the IRO which, in its 1947 budget, provided for the use of German reparation funds to resettle 100,000 Jewish refugees, with the funds to be transferred to the JOINT (Joint Distribution Committee, an American humanitarian organization that assisted Jewish refugees) and the Jewish Agency. All attempts to inhibit resettlement of Jewish refugees in Palestine via the IRO constitution having failed, the Arabs made a final attempt to keep the refugees in Europe in the first session of the UN General Assembly. The Arabs, backed by the British, were defeated in the attempt to make repatriation the exclusive function of the IRO or to include Jews in those slated for repatriation. Even when repatriation was argued on the highest moral grounds of equality, non-discrimination and the opposition to a Europe free of Jews, the Arabs and British were unable to succeed in targeting the Jews for repatriation.

11   Harbhajan Singh was a refugee who claimed refugee status but was

denied an oral hearing. In the Supreme Court of Canada decision of 4 April 1985, three judges on the basis of the Canadian Charter of Rights and Freedoms guarantees of fundamental justice, and three judges on the basis of the Canadian Bill of Rights (which provided that a person could not be deprived of a fair hearing in accordance with the principles of fundamental justice), decided that all refugee claimants were entitled to oral hearings.

12   Giddens (1990) was one of the first to point out the reflexive response to globalization and the stimulant of globalization on empowering individuals and groups, particularly women, minorities and movements focused on specific causes.

References

Abella, I. and Troper, H. (1982) *None Is Too Many*. Toronto: Lester and Orpen Denys.

Abu-Lughod, J.L. (1988) Palestinians: exiles at home and abroad. *Current Sociology*, **36** (2), 61–70.

Adelman, H. (1983) Palestine refugees: defining the humanitarianism problem. *World Refugee Survey*, pp. 20–7. Washington, DC: US Committee for Refugees.

Adelman, H. (1986) *Middle East Focus*, Guest Editor, *Palestinian Refugees*, **9** (2).

Adelman, H. (1988) Palestinian refugees, economic integration and durable solution. In A. Bramwell (ed.), *Refugees in the Age of Total War*, pp. 195–311. London: Unwin Hyman.

Adelman, H. (1991) Humanitarianism and self-interest: Canadian refugee policy and the Hungarian refugees. In *Studien Informatiecentrum Menschenrechten*, pp. 98–108. SIM Special No. 11.

Adelman, H. (1992) On UNRWA. Review article of Milton Viorst, *Reaching for the Olive Branch: UNRWA and Peace in the Middle East. Middle East Focus*, **14** (2), 11–15.

Adelman, H. (1994a) Refugees: the right of return. In J. Baker (ed.), *Group Rights*, pp. 164–85. Toronto: University of Toronto Press.

Adelman, H. (1994b) *Hungarian Refugees*. Toronto: York Lanes Press.

Adelman, H. (1995) The Palestinian diaspora. In R. Cohen (ed.), *Cambridge Survey of World Migration*, pp. 414–17. Cambridge: Cambridge University Press.

Adelman, H. (1996a) The right of repatriation – Canadian review policy: the case of Rwanda. *International Migration Review*, Spring, special issue, *Ethics, Migration, and Global Stewardship*, **30**, 289–309.

Adelman, H. (1996b) Indifference versus sentiment: humanitarian intervention in Zaire. *New Routes: A Journal of Peace Research and Action (Uppsala Life and Peace Institute)*, 1 (4), 3–7.

Adelman, H. (1997) Palestinian refugees. In L.Y. Luciuk and M.S. Kenzer (eds), *Under Threat: Essays on the Refugee Experience*. Lanham, MD: Rowan & Littlefield.

Adelman, H. and Sorenson, J. (eds) (1994) *African Refugees*. Boulder, CO: Westview Press.

Adelman, H. with Suhrke, A. (1996) *The International Response to Conflict and Genocide: Lessons from the Rwanda Experience, Steering Committee of the Joint Evaluation of Emergency Assistance to Rwanda*, vol. 2: *Early Warning and Conflict Management*. Copenhagen: Danida.

Baldwin-Edwards, M. and Schain, M. (eds) (1994) *The Politics of Immigration in Western Europe*. London: Frank Cass.

Brown, S. (1992) *International Relations in a Changing Global System: Toward a Theory of the World Polity*. Boulder, CO: Westview Press.

Bushrui, S., Ayman, I. and Laszlo, E. (eds) (1993) *Transition to a Global Society*. Oxford: Oneworld.

Chaconas, S. (1942) *Adamantios Korais: A Study of Greek Nationalism*. New York: Columbia University Press.

Claude-Valentin, M. (1995) *The EC Member States and Immigration in 1993: Closed Borders, Stringent Attitudes*. Brussels: European Commission.

Collinson, S. (1994) *Europe and International Migration*. London: Royal Institute of International Affairs.

Connolly, W.E. (1993) *Political Theory and Modernity*. Ithaca, NY: Cornell University Press.

Cornelius, W.A. Martin, P.L. and Hollifield, J.F. (1994) *Controlling Immigration: A Global Perspective*. Stanford: Stanford University Press.

Dakin, D. (1972) *The Unification of Greece 1770–1923*. London: Ernest Benn.

Diehl, P.F. (ed.) (1997) *The Politics of Global Governance: International Organizations in an Independent World*. Boulder, CO: Lynne Rienner.

E/REF/87, 30 May 1946. London: Public Record Office.

Featherstone, M. (ed.) (1990) *Global Culture: Nationalism, Globalization, and Modernity*. London: Sage.

Giddens, A. (1990) *The Consequences of Modernity,* Cambridge: Polity Press.

Habermas, J. (1995) *The Philosophical Discourse of Modernity,* tr. F.G. Lawrence. Cambridge, MA: MIT Press.

Hegel, G.W.F. (1977) *Phenomenology of Spirit*, tr. A.V. Miller. Oxford: Oxford University Press.

Held, D. (1995) *Democracy and the Global Order: From the Modern State to Cosmopolitan Governance*. Stanford, CA: Stanford University Press.

Hirsch, J.L. and Oakley, R.B. (1995) *Somalia and Operation Restore Hope: Reflections on Peacemaking and Peacekeeping.* Washington, DC: United States Institute of Peace Press.

Krasner, S.D. (ed.) (1983) *International Regimes.* Ithaca, NY: Cornell University Press.

Lefebvre, H. (1995) *Introduction to Modernity,* tr. J. Moore. London: Verso.

McNeill, W.H. (1992) *The Global Condition: Conquerors, Catastrophes and Community.* Princeton, NJ: Princeton University Press.

Marrus, M. (1985) *The Unwanted: European Refugees in the Twentieth Century.* Oxford: Oxford University Press.

Marx, K. (1963) Contribution to the critique of Hegel's *Philosophy of Right.* In *Early Writings,* tr. T.B. Bottomore. Toronto: McGraw-Hill.

Mittleman, J.H. (ed.) (1996) *Globalization: Critical Reflections.* Boulder, CO: Lynne Rienner.

Oxford University Press (1971) *The Compact Edition of the Oxford English Dictionary.* Oxford: Oxford University Press.

Pentsopoulos, D. (1962) *The Balkan Exchange of Minorities and Its Impact upon Greece.* Paris: Mouton.

Piper, R. (1996) *The Unknown Lenin: From the Secret Archives.* New Haven: Yale University Press.

Prunier, G. (1995) *The Rwanda Crisis: History of a Genocide.* New York: Columbia University Press.

Rengger, N.J. (1995) *Political Theory, Modernity and Postmodernity.* Oxford: Blackwell.

Richmond, A. (1994) *Global Apartheid: Refugees, Racism, and the New World Order.* Toronto: Oxford University Press.

Rieff, D. (1997) Case study in ethnic strife. *Foreign Affairs,* 76 (2), 118–32.

Robinson, J. (1947) *Palestine and the United Nations.* Westport, CT: Greenwood Press.

Toulmin, S. (1990) *Cosmopolis: The Hidden Agenda of Modernity.* Chicago: University of Chicago Press.

Wasserstein, B. (1979) *Britain and the Jews of Europe, 1939–1945.* London: Clarendon Press.

Weiss, T.G. (1995) Overcoming the Somalia syndrome – 'Operation Rekindle Hope?' *Global Governance: A Review of Multilateralism and International Organizations,* 1 (2), 171–86.

Weiss, T.G. (ed.) (1996) *The United Nations and Civil Wars.* Boulder, CO: Lynne Rienner.

Weiss, T.G. and Pasic, A. (1997) Reinventing UNHCR: Enterprising Humanitarians in the Former Yugoslavia, 1991–1995. *Global Governance: A Review of Multilateralism and International Organizations,* 3 (1), 41–57.

Widgren, J. (1993) Movements of refugees and asylum seekers: recent trends in a comparative perspective. In *The Changing Course of International Migration*, pp. 87–95. Paris: OECD.

Widgren, J. (1994) *The Key to Europe: A Comparative Analysis of Entry and Asylum Policies in Western Countries*. Stockholm: International Centre for Migration Policy Development.

Wiener, M. (1995) *The Global Migration Crisis: Challenge to States and to Human Rights*. New York: HarperCollins.

Wyman, D.S. (1968) *Paper Walls: America and the Refugee Crisis, 1938–1941*. New York: Pantheon Books.

Wyman, D.S. (1985) *The Abandonment of the Jews: America and the Holocaust 1941–1945*. New York: Pantheon Books.

Zacher, M.W. and Sutton, B.A. (eds) (1996) *Governing Global Networks: International Regimes for Transportation and Communications*. Cambridge: Cambridge University Press.

Zolberg, A., Suhrke, A. and Aguayo, S. (1986) *Escape from Violence: Conflict and the Refugee Crisis in the Developing World*. New York: Oxford University Press.

5

Sociocultural dimensions of war, conflict and displacement

Derek Summerfield

The pattern of modern conflict

The challenge to maximize our understanding of the experience of war, atrocity and displacement can usefully start with an overview of contemporary conflict. There have been an estimated 160 wars and armed conflicts in the Third World since 1945, with 22 million deaths and three times as many people injured (Zwi and Ugalde, 1989). There were on average 9 wars active in any year during the 1950s, 11 during the 1960s, 14 during the 1970s, and at least 50 currently. Torture is routine in over 90 countries. Five per cent of all casualties in World War I were civilians, 50 per cent in World War II, over 80 per cent in the US war in Vietnam, and currently over 90 per cent (UNICEF, 1986). In *The State of the World's Children 1996*, UNICEF states that in the past ten years, 2 million children have died in war, with 4–5 million wounded or disabled, 12 million made homeless and 1 million orphaned or separated from their parents. At present UNHCR counts 18 million refugees who have fled across an international border, a sixfold increase on 1970, but as many again are internally displaced and often no less destitute. This totals one person in 125 of the entire world population. Ninety per cent of all war refugees are in Third World countries, many among the poorest on earth. Between 2.5 and 5 per cent of the refugee population are unaccompanied children.

During the 1980s and 1990s there was serious conflict in Mozambique, Angola, El Salvador, Guatemala, Nicaragua, South Africa, Peru, Colombia, Ethiopia, Sudan, Somalia, Sierre Leone, Algeria, Liberia, Zaire, Rwanda, Burundi, Afghanistan, Iran, Iraq, Kuwait, Turkey, Azerbaijan, Russian Chechenya, Israeli Occupied Territories, Indian Kashmir, Sri Lanka, Indonesian East Timor, China, the Philippines, former Yugoslavia and Northern Ireland, among others. The two most publicized conflicts in the 1990s have been in Rwanda (where up to 14 per cent of the total population – almost all Tutsis – were slaughtered in just three months in 1994) and Bosnia (where 250,000 have died and 20,000 are still missing). Between 1989 and 1992 only three out of 82 violent conflicts were between sovereign states. In the first five cases mentioned above, a powerful neighbour played a key role in propagating violent conflict by proxy for its own geopolitical advantage.

A key element of modern political violence is the creation of states of terror to penetrate the entire fabric of grassroots social relations, as well as subjective mental life, as a means of exerting social control. It is to these ends that most acts of torture are directed, rather than to the extracting of information. The mutilated bodies of those abducted by security agents, dumped in a public place, are props in a political theatre meant to render a whole society a stunned audience. Not only is there little recognition of the distinction between combatant and civilian, or of any obligation to spare women, children and the elderly, but the valued institutions and way of life of a whole population can be targeted. It is depressingly clear that such strategies are highly effective. What in the 1980s was often called 'low-intensity' war, frequently played out on a terrain of subsistence economies, invariably had high-intensity conse-quences for its victims. The cheap hand-held automatic rifle has become a potent force in the lives of millions of people. In many places violence becomes a way of solving the problems of poverty. In Rio de Janeiro several thousand children are employed by drug traffickers, the only people who offer them a means of supporting themselves. Of course they are frequently the first casualties. In many settings there is an increasingly fine line between political and criminal violence, with security forces involved in unbridled profiteering, blackmarketing and extortion.

The recent circumstances of Mozambique serve to illustrate patterns commonly recurring in other conflict zones worldwide. Throughout the 1980s a war driven by Renamo guerrillas, sponsored by white South Africa, led to as many as 150,000 rural peasants being murdered in cold blood, 3 million others displaced, 200,000 children orphaned or separated from their parents, and the social fabric of large areas of the country left in tatters. Children as young as 8 were forcibly recruited into Renamo ranks and made to kill. Systematic use was made of public torture, often involving grotesque mutilations, and execution. Family members were forced to kill each other in turn, slowly, and usually for no clear reason. Women were made to kill, maim or even eat their own infants, with witnesses generally left to tell the tale. Exemplary violence, in this case with a ritualistic element, can be paralysing, even mesmerizing, and makes political persuasion redundant. In a hungry country the public destruction of foodstuffs by Renamo was also symbolically significant. The bodies of victims were thrown down wells to contaminate the drinking-water supply. A total of 1113 primary health centres – 48 per cent of the national total – were destroyed and looted, leaving 2 million people without access to health care of any kind. Mines were laid around hospitals, and in the massacre of 494 people at Homoine in 1987, pregnant women were bayoneted in the maternity unit and other patients kidnapped. Forty-five per cent of all primary schools were forced to close. In 1987 UNICEF estimated that Mozambique had the highest infant mortality rate in the world, with 320,000 children dying between 1981 and 1986 as a result of the war. There was general hunger, epidemics of measles (400 times more lethal in malnourished children), cholera, malaria and diarrhoea. Widespread rape and social breakdown are likely to have hastened the spread of AIDS (Cliff and Noormahomed, 1988). The damage to the social and economic resources of the country, which are now being further stretched by the structural adjustment policies of the World Bank, is scarcely calculable.

In Nicaragua 60,000 civilians (1.5 per cent of the total population, equivalent to 800,000 in Britain) were murdered, injured or abducted by US-sponsored Contra guerrillas during the 1980s. In El Salvador at least 70,000 rural peasants died at the hands of the army and its death squads during the same period. In 1982 Americas Watch pointed to the importance of mutilation killings in El Salvador, particularly decapitation of children, as mechanisms of social terror – as in Mozambique. In his Christmas 1983 address Rosa Chavez, the Auxiliary Bishop of San Salvador, said, 'It is a rare thing to die a natural death in this country. It is almost a miracle.' Extrajudicial executions, 'disappearances' and torture were equally institutionalized in neighbouring Guatemala (150,000 murdered in thirty years), which was often said to have no political prisoners because they were all dead. A 1981 Amnesty International report linked death squad activity there directly to the presidential palace.

In South Africa 24,000 children as young as 12 were detained between 1985 and 1989 without access to parents or lawyers, and many were tortured. In 1990, 450 street children were killed by death squads in the Brazilian cities of São Paulo, Rio de Janeiro and Recife alone (Logie, 1992). Children volunteered for, or were coerced into, an active role in armed movements in at least 20 conflicts worldwide in the 1980s. The consequences also include more hidden problems like sexual exploitation, substance abuse, informal justice, forced labour and crime. Some 10,000 teenage girls and young women are estimated to be in prostitution in Phnom Penh alone, a dramatic increase since 1989 (Boyden and Gibbs, 1996).

The issue of uncleared mines will increasingly loom as an obstacle to postwar reconstruction. There are 9 million each in Angola and Afghanistan, 5–10 million in Iraq, 4–7 million in Cambodia, 2 million in Mozambique and 90 to 100 million worldwide. Cambodia's 30,000 amputees represent 1 in every 240 persons, the highest proportion in the world. Amputees are in a particular plight in societies where most people earn a living by manual labour. Some estimates put the death toll in Afghanistan at 200,000 from mines alone since 1979, with 400,000 wounded (Arms Project and Physicians for Human Rights, 1993). The Red Cross estimates that mines kill 800 people and injure thousands every month. In a recent study of 206 communities in Afghanistan, Bosnia, Cambodia and Mozambique, 1 household in 20 reported a victim of a mine (a third of which were fatalities) (Andersson *et al.*, 1995); 1 in 10 was a child. Households with a landmine victim were 40 per cent more likely to have difficulty in providing food for the family. Up to 80 per cent of households had daily activities affected by landmines. A total of 54,554 animals had been lost, with a minimum cash value of US$200 per household. Without mines, agricultural production in the sample communities could increase by 88–200 per cent in Afghanistan and 135 per cent in Cambodia.

Sexual violation

Sexual violation is an endemic yet poorly visible facet of violent conflict (Swiss and Giller, 1993). The plight of 200,000 Southeast Asian women during World War II, abducted to provide sex 20 to 30 times per day for Japanese soldiers, has only recently been highlighted in the West. Eighty per cent of these 'comfort women' were Korean. For nine months in 1971, after the declaration of independence from Pakistan by Bangladesh and the entry of Pakistani troops to quell the rebellion, it is reliably estimated that between 200,000 and 400,000 Bengali women, 80 per cent of whom were Muslim, were raped by soldiers (Makiya, 1993). In Mozambique and elsewhere, women have been abducted and effectively enslaved in large numbers. In Iran, detained teenagers executed for political reasons have first been raped, denying them the automatic entry to heaven granted to virgins (Parliamentary Human Rights Group, 1994). Cambodian and Somali women have faced sexual violation before and during flight, and in refugee camps in Thailand and Kenya respectively, sometimes by camp authorities or local police. In India, women community organizers and human rights workers appear to be prime targets for rape. In Iraq under Saddam Hussein, there are licensed rapists employed as civil servants by the state. Many prisons in Iraq are reported to have specially equipped rape rooms. In Arab/Islamic culture, the honour of a family is located in the bodies of the women of that family, in their virginity, the clothes they wear and the modesty with which they deport themselves. The rape of a woman is thus a way of penetrating to the inner sanctum of her entire family's honour. Most recently, there were the well-publicized systematic rapes of Bosnian Muslim women by Serb militias. Under-reporting of rape by victims is probably universal because of the associated stigma, perhaps most pervasive in societies (as in Asia) in which virginity is regarded as a woman's single most important asset in securing happiness.

The role of women during war has been almost exclusively related to victim status. This has tended to obscure the extent to which women made significant contributions to political struggles in countries like Eritrea, Ethiopia and Nicaragua. But the attempted genocide in Rwanda in 1994 has shown women taking up a rather darker role, that of perpetrator. Educated women of every category, as well as peasants, participated in the genocide. Women teachers, civil servants, doctors, nurses and nuns made lists of people to be killed, handed over patients or others sheltering in hospitals or churches, betrayed colleagues, sang and ululated the killers into action, wielded machetes themselves and stripped the dead or barely living of their jewellery, money and clothes (African Rights, 1995).

Targeting of health workers and services

Violations of medical neutrality are a consistent feature worldwide and follow predictably from the way modern war is premised and played out. In Nicaragua, destruction of rural health clinics and targeting of their staff by Contra guerrillas was meant to demonstrate that central government could not protect what was valued by its citizens. Three hundred thousand people (15 per cent of the rural population) were left without any health care (Garfield and Williams, 1989). Many health workers were forced to operate in clandestine fashion in the countryside, burying their equipment and medicines at night. This much impeded the effectiveness of primary health work, like immunization, which depended on advance publicity. In El Salvador the extrajudicial execution or 'disappearance' of more than 20 health professionals in the first six months of 1980 set the tone for much of the decade. Soldiers made incursions into hospitals and surgeons were assassinated in mid-operation on suspicion that they were prepared to treat 'subversives'. The practice of medicine or community health care in rural areas was regarded by the military as linked to subversion, since the health worker was a source of advice and support to the peasant population. The bodies of health workers were left for discovery in a mutilated state – decapitated, castrated or with 'EM' (Spanish initials for 'death squad') carved in their flesh. This was exemplary brutality. In the Philippines, 102 health workers were subjected to extrajudicial killing or arbitrary detention between 1987 and 1989 by the army or government agents. Nurses in rural areas faced death threats, sometimes broadcast on local radio stations; these were intended to 'politicize' the clinics they ran and make local people afraid to attend (Summerfield, 1992). Hospitals in

Croatia and Bosnia have been repeatedly mortared by Serb forces and patients killed; at Vukovar 261 staff and patients were taken away for execution. In the Occupied Territories the Israeli army has fired into hospitals and arrested patients, refused to allow seriously ill Palestinians to reach hospitals during curfews, has assaulted, detained and tortured health workers and obstructed delivery of key medicines. The United Nations Relief and Works Agency reported that in 1990 alone, Israeli soldiers forcibly entered its clinics and hospitals 159 times (Physicians for Human Rights, 1993).

The US National Academy of Sciences says that Syria may have the highest number of health professionals and scientists imprisoned without trial in the world (Godlee, 1993). In 1980 the Syrian Medical Association passed a resolution reaffirming a citizen's right to free expression, denouncing violence and terror and calling for the release or trial of all detainees. The Assad government responded by dissolving this and other professional associations and arresting more than 100 doctors. Amnesty International understands that several were executed at an early stage but the Syrian government has never yielded to inquiries or pleas made on behalf of the rest. So too in Sudan, where Amnesty International documented in 1990 that more than 30 doctors were still being detained for having peacefully expressed their opposition to a military coup. They were said to have been tortured. The Iraqi government responded mercilessly to an attempted uprising in the Shiite south after the Gulf War. It paid special attention to those who had kept their hospitals open during the uprising. Fifteen doctors at the Jumhuri Hospital in Basra were executed on the spot and artillery fired at the building, crammed with 4000 civilians. At Saddam Hospital in Najaf, army troops molested female doctors and murdered patients with knives or threw them out of windows (Makiya, 1993). Other doctors were executed in public by firing squads. In Indian Kashmir, a persistent pattern of extrajudicial abuses, and impunity for the perpetrators, strongly suggests official policy. In February 1993 Dr Farooq Ahmed Ashir, Chief Orthopaedic Surgeon at Srinagar's Bone and Joint Hospital, was shot dead at an Indian army checkpoint. He had recorded numerous cases of torture and assault on civilians, giving evidence to Asia Watch and Physicians for Human Rights. Professionals who see health in its widest sense – who are concerned not just with what makes an individual sick, but what makes a whole society unhealthy – cannot but raise questions which oppressive regimes find subversive.

Even international peacekeeping operations are not immune to violations of the Geneva Convention regarding the neutrality of medical services. On 17 March 1993, UN forces in Somalia, in pursuit of the warlord General Aideed, deliberately attacked Digfa Hospital in Mogadishu. Nine patients were killed and there was extensive destruction of scarcely replaceable equipment and supplies. The hospital was immediately evacuated, decanting hundreds of patients into the war-torn city; it is not known how many more died as a result.

Targeting of cultural forms and traditions

Another key dimension is the crushing of the social and cultural institutions which connect a particular people to their history, identity and lived values. Middle East Watch documents that the Iraqi government campaign against Iraq's Kurdish population in the 1980s amounted to genocide within the meaning of the Genocide Convention of 1951 (Middle East Watch and Physicians for Human Rights, 1993). This included the use of poison gas – a mixture of mustard gas and nerve gas – dropped by aircraft, most notoriously on the town of Halabja in 1988, where 5000 civilians were killed. In all, 182,000 Iraqi Kurds have disappeared after mass removals in the style of Nazi Germany or Stalinist Russia; most are believed dead. Their villages, with every building razed by explosives, have ceased to exist. Since their invasion in 1977 the Indonesian authorities have murdered an estimated 200,000 East Timorese, an ethnically distinct people. This is nearly one-third of the total population. The Pol Pot regime in Cambodia murdered between 1.5 and 3 million people, 20 to 40 per cent of the total population, in only four years from 1975. It made a determined effort to reconstruct Cambodian society and culture, to rewrite its history, social structures, beliefs and values. A great deal of documentation on Khmer culture perished, as did dancers, craftsmen, women who could weave traditional designs and, in a deeply religious land, more than 90 per cent of Buddhist monks. So too did anyone found to speak French or even those wearing spectacles, since these were considered marks of the educated and modern. In Guatemala, 440 Indian villages were wiped from the map during the 1980s, regarded by this victimized population as part of a 500-year-old attack on their Mayan culture. The Serbs did not invent ethnic cleansing! At least 1.5 million people died in the Sudanese civil war during the 1980s; repeated large massacres of Dinka civilians were poorly reported in the outside world.

In Turkey, the Kurdish culture and language have long been suppressed and children must speak Turkish in school, a persecution which has fostered violent revolt by Kurdish activists. It was protest against Afrikaans as the medium of education, regarded as the language of the oppressor, which sparked the Soweto riots of 1976 in which around 500 black children were shot dead by the authorities. In Iraq, Saddam Hussein mounted a devastating assault against Shia cultural and religious life in early 1991 (Makiya, 1993). Within a few weeks some 5000 religious scholars and students from Najaf alone had been arrested and all the religious schools shut down. Many were executed. Mosques and their ancient cemeteries were levelled; the Golden Dome of the Shrine of Ali was hit by artillery fire and the interior ravaged. The cultural offensive against holy sites, seminaries and libraries continued long after the fighting in the cities was over. Ancient treasures that had survived centuries were looted or transported to Baghdad, representing gifts accrued over a period of a thousand years. The libraries of the religious schools and seminaries of Najaf, Kufa and Kerbala were burned, together with their ancient manuscripts. It is possible that the scale and organized character of the assault has ended a thousand-year-old tradition of religious scholarship and learning, with unpredictable future consequences. In Bosnia, hundreds of mosques have been intentionally destroyed by Serb militias and the educated among their prisoners reportedly singled out for execution. So too in Rwanda. When the army took over in Argentina in 1976 their attacks on the progressive professional sector included the burning of books from the university, Freud as well as Marx.

The social experience of war

War and the social fabric

The debate about the effects of war and other extreme experiences on human beings veers in the West towards an individual rather than a collective focus, and towards individual pathology in body or mind. How applicable is this to non-Western populations worldwide? Many of their ethnomedical systems do not logically distinguish body, mind and self and therefore illness cannot be situated in body or mind alone. Social relations are understood to be key contributors to individual health and illness, and the body is thus seen as a unitary, integrated aspect of self and social relations. It is dependent on and vulnerable to the feelings, wishes and actions of others, including spirits and dead ancestors (Boyden and Gibbs, 1996). The maintenance of harmonious relations within a family and community is generally assigned more significance than an individual's own thoughts, emotions and private aspirations. Thus the emphasis tends to be on a sociocentric notion of a person rather than an egocentric one as in the West. Perhaps the primary psychic impact of war for survivors is their witnessing the deliberate destruction of their social, economic and cultural worlds, ones which define their identity, roles and values. Some torture survivors say that this is not the worst thing that has happened to them. They cite other experiences, like the ominous disappearance of a brother, witnessing the gruesome death of people they valued, the crushing of their community or cause, as having affected them more. As the psychologist Martin-Baro (1990) wrote of his own country, what was left traumatized was not just Salvadorean individuals but Salvadorean society. Like any traumatic experience, victims come to terms with war as a function of what it means to them, meanings that are socially, culturally and of course politically defined. This is a public, collective and evolving process.

Many targeted communities must contend with war based on the psychology of terror, one in which to keep silent is an essential survival mode. In El Salvador or Guatemala, terror was intended to be felt but not named. To give voice to it, to say what had happened, to name the victims or even to be related to them, was to be regarded as subversive and a target for more. Even public utterance of terms like 'health' or 'organization' was dangerous because the military regarded these as code words for resistance. People were forced to deny their own reality, to swallow their own words. Concepts of innocence and guilt lose their distinctiveness, no one can realistically feel safe and it becomes hard to hold onto assumptions about a reasonably predictable world upon which a rationally planned life depends (Zur, 1994). In El Salvador the collective memory of the massacre of 30,000 peasants in 1932 was effective in suppressing even verbal dissent for over a generation: whenever peasants began to talk about their social grievances, others brought up 1932 again. These forces may make it impossible properly to mourn and honour the murdered and disappeared, reinforce everyone's sense of isolation and mistrust, and interfere with long-held Mayan forms of organizing. These include storytelling, which is a traditional Mayan psychological resource. In Mozambique, Renamo terrorism seemed intended to instil an incapacitating fear into the population by conjuring up a vision of inhumanity and maniacal devotion to the infliction of suffering which set them beyond comprehension, outside the realm of social beings and hence beyond social control or even resistance (Wilson, 1992).

In the Philippines, women raped by soldiers during 'low-intensity' offensives may end up as prostitutes in Manila. The definitive injury rape has inflicted on them, a catastrophic one, is social, because there is now no place for them in their rural communities.

Perhaps the most extreme predicament is when a social group finds that what has happened to it is incomprehensible and that its traditional recipes for handling crisis are useless. Meaninglessness leaves people feeling helpless and uncertain what to do. Frequently at stake are the cultural and social forms which for a particular people define the known world and its values. In Africa, Asia and Latin America there are subsistence peoples who may not be able to imagine personal survival if their way of life does not survive. Indeed, there are no socially defined ways of mourning a lost way of life. Almost all contemporary war targets those structures which hold the social fabric together: community organizations, trade unions, health and education institutions, religious leadership. When this happens the social fabric may no longer be able to perform its customary role in buffering the effects of crisis on its citizens; coping strategies which have served in previous crises may be undermined.

Culture and identity

Guatemalan Indians, hunted by 'low-intensity' warfare, felt that their collective body had been wounded, one which included the ants, trees, earth, domestic animals and human beings gathered across generations. Mayan origin myths are linked to land and maize (Lykes, 1994). To them the burning of crops by the army was an attack not just on their physical resources, but on the symbol which most fully represented the Mayan collective identity, the people of maize. To them it was genocide. For the internally displaced, the war played havoc with their traditions. It was hard to pray to a local deity when you no longer lived near the geographical feature associated with it.

In the Sudanese civil war, disruption of the traditional cycle of animal husbandry has brought social breakdown to the pastoralist Southerners. Cattle are crucial to them, being a form of currency not just in trading but in rituals and disputes. Tribal marriages can no longer be arranged because of dislocation and lack of cattle (the only traditional dowry); women are driven to prostitution in the towns, something previously unheard of. Because of the endemic killings and rape in the countryside, security conditions have become prime determinants of social behaviour, to the extent that families with noisy children are pushed out. Half this population has been forced to abandon villages regarded as ancestral places, seeking precarious safety in urban areas where their traditional skills are worthless. One study of teenagers displaced to Juba showed the resulting cultural estrangement and loss of social identity: none could write a history of their clan and many did not even know the names of their grandparents or the village their clan came from. Not one could name any traditional social ceremonies (Panos Institute, 1988).

In Mozambique, fleeing survivors are haunted by the spirits of their dead relatives, for whom the traditionally prescribed burial rituals have not been enacted (Harrell-Bond and Wilson, 1990). In Vietnam the 300,000 still missing nineteen years after the war with the USA ended are considered wandering souls for the same reason. Eisenbruch (1991) has described what he calls culturally bereaved Cambodians in the USA, who continue to feel guilty about abandoning homeland and their unfulfilled obligations to the dead, are haunted by painful memories and are unable to concentrate on the tasks facing them in an alien society. He pointed out that Cambodian adolescents in Australia, where there was less pressure to conform and where they were able to practise some traditional ceremonies, adjusted better than those in the USA. We must take account of the diverse ideologies and identities worldwide which govern the repertoire of explanations available to a particular people. These include Hinduism, Islam, Buddhism, Marxism, and for the Guatemalan Mayans a choice of three: animism, Catholicism and the politics of oppression. In Cambodia the word 'torture' derives from the Buddhist term for karma, an individual's thoughts and actions (often bad) in a prior existence which affect life in the present. Thus survivors can feel somehow responsible for their suffering (Mollica and Caspi-Yavin, 1992). In Mozambique both the Renamo guerrillas and government forces sought to heighten the impact of their military efforts by incorporating traditional sources of ritual power: ancestors' spirits and myths of male invincibility, including ceremonies conferring 'vaccination' against bullets. The rural peasantry did the same thing to bolster their capacity to resist Renamo violence. Thus a war driven by South Africa's destabilization policies has been imbued by local understandings and worldviews, becoming in part a 'war of the spirits'. This spiritual revitalization and other cultural shifts may outlast the war, with as yet unknown effects upon the social order (Wilson, 1992).

There is considerable plasticity and adaptability in the way people draw on their belief systems. The Mayans believe in ancestor spirits but are also devout Catholics. They attend for immunizations but also use plants and roots traditionally applied to differing ailments. So too in Zimbabwe: when in 1980 I worked as a government medical officer in the war-affected southeast, I found that local healers and diviners were in professional competition with our services. Patients regularly switched from one to the other and a man once asked me if he could take his desperately ill child from the ward to a traditional fontanelle ceremony and bring him back in time for the next penicillin injection.

Turton (1991) has studied the Mursi tribe of southwestern Ethiopia for more than 25 years. He describes how the Mursi see warfare not so much as a means by which they seek to extend or defend their territory, but as a means by which the very notion of their separate political identity is created and kept alive. Warfare traditionally has been a pervasive feature of their social organization and external relations and is thus not necessarily a breakdown in 'normal' political relations, but their very underpinning. It is at the heart of the balance that they have struck with neighbouring tribes over time. This balance or reciprocity may of course be dramatically altered by, in the Mursi case, a neighbouring tribe acquiring numbers of modern automatic weapons (spilling over from the Sudanese civil war).

Thus culture is impacted on by war, but also engages with it. Despite the assault on their way of life, the Guatemalan Mayans have emerged with a strengthened cosmology. The upheavals saw many seek new refuge in the old traditions, shamans and deities. Communities in flight petitioned the mountain spirits for the right to pass through their domain, and to take on a guardian angel role. At the same time there was a growth in politically conscious grassroots organization in exile, a preparedness to write, speak and campaign openly while remaining on a platform of Mayanness (Wearne, 1994). The aftermath of war in Uganda has seen an erosion in the power of traditional elders and their wisdom. The refugee experience has undermined their influence since they have not been in a position to negotiate bridewealth payments as of old. There has also been the appointment of ritually insignificant men as government chiefs. One of the reasons why the explanations of affliction offered by the elders were taken less seriously is that the intervention of ancestors, for whom they were interlocutors, was no longer considered to be the problem. Surely the ancestors would not have left people to suffer so much for so long, to witness such atrocities and the death of their children. The ancestors induced suffering for moral purposes but surely there were malign forces at work here? This meant witchcraft, in the form of young women seen to be possessed by wild and new spirits, including the ghosts of those slaughtered and left to rot in the bush rather than buried in the ordained manner. Witch killing can be seen in terms of the basic social need to make sense of suffering, to enforce social accountability and the emergence of a sustainable mode of communal order. The advent of AIDS, accelerated by war, was another challenge too much for the capacity of the elders to regulate and explain events. New forms were needed, with AIDS viewed as a 'poison' encompassable by beliefs drawn from witchcraft, Christianity and biomedicine (Allen, 1996). From Somalia too come accounts of the waning influence of traditional sources of wisdom.

Even concepts generally thought of as relatively fixed, like ethnic identity, have a capacity for fluidity that war may particularly mobilize. The collective arousal of a political crisis within a society, where one man's opportunity is another's danger, can make for rapid shifts and polarizations which confound what has gone before. During the years of the then Yugoslavia, its citizens did not routinely feel that their bottom-line identification was as 'Serb' or 'Croat' or 'Bosnian Muslim'. There were other identities, based on occupation or political affiliation or other role, which were more relevant to daily life than ethnicity. A man might have seen himself as much a 'carpenter' or 'communist' as he did 'Catholic Croat', yet it was this last which came to define him after the civil war started, whether he liked it or not. In South Africa, Zulu identity – which had never before been an issue in the anti-apartheid struggle – was manipulated by Zulu politicians and by elements of the white political and military establishment; both parties feared a loss of influence in the transition to black democratic, and non-tribal, rule. Between 1990 and

1994, 14,000 people died in the massacres that ensued. Enmities have not subsided with majority rule, and killings continue. In Somalia the dictator Siad Barre cemented his 22-year rule, which ended only in 1991, by playing on clan differences. The aftermath has been one of Somalian sovereignty and society pulled apart by centrifugal forces, perhaps permanently.

The capacity to draw on social or religious ideals, and on co-operative effort and solidarity, can bolster psychological and physical defences in even the most extreme situation. The most telling recent evidence of this emerged from a secret military prison, Tazmamart, in Morocco. For eighteen years 59 men were held incommunicado and in almost complete darkness in small single cells which they never left. They were exposed to extremes of temperature, poor food, little water and no medical care. They were split between two separated wings of equal size. In one wing, where prisoners had structured their time with joint activities from their cells, including recitations from memory from the Koran, 24 survived. However, in the second wing, where this did not happen and there was always chaotic argument and tension, only 4 survived (Van Ginneken and Rijnders, 1993).

The role of political meaning

Bettelheim (1960) noted at Auschwitz that those incarcerated as communists rather than as Jews could draw on their political ideals to better withstand what was happening to them. In Nicaragua, war-maimed young men were fortified by the belief that they had made a worthwhile sacrifice for the social values at stake in the war and were recognized by their society as having done so. Disability had a positive image (in stark contrast to, for example, Cambodia, where amputees are stigmatized because wholeness of body is a key value in the Buddhist worldview). But such beliefs, and the strength people draw from them in adversity, may change as circumstances change: some of these same men had later been sufficiently disappointed by the electoral defeat of the Sandinista government to abandon the sense of having suffered in a good cause. They now feared it had all been in vain and for a second time were having to come to terms, different terms, with their physical disability and other losses. On the other hand, it is relevant to the grief of the wife of an activist assassinated by a South African death squad that his cause has had a positive outcome in a more egalitarian society, and if there is public acknowledgement of what this struggle cost. This is a key theme: the societal validation on offer for those who have suffered. The case of the US Vietnam war veterans is instructive. These men returned to find that their nation, and even their families, had disowned their own guilt for the war and were blaming them instead. Attended by feelings of shame, guilt, betrayal and a sense of wasted sacrifice, the trauma of the war continued for them back home (belatedly validated by a diagnosis of post-traumatic stress disorder). In stark contrast, British Falklands war veterans came home to national acclaim for an honourable job well done (Summerfield and Hume, 1993).

Thus it is simplistic to see those exposed to political violence as merely helpless victims, unable to act on their environment. Violent crises constitute positive challenges for some, even if they expect to suffer. This is also true of children. 'Childhood' is a cultural construction: in the West, it is often seen as a time of innocence, passivity and vulnerability, a time requiring protection and nurturance. But such constructions vary across cultures, and indeed within the same one over time (not much more than a century ago, after all, children were working in British coal-mines). Children are not just passive recipients of experience, but also active negotiators of it. In wartime they too may have values and causes, and act on them. In Gaza, strong identification with the aspirations of Palestinian nationhood seems to have offered psychological protection to children facing high levels of violence from the Israeli army. The more they were exposed to political hardship, the more they deployed active and courageous coping modes (Punamäki and Suleiman, 1990). This did not mean they did not also have fear, grief and nightmares, and suffer from bed-wetting. Similar observations have been made in South Africa about young black activists (Dawes, 1990). However, wars also disturb traditional hierarchies and authority structures, not least within the family. It is noteworthy that in Gaza, Soweto and Cambodia, parents have complained that children no longer have proper respect for them and other elders.

Refugees and asylum-seekers

The pressures on asylum-seekers

Perhaps as few as 5 per cent of all refugees migrate to Western countries, though there have been substantial rises in flows into Europe in recent years. The insecurities of such asylum-seekers about their prospects for official refugee status are increasingly intrusive now that Western governments are moving in concert towards much more dismissive practices. Such attitudes from rich nations are shaming when one considers that over 90 per cent of all refugees are being harboured by some of the poorest societies on earth: Malawi, Pakistan, Zaire, etc. Some of the Guatemalan and El Salvadorean asylum-seekers forcibly returned by the USA in recent years have been later documented as victims of death squads. In the UK, over 75 per cent of all asylum-seekers are now being refused and the government is claiming that war-torn countries like Sri Lanka and Algeria may be 'safe' to return to. Determined campaigning is required to ensure governmental respect for the rights of asylum-seekers embodied in international conventions and protocols.

Asylum-seekers have a point of view on us as we have on them; we are points of reference in the situation they survey, not least at a time when so many of theirs have been lost to them. We may sentimentalize them but it is not in their interest to do the same to us. They may see it as a matter of survival that they take a strategic view of what advantages may accrue in their dealings with us, and this too is part of the dynamics of intervention. An asylum-seeker with a history of torture may pick up the fact that doctors are interested in his psychology and that adjusting how he presents to accommodate this might gain him a medical report, and thus an increased chance of full refugee status or of housing. In some situations the imperatives of asylum-seeking demand desperate measures. A mother may even hide the death of one of her children in a refugee camp so that the others have an extra ration of food to share. A Bosnian woman can falsely claim she was raped when this is a passport to a country abroad.

Asylum-seeking in a country with a distinctly different culture brings contact with different sets of meanings assigned to particular life events. For example, torture has been endemic in Turkey and is well enough understood, but not all ill-treatment there is considered torture by everyone. Kurdish men are routinely assaulted during interrogation in police stations, including beatings on the soles of the feet (*falaka*). Such treatment is part of the victimization of this persecuted ethnic group, but also of their capacity to endure and resist. When some finally seek refuge in the West, they can find their experiences reinterpreted *in toto* as torture. Though, as noted above, this may confer short-term advantages, it brings exposure to a medicalized trauma discourse which too routinely associates torture with long-term mental effects and damage. They would not have subscribed to these ideas back home. The impact of this on their attitude to themselves, on their capacity to feel whole and effective, has not yet been studied.

The psychological impact of torture or war on an individual is not a thing apart. Whatever the experiences from which they have fled, refugee demeanour and presentation will be shaped by the context in which they find themselves. A comparison between refugee reception in Sweden and Britain is instructive here. In Sweden, new arrivals are generally housed in hostels away from the urban centres. They are spared the anxiety of seeking out health care, legal advice, schooling and language lessons since these provisions are built-in on site. This comprehensive if rather paternalistic system expects asylum-seekers to be accepting, quiescent and patient while their claims are being processed by the immigration authorities. In contrast, new arrivals in Britain must fend for themselves, albeit with largely unfettered movement in the cities. The availability of accommodation and other services is often patchy and difficult to access. This situation requires asylum-seekers to be active, tenacious and feisty if they are to manage, attributes that would have served them poorly if they turned up in Sweden instead. It is adaptive for refugees to appraise their new situation, and to comport themselves in ways which take account of both the demands on them and the opportunities available.

The social experience of refugeedom

Too often the pronouncements of government seem to collude with the increasingly negative connotations attached to the word 'refugee'; in the UK this process is vigorously promoted by the more right-wing tabloid press. The fate of Cambodian refugees who survived Pol Pot but succumbed to firebombs in New York, and the spate of attacks against refugees in Germany, are but extreme examples of racist and discriminatory experiences that many need to weather regularly. On the other hand, host countries and their institutions, and those of the general public who are fair-minded and friendly, can play a highly positive role in allowing survivors to put horrific experiences behind them and to rebuild.

There are concerns about whether refugees have proper access to health services but insufficient data on how much their patterns of utilization carry the stamp of their past war experiences, and how much the complications of refugeedom itself. Their encounters with health professionals may be hampered by lack of interpreters and ignorance of cross-cultural factors. Medical settings do represent a place to turn to at a time when they have few others, but their presentations may be driven by deeper dilemmas: disrupted life projections, loss of status, alienation in a strange culture, intergenerational conflict. For example, some Turkish Kurdish women in London, often frequent attenders at their GP surgery with non-specific ailments, eventually confide that they find Britain an alien place where they cannot live a normal life, even after five years or more there (R. England, 1996 personal communication). They paint a picture of fractured family networks, high unemployment, domestic violence, a sense of isolation and concerns over parenting. Some of their daughters present to the GP with abdominal pain or school refusal, expressions of adolescent turmoil about being caught between two worlds. Some are expected to return to Turkey for an arranged marriage and are brought to the doctor for a virginity test. It is interesting that despite the stigma they attach to mental ill health, some mothers have started to say that they have 'psychological problems'. Their adoption of this term reflects their awareness of the language of distress most likely to be acknowledged in their new cultural milieu. What these women are attesting to is a still broken social world. Beyond a certain point, medical, psychological or social welfare interventions cannot provide specific antidotes to a profound predicament of this kind.

However, many other refugees, particularly younger ones, are able to master the crisis of exile, and to see it as an opportunity for education, work and new lifestyles and freedoms. The range of refugee trajectories over time must be acknowledged, and their relationship to the meaning of exile. Those who were social activists, who have a firm political view on why they were persecuted, may behave differently from others who see themselves more as unlucky bystanders. Iraqi Arab refugees in Western Europe have defined 'refugee' as someone who could not go home. In contrast, Iraqi Assyrian refugees have seen 'refugee' as someone who had no home, and did not view themselves as having 'lost' Iraq. Because of this they had much more of the attitude of a settler in their new environment (Al Rasheed, 1994).

It is a hypothesis worth empirical testing that the high unemployment levels prevailing across Western Europe since the 1980s have had a significant influence on the struggle to build a new life in exile. In earlier decades, when labour-short countries were welcoming towards economic migrants, survivors of persecution had an alternative to claiming political asylum if they so chose. In Sweden, Eastmond *et al.* (1994) highlighted one facet of this shift, noting that in the 1970s the official approach to refugee assistance focused on material support and rapid labour market integration. There was little talk of psychological needs. Today, there is considerable interest in 'trauma' and in psychological services for refugees, but there are no jobs for them. These authors go on to query whether this new focus might unwittingly set up and maintain sick roles as traumatized victims, promoting helplessness, in the absence of other structures through which to reconstitute a meaningful life.

The wider context: the world order and the question of justice

History has shown that social reform is the best medicine: how far can we move beyond mere 'binding of wounds' to speak out for the wider rights of the disadvantaged and persecuted? It has been noted, for example, that medical associations in countries which routinely torture their citizens are often remarkably passive about such issues (British Medical Association, 1992). It may be no coincidence that the most trenchant criticism of medical approaches to trauma has come from oppressive societies, notably in Latin America, where assistance to victims is unavoidably also human rights work. Such critics charge that the narrow application of the scientific method can amount to reductionist medicalizing, with health and illness being separated from their social roots. Post-traumatic symptoms are not just a private and individual problem, but also an indictment of the social context that produced them. In El Salvador, which has long had one of the most atrocious human rights records in the western hemisphere, Martin-Baro (1990) saw psychosocial trauma there as the normal consequence of social systems based on exploitation and dehumanizing oppression. He described how destructively polarized choices imposed themselves on the developmental processes of Salvador-ean children who had to grow up with this social 'normal abnormality', a climate of unremitting state terror, militarization of social life and institutionalized lying. The response of the Salvadorean military to this analysis, in one sense a confirmation of it, was to assassinate him in November 1989.

Much political violence in the developing world is rooted in gross social inequities. Extrajudicial execution and torture are the most eloquent expressions of the refusal or incapacity of those in power to fulfil the basic needs and aspirations of all of their citizens. Most victims are the poor and those who speak for them, or members of persecuted ethnic minorities with few advocates in the West. Grossly inequitable patterns of land ownership (for example, in Guatemala 75 per cent of all land is owned by 2 per cent of landowners) is almost invariable in violent societies, particularly in Latin America. The Western multinational economy has an implicit investment in developing-world workforces which are leaderless, fragmented and cowed, and thus docile and cheap. The sales made by the world's four largest corporations exceed the gross national product of the whole of Africa. What structures are available to make such power accountable to more than just the corporations' shareholders?

Western governments tacitly insist that human rights considerations should not significantly influence the alliances they choose in the developing world: people without power, even in their millions, are *ipso facto* strategically unimportant and therefore ignorable. Thus regimes serving Western geopolitical interests provoke at best mere routine denunciations when they murder and torture their citizens. Because of its ideological opposition to 'communist' Vietnam, the West opposed Vietnam's 1978 invasion of Cambodia, even though it toppled Pol Pot. Indonesia, the Philippines, Zaire, (white-ruled) South Africa, Chile, Brazil, Haiti, Turkey, Israel all enjoyed Western support and friendship in the 1980s, despite grossly exploitative and repressive policies towards sectors of their own societies. Eyewitness accounts of the bayoneting of children in the El Mozote massacre of 794 Salvadorean villagers by the (US-trained) Atlacatl battalion on 11 December 1981 were dismissed in the USA as communist propaganda. Proposed bills which would have required the Salvadorean government to show progress in human rights if the USA was to maintain its military aid (US$1 million per day throughout the 1980s to this small country of only 5 million, largely impoverished, citizens) were consistently blocked, even as peasant massacres continued unabated. From neighbouring Honduras, there is now evidence that the US CIA trained Battalion 3-16, a secret unit responsible for the torture and murder of many of the 184 trade unionists, human rights activists and students who disappeared between 1981 and 1984.

The British government continued to allow, indeed covertly encouraged, the sale of arms-related material to Iraq, even though it was public knowledge that the Iraqi government was using poison gas and other genocidal actions against the Kurds. Spending on arms in 1992, US$815 billion, equalled the combined income of 49 per cent of the world's population. In the UK in 1990, 44 per cent of total spending on research and development was for military purposes (Germany 13 per cent, Japan 5 per cent). Ten years ago the Brandt report pointed out that the most dynamic transfer of sophisticated equipment and technology from rich to poor countries was of arms. What is the tacit human rights message accompanying such massive transfers of state-of-the-art weaponry in the name of 'national defence' to those with power to abuse in the Third World? Average expenditure per capita on arms in the developing world is US$38, compared to US$12 on health (Siward, 1989).

Allied to this is the vital question of official reparation for human rights crimes. Victims may better become survivors if some part of the legacy of the past can be addressed; better still if this takes an official form, like a war crimes tribunal or financial compensation. After World War II, Germany apologized to its victims (and has continued to do so) and made financial restitution. Japan, which has largely failed to do either or even to give an open account in the history books used by its own schoolchildren, left its victims shorn of the full recognition they deserved. British ex-servicemen survivors of Japanese death camps, Korean ex-'comfort women' and others are still campaigning on this account, and would not countenance the presence of Japanese officials at ceremonies commemorating fifty years since the end of World War II. Japan's continued refusal to apologize is part strategic – it fears demands for financial compensation – but also cultural. Filial piety is a particular virtue in Asian societies and the Japanese feel it would be sinful to apologize for World War II because they would be blaming their ancestors, and also Emperor Hirohito, who was considered a deity at the time. There is also their long-held sense of cultural superiority over other Asian peoples.

The first genocide of the twentieth century, of up to 1.5 million Armenians by Turkey in 1915, is still officially denied *in toto*. The USA has expressed not a word of regret for the death of several million people and the ecological devastation wrought in Vietnam between 1964 and

1975, and until recently continued to stigmatize the country and impede its reconstruction. The same can be said of (white) South Africa, whose undeclared wars against Mozambique and Angola in the 1980s have virtually destroyed them as viable nations. In recent years, ostensibly democratizing civilian governments have replaced brutal military regimes in Uruguay, Chile, Argentina and, most recently, El Salvador, and yet have been reluctant to allow full investigation into past human rights offences or have given retrospective amnesty to the perpetrators. A government which refuses to own up to atrocious acts committed by agents in its name seems still to insist that the extrajudicially executed, tortured and 'disappeared' are the guilty ones, and denies their relatives the public acknowledgement they need to make proper sense of their losses.

Constructions of 'war' by the humanitarian field: some issues

Suffering is at the centre of the social order and in this sense is 'normal'. Violent conflict is part of social experience and memory (Davis, 1992). It cannot be assumed that experiences of war are necessarily discontinuous from those arising out of other sorts of social destabilization and deprivation. There are 150 million children under 5 years old in the world with chronic protein–calorie malnutrition; their suffering is not necessarily less 'violent' or 'traumatic' than that occasioned by bombs and bullets, yet we talk of the trauma of war but not of the trauma of poverty and powerlessness. Westernization benefiting only an economic and military élite, unbridled exploitation of natural resources, chaotic urbanization and the plight of impoverished, landless peasants are all linked to the withering away of traditional self-sufficient ways of life in many parts of the world. In Cambodia, for example, neo-liberal economics reflecting the dominant Western order is undermining the integrity of the social and family fabric, and deepening poverty, no less effectively than did the violent upheavals of the Pol Pot period and the lower-level violence since then (Boyden and Gibbs, 1996). So too in Mozambique, where International Monetary Fund and World Bank structural adjustment has impeded the rebuilding of social and health services destroyed in the war; far too many are even poorer than before. The replacement of traditional cultural and spiritual beliefs by Western norms and values is cited by Cambodians as a contributory factor in this weakening of social networks, and of other concerns like the waning of parental authority over children.

Orthodox analysis in the non-governmental organizations (NGOs) involved in humanitarian work has held a relatively sharp distinction between relief and development, with disasters which create a need for emergency relief viewed as time-limited interruptions to the favoured task of development work. Duffield (1995) reminds us that in many parts of the world, war is not an extraordinary and short-lived event to be seen as extrinsic to the way a society functions in 'normal' times. It has become a given, something constant and internal that colours the whole web of political, socioeconomic and cultural relations across a society, and the daily calculations and activities of its citizens. As an example he cites Sudan, where the combined effects of an endemic civil war, successive famines and falling income from staple exports have brought it to a state of 'permanent emergency' marked by end-to-end relief operations. All over Africa, NGO resources which might have gone to development work have been diverted to relief operations. There has been less government–government assistance and much more channelled through UN agencies and NGOs, to the extent that NGOs have been replacing the state in the provision of basic welfare services. This gives them considerable clout. The backdrop to these shifts is the increase in the number of ongoing wars from 34 in 1970 to 56 in 1995 (90 per cent of them internal). The nation-state itself is under pressure: the poorest 20 per cent in the world are now 70 times poorer than the top 20 per cent (twice the difference of a generation ago); there are huge numbers of displaced peoples and a global rise in food insecurity. It is likely to become increasingly difficult to distinguish the effects of war, of environmental degradation and of global economic policies that mean structural poverty for the overwhelming majority. Their cumulative effects are devastating. A recent report from the WHO warns of a health catastrophe: life expectancy in the world's poorest countries is likely to fall by the year 2000, one-fifth of the 5.6 billion people on earth live in extreme poverty, one-third of the world's children are undernourished and half the global population does not have access to essential drugs (World Health Organization, 1995).

Duffield (1995) argues that the social and political economy of permanent emergency is complex and still poorly understood, but will be an important policy issue for the humanitarian field. There are losers in war but also winners, who may be an entire social sector or ethnic group and who take over the assets of the losers. For these people war is far from 'irrational', as it is sometimes termed, and indeed might be the only way they can achieve their desired ends. Without the brutality that drove ethnic cleansing, the Bosnian Serbs would not have the territory and political recognition they have today. The nature of humanitarian intervention is itself part of, and a contribution to, the complexity of modern emergencies. It is subject to influence, and indeed distortion, by donor priorities and fashions, as well as by wider political forces. It has negative side-effects as well as benefits. The conventional paradigms of 'relief' and 'development' are having to be rethought, and the argument that constructions of 'rape' or 'torture' are simplistic and decontextualizing may in many respects apply to 'war' as well.

World religions have struggled with the question of pain and suffering for centuries but in the twentieth century it is medicine and psychology that have come to dominate the language of distress in the Western world. Western ideas, which include our concepts of health and healing, are cultural products and are being globalized, often displacing indigenous forms of knowledge and coping. Thus the health and humanitarian fields are not exempt from consideration of issues of power and ideology. It is important that we reflect on our own assumptions, frequently unexamined, about the effects of war and atrocity on human beings in order that we do not unwittingly impose them on those we want to assist. As high as possible a level of scholarship about the interplay of political, social and cultural forces operating in a particular war zone will improve our capacity for accurate empathy with those affected, encouraging them to express themselves in their own terms and minimizing the likelihood that we will misunderstand them when they do so. This will minimize the chance of unwanted and wasteful assistance projects. The core question is, who has the power to define the most pressing problems? Too often those most affected are at a disadvantage here since they have so little influence.

Conflict impinges on every facet of life: economic, social, cultural, family. These effects should be seen as interactive and dynamic, rather than discrete strands to be analysed within the specialist disciplines of economics, sociology, anthropology, medicine and psychology. We should also pay attention to the output of local historians, poets and scholars. As far as health work is concerned, some projects in war zones will obviously be uncontroversial. However, we must also recognize that the scientific framework claims to objectify disease but that models which individualize ill health must mean its decontextualization from the social and cultural environment in which it is embedded. The current fashion for war trauma projects based on Western psychological concepts applied to non-Western populations in various war zones worldwide seems at risk of ignoring local norms and traditions, and the coping mechanisms based upon them. There is no one psychology to be considered universally valid (Bracken *et al.*, 1995). For the vast majority of survivors 'traumatization' is a pseudo-condition, a reframing of the ordinary distress and suffering engendered by war as a technical problem to which technical solutions (like 'counselling') are supposedly applicable. The direction of survivors' concerns is generally not inwards, towards their emotional lives, but outwards, towards their shattered social world. I have critiqued these issues at length elsewhere (Summerfield, 1996). Refugeedom too is not a thing apart, and the social theories we apply to refugees must also encompass their place in the world of non-refugees, and in a world order that does not enshrine basic rights for the least protected peoples on earth.

The core question is surely the role of a social world, invariably targeted by war (but equally vulnerable to Western-led economic policies) and yet embodying the capacity of survivor populations to manage their suffering, adapt and recover. It is crucial that the humanitarian field puts at centre stage their own expressed priorities – not least, calls for reparation and justice – and sees their knowledge as the basic frame of reference within which appropriate assistance projects are shaped. Some of their priorities may relate as much to the prewar backdrop – particularly poverty and marginalization – as to the supposedly direct effects of violence. Their needs are perhaps more typically for material assistance than for imported expertise, but certainly for the solidarity of those in the West in a position to pressurize those with influence in the political and economic order. Social healing and the reconstruction of valued ways of life and institutions cannot be managed by outsiders.

References

African Rights (1995) *Rwanda Not So Innocent: When Women Become Killers*. London: African Rights.

Allen, T. (1996) A flight from refuge. In T. Allen (ed.), *In Search of Cool Ground: War, Flight and Homecoming in Northeast Africa*, pp. 220–61. London: James Currey.

Al-Rasheed, M. (1994) The myth of return: Iraqi Arab and Assyrian refugees in London. *Journal of Refugee Studies*, 7, 199–219.

Andersson, N., Palha da Sousa, C. and Paredes, S. (1995) Social costs of landmines in four countries: Afghanistan, Bosnia, Cambodia and Mozambique. *British Medical Journal*, 311, 718–21.

Arms Project of Human Rights Watch and Physicians for Human Rights (1993) *Landmines: A Deadly Legacy*. New York: Cambridge University Press.

Bettelheim, B. (1960) *The Informed Heart*. New York: Free Press.

Boyden, J. and Gibbs, S. (1996) *Vulnerability and Resilience: Perceptions and Responses to Psycho-Social Distress in Cambodia*. Oxford: INTRAC.

Bracken, P., Giller, J. and Summerfield, D. (1995) Psychological responses to war and atrocity: the limitations of current concepts. *Social Science and Medicine*, 40, 1073–82.

British Medical Association (1992) *Medicine Betrayed: The Participation of Doctors in Human Rights Abuses*. London: Zed Books.

Cliff, J. and Noormahomed, A. (1988) Health as a target: South Africa's destabilisation of Mozambique. *Social Science and Medicine*, 27, 717–22.

Davis, J. (1992) The anthropology of suffering. *Journal of Refugee Studies*, 5, 149–61.

Dawes, A. (1990) The effects of political violence on children: a consideration of South African and related studies. *International Journal of Psychology*, 25, 13–31.

Duffield, M. (1995) The political economy of internal war: asset transfer, complex emergencies and international aid. In A. Zwi and J. Macrae (eds), *War and Hunger: Rethinking International Responses to Complex Emergencies*, pp. 50–69. London: Zed Books/Save the Children Fund.

Eastmond, M., Ralphsson, L. and Alinder, B. (1994) The psychological impact of violence and war: Bosnian refugee families and coping strategies. *Refugee Participation Network*, 16, 7–9.

Eisenbruch, M. (1991) From post-traumatic stress disorder to cultural bereavement: diagnosis of Southeast Asian refugees. *Social Science and Medicine*, 33, 673–80.

Garfield, R. and Williams, G. (1989) *Health and Revolution: The Nicaraguan Experience*. Oxford: Oxfam.

Godlee, F. (1993) Syria accused of torturing doctors and scientists. *British Medical Journal*, 306, 1089.

Harrell-Bond, B. and Wilson, K. (1990) Dealing with dying: some anthropological reflections on the need for assistance by refugee relief programmes for bereavement and burial. *Journal of Refugee Studies*, 3, 228–43.

Logie, D. (1992) The great exterminator of children. *British Medical Journal*, 304, 1423–6.

Lykes, M.B. (1994) Terror, silencing and children: international multidisciplinary collaboration with Guatemalan Mayan communities. *Social Science and Medicine*, 38, 543–52.

Makiya, K. (1993) *Cruelty and Silence: War, Tyranny, Uprising and the Arab World*. London: Jonathan Cape.

Martin-Baro, I. (1990) War and the Psychosocial Trauma of Salvadoran Children. Posthumous presentation to the Annual Meeting of the American Psychological Association, Boston.

Middle East Watch and Physicians for Human Rights (1993) *The Anfal Campaign in Iraqi Kurdistan: The Destruction of Koreme*. New York: Human Rights Watch.

Mollica, R. and Caspi-Yavin, Y. (1992) Overview: the assessment and diagnosis of torture events and symptoms. In M. Basoglu (ed.), *Torture and Its Consequences*, pp. 253–74. Cambridge: Cambridge University Press.

Panos Institute (1988) *War Wounds: Development Costs of Conflict in Southern Sudan*. London: Panos Institute.

Parliamentary Human Rights Group (1994) *Iran: The Subjugation of Women*. London: Parliamentary Human Rights Group.

Physicians for Human Rights (1993) *Human Rights on Hold: A Report on*

Emergency Measures and Access to Health Care in the Occupied Territories. Boston: Physicians for Human Rights.

Punamäki, R.-L. and Suleiman, R. (1990) Predictors and effectiveness of coping with political violence among Palestinian children. *British Journal of Social Psychology*, **29**, 67–77.

Siward, R. (1989) *World Military and Social Expenditures*. Washington, DC: World Priorities.

Summerfield, D. (1992) Philippines: health, human rights and 'low-intensity' war. *Lancet*, **339**, 173.

Summerfield, D. (1996) *The Impact of War and Atrocity on Civilian Populations: Basic Principles for NGO Interventions and a Critique of Psychosocial Trauma Projects*. Relief and Rehabilitation Network Paper 14. London: Overseas Development Institute.

Summerfield, D. and Hume, F. (1993) War and post-traumatic stress disorder: the question of social context. *Journal of Nervous and Mental Disease*, **181**, 522.

Swiss, S. and Giller, J. (1993) Rape as a crime of war: a medical perspective. *Journal of the American Medical Association*, **270**, 612–15.

Turton, D. (1991) Warfare, vulnerability and survival: a case from southwestern Ethiopia. *Disasters*, **15**, 254–64.

UNICEF (1986) *Children in Situations of Armed Conflict*. E/ICEF.CRP.2. New York: UNICEF.

UNICEF (1996) *The State of the World's Children*. New York: Oxford University Press.

Van Ginneken, E. and Rijnders, R. (1993) *Tazmamart: fort-militaire secret du Maroc: conséquences d'un internement de 18 années*. Amersfoort: Johannes Wier Foundation for Health and Human Rights.

Wearne, P. (1994) *The Maya of Guatemala*. London: Minority Rights Group International.

Wilson, K. (1992) Cults of violence and counter-violence in Mozambique. *Journal of Southern African Studies*, **18**, 527–82.

World Health Organization (1995) *Bridging the Gaps*. Geneva: WHO.

Zur, J. (1994) The psychological impact of impunity. *Anthropology Today*, **10**, 12–17.

Zwi, A. and Ugalde, A. (1989) Towards an epidemiology of political violence in the Third World. *Social Science and Medicine*, **28**, 633–42.

6

The experience of refugees as recipients of aid

Barbara Harrell-Bond

Introduction

This chapter is written from the perspective of an anthropologist observing those who provide aid to refugees and their relationships with those who receive it. The aim is to explore the refugee experience of being helped, and relationships between refugees and those who help them, in order to raise the possibility that the modalities of distributing aid, or the 'helping', may themselves undermine the personal coping resources of individuals. Is it possible that the way refugees are 'helped' is one source of debilitating stress for those who are in a position where they have no alternative but to receive?

Was Marcel Mauss (1925) correct when he said that the gift debases the one who receives, especially when there is no intention (or ability) to reciprocate? It was Mauss who taught us that unequal power is the essence of the relationship between the giver and the recipient – until the gift is reciprocated (Voutira and Harrell-Bond, 1995). There is a great deal of rhetoric about 'empowering' refugees, particularly the women, but very little discussion of the use (and abuse) of power by those who distribute aid, or who has the power to decide who should be 'empowered'.[1]

There is considerable literature about the resettlement process, or adaptation, itself as a source of stress (e.g. Beiser, 1993). Indra (1988, 1993) has focused specifically on the problems which arise in the asymmetrical relations which exist between refugees and their sponsors in Canada. Her comparisons of the experiences of the privately sponsored refugees with those assisted through the fairly impersonal state-run programme suggested to her that the 'social psychological effects' for the privately sponsored refugees 'may have been somewhat inferior' (1993, p. 229).

[W]hile private sponsorship [in Canada] was a remarkable example of altruistically motivated giving marked by high levels of sponsor commitment and sacrifice it was also a highly political process. That process was grounded in an ideal western concept of charity that was practically expressed in highly symbolic forms of asymmetrical social exchange for which refugee individuals could rarely find a personally and culturally acceptable model. (Indra, 1993, p. 230)[2]

One might have thought that the availability of such literature would have already alerted social scientists to the need to pay more attention to the stress associated with the experience of the disempowerment through being helped, so characteristic of the process of becoming a refugee. Much of the literature concerned with refugee mental health focuses, however, on the impact of violence, torture and uprooting (Ager, 1993). It tends to attribute the mental health problems of refugees to the losses, including loss of culture, experienced as a result of flight (e.g. Baskauskas, 1981; Marris, 1986; Aron, 1988; Eisenbruch, 1984, 1990; Ager, 1993), or on the violence and/or torture individuals suffered which led to their flight. There are a growing number of centres which provide therapy to 'victims' of torture. In fact, a near-global industry has emerged to deal with this phenomenon (Bracken *et al.*, 1995; Summerfield and Hume, 1993; Summerfield, 1991, 1997).

There are also studies which examine the impact of the stresses of adaptation that follow flight and settlement. For example, a study of Somalis in London found that of the different 'risks' of impoverishment relating to displacement (Cernea, 1995), insecure *housing*, not war experiences, torture, detention, nor death of relatives, was the most significant variable predicting which refugees would report mental health problems (Dahoud and Pelosi, 1989, 1991; see also Spitzer, 1989). There are other studies which focus on the relation of minorities *vis-à-vis* mainstream society (e.g. integrated, assimilated, or marginalized) and the implications of these relationships for mental health outcomes (e.g. Berry, 1991; Berry *et al.*, 1992; see also Chapter 7).

I have found few studies, however, that relate the mental health of refugees to their experiences during the 'liminal' stage of their transition from flight to resettlement that takes place in the context of camps, particularly for refugees in the South. Despite their ostensible 'temporary' nature, these settings have become the main 'living environments' for many refugees for many years. In this respect, the conditions of refugee mental health remain fundamentally under-researched and thus under-determined (Voutira and Harrell-Bond, 1995).[3]

Beiser *et al.* (1989), however, conducted a study which related the mental health problems of Vietnamese refugees to the experience of stress associated with the relative harshness of the camp situations in which they lived prior to being resettled in Canada:

Although it has not been prominent in studies of the refugees experience, we have found the 'stress process' a useful frame of reference. Stress is an event or experience that challenges one's usual coping patterns, thus requiring a new adaptation. Since the capacity to adapt to challenge is finite, massive stress or an accumulation of stressors sometimes overwhelm the individual, resulting in an increased vulnerability to illness. (p. 184)

These findings of Beiser *et al.* concerning Vietnamese people settled in Canada suggest that the more authoritarian the camp administration, the less control refugees had over their own lives in these camps, the more likely they were to manifest symptoms of mental ill health in the process of their adaptation to Canada. Such observations tally with the model of camps as Goffman-like (Goffman, 1961) 'total institutions' and with observations of the impact of their authoritarian structure on the coping strategies of the 'inmates' (Waldron, 1987; Hyndman, 1996, 1997). As Hyndman (1996, p. 23) observes from her fieldwork in Dadaab camp:

In refugee camps power is exercised through both coercion and discipline. Kenyan police guard the camps ... while the 'humanitarian international' literally organises the field: building camps in a grid style; generating systems to meet refugees' basic needs in an orderly way; and checking refugee cards to ensure a match between family size and their given rations.

Psychologists are well aware that adverse experiences at different stages in the development cycle have consequences for mental health. There are many allusions to, and some research on, the particular hardships of refugees disaggregated by age and gender.[4] Most of the research (Ager, 1993; see also Chapter 7) has been conducted in industrialized countries among 'resettled' refugees.[5] What is not known is how growing up or living out one's old age as a camp refugee dependent on international aid for survival impacts on these different age groups; for example, on children, adolescents and the elderly.

Gender may be another critical variable (see Chapter 8). There are many publications which are concerned with the way the hardship of refugee life differentially impacts on women (e.g. Ager *et al.*, 1995; Kay, 1987; Voutira *et al.*, 1995; Hyndman, 1996). Yet *is* there good evidence that being dependent on assistance for survival, or being the recipient of help from strangers, differentially affects men and women? Time is another factor which Beiser has identified as a factor in reducing the effects of harsh experiences (1987), but Ager (1993) has reviewed some contradictory findings.

Perhaps as important in the way situations are perceived as stressful are differences in educational levels and social class backgrounds (Ritchie, 1992; Reeves, 1997). Margaret Reeves, in her article 'Could Oxford dons survive?', describes the 'particular challenge' of surviving camp conditions faced by highly educated Rwandans. One expressed his suffering in their goodbyes when he asked, 'Can you leave me a book? I feel my mind is dying here.' Another factor which may affect a refugee's capacity to cope is his or her religious belief,[6] or commitment to a political cause. One 'victim' of detention and torture from Argentina told me how he hated the 'how sorry' statements of helpers. 'We knew *why* we were detained. We knew why we were being tortured.' He explained how such statements of sympathy could undermine the very identity of someone who has had the courage to suffer for principles.

What is important to emphasize is, as Beiser *et al.* have noted: 'most refugees do not become mental health casualties.... The hope is that increased understanding of the components of stress, as well as of the factors which mitigate risk, will make possible the development of successful and timely mental health interventions' (1989, p. 183). Enormous amounts of money are invested in so-called psychosocial interventions, but, unfortunately, few are informed by research (Ager, 1993).

Is dependence on aid a source of stress for refugees?

Is one of the major sources of stress the experience of being helped?

> [S]ocial service deliverers customarily create an image of 'the refugee' in such a way that as 'experts' they can take custody of them. Individuals are made into 'clients' by being categorised impersonally. Policy is decided deductively and unilaterally, with little input from refugees themselves. This creates a 'non-reciprocal causal epistemology' among practitioners in which cause and effect ... is self-evident, in which refugeeism is constructed as a social problem and where there is a standardised prescription of how experts should act in order to ensure their clients' salvation. (Indra, 1993, p. 234)

Given the wide variety of pre- and post-flight experiences, a sophisticated research design would be required to corroborate the underlying 'hypothesis' of this discussion, that one of the intervening factors is the structure of aid to refugees itself. All human beings are dependent on others to a greater or lesser extent; the issue is not being 'helped' *per se*, but the relative powerlessness of the recipient *vis-à-vis* the helper. In this sense, research would test whether one of the major sources of debilitating stress is the very *structure* of the aid regime for refugees.

Research could be designed to compare the mental health outcomes of the assisted (that is, refugees in camps in the South or 'on welfare' in countries of resettlement) and those of unassisted refugees (Hansen, 1982,

1990). Since most refugees in the world do not receive official assistance –
they settle themselves among their hosts, often with kin or at least co-
nationals – such a study of mental health outcomes is conceivable.

There are other groups of refugees that would be even more interesting
for comparison than the so-called spontaneously settled refugees, who, at
least in many African countries today, are increasingly subjected to police
and military swoops aimed at forcing them into camps (Hannan, 1997;
Africa Rights, 1997).[7] These are refugees who manage their own
assistance: the Saharawi in Algeria (Harrell-Bond, 1981; Lawless and
Monahan, 1988) or the Tibetans in India (Subba, 1990).[8] In both these
cases external aid is channelled through the governments-in-exile which
have been recognized by the host government.[9]

If it were possible for us to know that altering the existing power
relations which obtain in assistance programmes organized by international humanitarian programmes eliminated a significant source of stress
in the refugee experience, what would it cost to change these? The
resistance of some humanitarian workers to the introduction of 'self-
management' or 'democracy' into Dadaab camp in Kenya suggests that
international agencies have very strong interests in maintaining the
distinct type of social environment of the camps they run in order to keep
control over the distribution of aid (Hyndman, 1996, 1997; Harrell-Bond
et al., 1992; Voutira and Harrell-Bond, 1995). Sidney Waldron is another
person who has identified the 'class structure' of refugee camps as a
source of 'grave damage to all involved' (Waldron, 1992; see also
Waldron, 1987).[10]

I am indebted to the Saharawi refugees whom I visited in 1981 for being
the catalyst for the work which I have done since 1982. It was my visit to
their camps near Tindouf and subsequent discussions with Oxfam staff in
Oxford that led me to ask whether or not a major problem facing refugees
is their helpers. It is not that refugees do not need help; they do. The
problem, it is suggested, is the kind of help they receive, the way help is
provided, and the role which they are forced to assume to get it.

What do refugees say about being 'helped'?

A search of Oxford's Refugee Studies Programme (RSP) library for
examples of refugees' oral testimonies of their experiences of being
assisted brought forward several examples of agency publications. The
refugee 'voices' expressed in these works concentrate on 'the sadness of
exile', the 'longing for home', and how 'grateful' refugees are to those
who have come to assist them (see UNHCR, 1997).[11]

Assistance programmes for refugees in the South often depersonalize
refugees. Humanitarian assistance is planned on the assumption that the

affected populations are homogeneous, undifferentiated masses. As one aid worker observed, 'Dignity is the vital ingredient missing when basic physical needs are delivered in a mechanistic and impersonal way. Respect for human dignity is too often the first casualty in emergency responses to refugees' (as quoted in Needham, 1994). Somali refugees point out that headcounts which require them to be rounded up inside fenced lots do not 'respect basic human dignity'. For them, this experience common to refugees in most camps 'reminded them of the slavery under Arab rule' (Hyndman, 1996, p. 101).

In relation to the aid workers, individuals become nameless numbers, not faces.[12] 'Individual cases', or 'ICs' as they are referred to by agency staff, are the bane of every humanitarian agency office. Field staff are overworked and not trained to cope with most individual problems that present themselves. Their sense of frustration may account for the amazing levels of hostility which one so frequently observes in their relationships with refugees. On one occasion I observed a refugee literally waiting seven days for an appointment outside the UNHCR office in Yei River District. Listening and resolving his problem took exactly ten minutes once he finally got his turn to enter the office.

Some refugees decide to get attention by dramatizing their frustrations. In one notorious case during my research in southern Sudan, one threatened to hang himself if not immediately allowed to talk with someone about his particular problem. The overworked official on duty, preoccupied with accounts, advised him to 'proceed'. He did, and it was only at the very last moment, as the refugee was about to step off his makeshift gallows before the spellbound audience of other waiting refugees, that this exasperated expatriate surrendered to the psychological pressure and agreed to grant an 'audience'.

Another refugee who was trying to get attention to his problem through behaviour perceived as bizarre was accused by an aid worker of being 'mad'. After insisting on an examination and receiving a medical certificate verifying his sanity, this Ugandan decided to sue UNHCR for libel. Offering to 'settle out of court', in his written submission to UNHCR, he listed what he would accept as compensation: clothing, shoes, spectacles and neckties. He concluded, 'With all these I will be sure to appear like a man and a living man. Not a statue or a picture' (Harrell-Bond, 1986, p. 308).

To what extent is *inappropriate* aid a stress factor?[13] Take the bundles of used clothes that arrive in a refugee camp, for example. There are rarely enough suitable clothes for men and southern Sudan can be extremely cold. There is, apparently, a great surplus of nylon quilted women's dressing-gowns (bathrobes) donated to refugees. These appeared to be the only garments available to Ugandan men to wear to keep warm.[14] To take another example, food in camps is not only too little for survival, it is often totally unfamiliar. Often refugees do not know how to prepare it and it is difficult to get children to eat. It does not require an anthropologist to explain how difficult it is to adapt to foreign foods.

Some Bosnian refugees articulated their reactions to the inappropriate contents of their food packages as evidence that the donors did not *respect* them enough to bother to consider them as 'fellow human beings'. This reference to a sense of lack of 'respect', and the other words refugees use to describe how it feels to be a recipient of aid, are themselves telling: 'humiliated', 'degraded', 'shamed', 'disgraced'. The memories of parti- cular incidents of feeling humiliated apparently can last a lifetime.

One Palestinian refugee, now 46 years old and a father of five children, still recalls his experience as a 7-year-old child. It happened at the end of his first term. There was a prize-giving ceremony. At the end of it the headmistress said, 'and finally, a special prize for little Ahmed, for though his clothes are old and torn, they are always clean'. Ahmed had to walk up in front of his forty classmates to receive a certificate.

> After telling me this story, Ahmed decided that this had been the most defining traumatic moment of his life. In this context, it is worth noting that Ahmed has lived through not only the loss of his country, but over thirty years of Israeli occupation. He was determined that his children would never suffer the same humiliation. (Louise Weighill, personal communication)

Some refugees equate their experience of requiring help with the pain of being dependent:

> How does it feel to depend on others for all of your basic requirements? Has it occurred to you what you would have to do if your wife or child was sick and you have to obtain a reference letter prior to taking them to hospital? What would you do when for some reasons, you cannot see the doctor you are referred to? I can tell you what you would have to do. You would have to return the next day because you cannot afford to see another doctor. How would you feel when the nearest maternity hospital for your wife to deliver is more than fifty kilometres away? You will also pray that her labour starts during the daylight. (Anon.)

Frequently refugees describe the behaviour of the helpers they meet as patronizing and condescending. One refugee, a university student from the now Democratic Republic of Congo, described his experiences in Sweden, where he was said he was treated 'like a baby'. He acted out for me how one of his 'helpers' spoke to him: 'Now this is how you pick up a plate. This is the way you place it on the cupboard.' He went on, 'They tried to make me feel as if I were back to zero.' Even though he learned about a more appropriate language class in Uppsala, preparing foreign students for entering university (as he expected to do), he was forced to learn Swedish with a group of mixed ages which included persons who were pre-literate. 'They would *not* allow me to work things out for myself.'[15]

Is the common experience of suffering loss of status or 'declassing' in relation to helpers another source of stress for refugees? Perhaps for most refugees in the world, the first time they receive rations in a camp or 'dole' money from a state institution may also be the first time in their lives they have received help from a stranger. This was certainly a blow to one refugee who had previously been a manager of a refugee camp in the Sudan before seeking asylum in Europe. On the second day of his arrival, he was shocked to find himself queuing along with the poor and homeless, some of them obviously mentally ill, 'drugees' and alcoholics. As he described it, 'All of a sudden my role changed ... [to that of a] vulnerable person and [I am] viewed as an object of philanthropy ... becoming a refugee means lowering one's social and economic status.... It is synonymous with losing self-esteem and self-confidence' (interview, Dublin, June, 1997).

Rather than viewing themselves as heroes who have stood up to, and escaped from oppressive regimes, today many refugees are very reluctant to admit their status. Rather than perceiving themselves as persons who have rights under international humanitarian and human rights law, many feel they are obligated for *any* help they receive.[16]

That refugees are expected to appreciate whatever is offered is expressed by aid workers in different ways. At a conference at the RSP, where the menu of one meal was World Food Programme (WFP) rations, an agency worker was reminded by a refugee sitting beside him that 'What we are eating is a whole day's ration, not just one meal.' The response was, 'If you refugees are not grateful for what we are doing, we should just stop.' Hyndman (1996) found that Somalians also have a reputation for 'talking back' to relief workers, 'rejecting the charity script of the needy and grateful'. Is that the reason why, as one Red Cross worker told her, 'the Somalis are hated by every delegate' (p. 117)?[17]

In introducing his book *From Citizen to Refugee*, which he says includes the story of those who 'refused' to become refugees, Mamdani notes that he used the term 'refugee' with some hesitation:

Contrary to what I believed in Uganda, a refugee is not just a person who has been displaced and has lost all or most of his possessions. A refugee is in fact more akin to a child: helpless, devoid of initiative, somebody on whom any kind of charity can be practised, in short, a totally malleable creature. (Mamdani, 1973, Preface)

When refugees were still 'people'

After World War II, the policy of host states for refugee assistance and settlement was largely based on the logic of integration through the labour market (Skran, 1995). Refugees fleeing communism were not regarded as helpless. They were Europeans. In the context of the Cold War, they represented votes for liberal democracy. The reception of refugees was also influenced by postwar appeals which had emphasized the unique potential of arriving refugees for the economic growth of their host's economy (Harrell-Bond, 1985).[18]

Consequently, there was little concern with state provision of social and psychological support to assist them in the process of their adaptation in the 'new lands' (Harrell-Bond, 1985). Even when the Allied forces were responsible for providing for the 60 million refugees after the war, the approach was to place responsibility for all administration of the camps into the hands of the people themselves, 'Self-government was recommended for the centers ... for the time-honoured reasons that the best welfare officer is the man who can teach the people to dispense with his services' (Proudfoot, 1957, p. 163).

Before visiting the Saharawi in 1981 (Harrell-Bond, 1981), my only previous experience of refugees was working for a few months in 1956–7 as a resettlement officer, assisting some of the Hungarians arriving in Los Angeles. Once these refugees arrived at the military base in New York State from a reception centre in Austria, their settlement in various parts of the USA became the responsibility of their sponsors, most often evangelical church groups or individuals.

At the time, the survival of Hungarians in the USA depended mainly on their finding employment. There were no formal government-funded welfare programmes or language-training facilities for these refugees. Assistance was provided by Catholic and Lutheran church organizations. I worked for the Church Federation of Los Angeles, an ecumenical body. Those who came to my office for assistance were those who had fallen through the net of the denominational programmes. In short, most assistance was contingent on the individuals' identity and their membership in a particular confessional group, and/or their willingness to conform to its strictures.

The level of confidence that Hungarian refugees could 'make it', with little more help than transport to freedom, was most dramatically demonstrated by one church-sponsored programme I observed in Los Angeles. Many of 'their' Hungarians were simply met at the airport; goodbyes were said after they had been checked into a cheap hotel. Since the mounting bill was theirs to pay, these refugees wasted no time in trying to find employment of any kind. Others sponsored by evangelical churches or families were usually provided furnished accommodation, the rent being paid by the sponsors for a short period of time. However, in most of these cases these beneficiaries were then expected to attend church services, and sometimes perhaps mid-week prayer meetings too. Since most Hungarians were not prepared to conform, and the booming postwar economy of the arms race allowed for some options, relationships with such sponsors were frequently short-lived.

My office at the Church Federation, an umbrella organization for Christian churches, received the 'problems' – or should I say, those who did not, or were not prepared to, conform with the helpers' norms or expectations. These included people who had not registered themselves as Catholics or Lutherans (or at least Protestants), couples who were 'intermarried', and people who professed no faith at all. I also assisted individuals who found the conditions of adaptation too severe and who requested to be enabled to return to Hungary.[19]

Dashed hopes about life in exile may be another source of stress in relationships between refugees and aid workers. Some Hungarians did arrive with unrealistic expectations about what life in exile in the USA would be like. One such case was a Hungarian man who spoke enough English to shout while pounding my desk that he wanted 'big house, big car, work five hours a day'. His sponsor had arranged a small flat for him to rent and a full-time job in a shop. I had to explain that in America people had to earn money to acquire these things and that some people worked for *more* than the eight hours a day to which he was objecting. However, I went on, if he was finding this arrangement too difficult (since by now I learned that I could), if he preferred, my government could arrange for him to return to Hungary. He decided to remain and work until he could buy his own car and house.

Incompatible values were a frequent cause of conflict, if not stress, in relationships between Hungarians and their helpers. Some were actually rejected (and *ejected*) by sponsors because they had failed to 'appreciate' the help they were receiving or were perceived as refusing to make the effort to 'fit in'. For example, one 19-year-old Hungarian was accommodated in the home of his sponsor. Speaking no English and still unemployed, he spent his time watching television and smoking, using the toilet for his stubs. One day the exasperated housewife handed him a towel and asked him to wipe the dishes for her. He drew himself to full height, threw the towel on the floor and announced, 'I, Hungarian man. Dishes, *woman's* work.' He was promptly driven to my office with his luggage. I was informed, 'You can keep your Hungarian *man*!' Fortunately, I did not need to 'keep' him; both employment and a place to live on his own were found.

As noted, refugees were expected to *conform* to the values of their sponsors with little or no information about what was expected or acceptable to them.[20] There was little or no effort on the part of the American sponsors to understand the Hungarians, or Hungarian.[21] In the

1950s Americans were perhaps even less 'worldly wise' than they are today. For example, one church offering to help Hungarians settle in Los Angeles learned of an engaged couple who needed a sponsor. Thinking how romantic it would be to hold a wedding ceremony in their beautiful Presbyterian church, the congregation pitched together to raise the money to rent and furnish *two* flats. When they arrived in Los Angeles from the military camp in New Jersey where Hungarians were first housed on their arrival in the USA, the couple promptly moved in together into one flat. The final straw came when the woman approached a surgeon, a deacon in the church, requesting him to perform an abortion, illegal at the time. The troubled clergyman came to the Church Federation for help. Together with a lawyer, the first Hungarian whom I met who could speak English,[22] the woman was interviewed in *their* flat. Completely unconscious that her lifestyle was a matter of anyone's concern, much less their business, in no uncertain terms she expressed her fury at the refusal of the doctor to perform the abortion, but announced to us that she had 'taken care of the matter herself'. She then requested that it be arranged for her to go to Reno, Nevada, or Mexico. What for? In her eyes, for a small detail, a 'divorce'! The couple could not marry until her partner obtained a divorce from the wife he had left behind in Hungary! They continued to cohabit, against the norms of their sponsor, the religious organization that was supporting the process of their integration. Perhaps it should not be surprising, this being the period of 'McCarthyism', to learn that not much later this man was identified as a communist spy who had infiltrated the USA along with the freedom-fighters, and he was summarily deported.

Over the years I maintained contact with those Hungarians with whom I had developed a personal relationship. Although I do not know enough to generalize about Hungarian patterns of adaptation, there is theoretical literature to support the impression that, like other post-World War II East European refugees, Hungarians drew their strength from ethnic networks and the cultural associations which existed or that they formed (e.g. Marx, 1990; Indra, 1988, 1993).[23]

The 'repackaging' of refugees

My visit to the Saharawi in 1981 forced me to come to grips with a radically different context of aid intervention, one situated in the so-called Third World. My trip to the Saharawi camps near Tindouf, Algeria, was originally undertaken simply to supplement information for writing on the war over the Western Sahara that had begun with Morocco's invasion in 1975 (Harrell-Bond, 1981).

My previous experience of assisting Hungarian refugees was undertaken in the context of 'my own society' where refugees were largely defined as victims of communism and 'votes for democracy', or, when they did not conform, as possible spies and 'infiltrators'. It did not prepare me for the negative perceptions of refugees which I found in the sparse literature, mainly unpublished agency reports, on refugees in Africa.

From my reading, I discovered that the 'packaging' of refugees had dramatically altered. The documents I obtained from agencies emphasized images of helpless, starving masses who depend on agents of compassion to keep them alive. It was assumed by humanitarian agencies that refugees always require relief and that this assistance must come from outside the host country. Moreover, it was – and continues to be – assumed that, left to their own devices, 'Third World' refugees would remain perpetually dependent on relief; outsiders are therefore needed to get the refugees to be self-supporting (Hyndman, 1997).[24]

Such assumptions are rooted in modernization theory, which has remained the dominant paradigm for understanding poverty and underdevelopment in Africa (see Ake, 1996 and Chapter 4 in this volume). In short, this approach to development was based on the understanding that economic growth required a total revolution of African societies, of their values, their social organization and of the way they earned their living. These changes would be best brought about if people were uprooted from their familiar environments and resettled under conditions where they would be more receptive to new ideas and where any resistance to adapting to the new methods of, for example, mechanized agriculture could be overcome by *managing* the process of adaptation, making it the condition of obtaining the means of survival, access to land (Daley, 1989).

UNHCR became involved in assisting refugees in the heyday of efforts by the World Bank and others to modernize African peasants, and it was advised by the same persons as those advising the Bank. Although its aim was to make refugees self-sufficient, UNHCR saw refugees through the lens of modernization theory. Thus it should not be surprising to learn that according to the agencies, the best way to make refugees self-sufficient is to put them into camps where they can be managed and that the agencies continue to resist the suggestion that refugees are capable of managing themselves (see Hyndman, 1997).

There were three phases to this strategy.[25] First, refugees are transported to camps, given relief and expected to inhabit houses built for them, or to build their own. During the second stage they receive tools and seeds; they are allocated plots of land and primary education is organized. During this period refugees are expected to be motivated to work – to get on their own feet quickly – by being warned well in advance that there will be a gradual reduction of food rations after the first harvest. In the third stage, aid is withdrawn on the grounds that by this time, refugees will be self-sufficient and integrated into the host economy.

For the most part, results have been disappointing, but the responsibility for these failures is laid at the feet of the refugees themselves (Waldron, 1987). During the period of receiving assistance, it is believed, refugees adopt attitudes and behaviour which impede their progress towards self-sufficiency. Thus, by the time it is possible to introduce long-term solutions, the 'dependency syndrome' has already become entrenched. But, as Waldron (1992, p. 6) has noted,

> a dependency syndrome does not derive from any psychological weakness.... Rather, in the context of the model of stratification employed here [in refugee settlements], such 'dependence' may be described ... as, simply, the adjustment of the enclosed refugee population to the long-term conditions of a direct delivery, donor economy. To blame refugees for adapting to the social and economic structure of the refugee settlement is illogical and unfair. Moreover, the common use of dependency in refugee contexts has strong moral overtones which condemn refugees for 'freeloading', rather than spontaneously breaking out of the class and control structure imposed upon them.

Nevertheless, a kind of working hypothesis has developed among humanitarians: 'The more you give, the more dependent people become.'

Underlying all such explicit and implicit assumptions concerning the role of assistance programmes for refugees is the fundamental belief that aid, in and of itself, has to the power to move populations. Aid, it is believed, can attract people from point A to point B and back again to point A (Aga Khan, 1981).

Humanitarians thus face a dilemma. To prevent mass starvation, aid is obviously needed. Yet to provide assistance risks the danger that yet more people will be attracted across borders. A delicate balance must be struck. Aid should thus be evenly distributed on a per capita basis and assistance should not be so generous that refugees seem better off than their hosts. In practice, the measure of this level seems to be that of the very poorest members of the host society. Too much assistance, and refugees will refuse to work for themselves; too little assistance, too many die and the humanitarian community gets a bad name. The isolation and alienation of humanitarian workers from the local reality shields them from evidence which would contradict such assumptions, but the belief that meagre rations, plastic sheeting for shelter, dinnerware, a hoe and a *panga* cause hundreds and thousands of people to flee ancestral homelands to seek refuge beggars belief.

When repatriation is deemed to be in the political interest of the country of origin, the host or the donor governments (who wish to decrease or terminate financial obligations), or all of them, aid is gradually reduced or cut off and inducements are handed out on the other side of the border. These 'inducements' are no more than the relief packages which are provided to refugees.

The control of this powerful tool of manipulation has been delegated by donor governments to humanitarian agencies. The questions asked by agencies are: how much, what kind of aid, where, who, and when? What is never questioned is who should be responsible for these decisions. The result of the failure to ask this question leads to misallocation of scarce resources and misapplication of aid. If aid were to come from inside the host country, or if management responsibilities were shared with hosts and refugees, the monopoly on power, held by the outsiders, would be broken.[26]

Socializing refugees: the impact of the gift

As noted earlier, to understand the experience of refugees as recipients of aid requires an examination of the dynamics of giving and receiving. This is a subject very close to the hearts of anthropologists who have been studying societies based on norms of reciprocity and exchange, or in the process of transition and adaptation of these norms to those of the 'global culture'. As Marcel Mauss discovered, the act of giving is not simply mechanical; the gift defines the status and power relationships which exist between the giver and the one who receives it (1925).

Mauss's significant anthropological insight was that great or small acts of generosity are seldom free from self-interest, whether the gift is given by a state or by individuals. The giving of gifts demands reciprocity, whether in material or in symbolic (e.g. spiritual reward) terms. The act of receiving places the recipient in a position of obligation, an inferior position *vis-à-vis* the benefactor until the gift has been reciprocated. In Islam, for example, 'rulers are strongly warned against accepting gifts offered to them' (Uthman, 1978). Indeed, as Mauss put it, the gift not repaid debases the man who accepted it, particularly if he 'did so without thought of return' (Harrell-Bond *et al.*, 1992, p. 207).

In the case of the Hungarians in 1956, and even the Czech refugees in 1968, humanitarian organizations were able to base their appeals for funds on anti-communist sentiments, but once refugees were originating from the South, what else was left besides human misery to trade upon to raise funds?

Agencies vary in the degree of dignity with which they transmit images of refugees, but all rely on funding from a public which responds to media portrayal of extreme human suffering, starvation and helplessness. Pictures depict refugees in postures of submission, despair and utter destitution. While some agencies are concerned about the risks of satiating the public with fundraising and advocacy appeals based on the image of the starving child, this form of marketing of refugees continues.

The image of helpless refugees, desperately in need, reinforces the view that outsiders are needed to help them. This view underpins the willingness to give humanitarian aid. A survey carried out by NGOs reported by Beristain and Doná (1997) found that 'every second person interviewed maintained that Europe's relationship to the South is based on the South's need for aid' (p. 37). As Beristain and Doná also note, this stereotyping of refugees as passive and powerless victims influences both the way in which humanitarian aid is organized and interpersonal relations between those who come to 'help'.

The standard image of the helpless refugee also reinforces the view of their incapability, motivating people from all walks of life to offer their services. Refugees attract 'volunteers', often people with no specialized training, who often behave as though they 'need refugees more than refugees need them'. As Steen (1993, quoting de Voe, 1986) notes, their 'benefaction is not altruistic but virtually overwhelming in its creation of uncertain but felt obligations placing refugees in an unequal position in relation to their benefactors' (p. 9). Unable to repay such obligations, refugees feel compelled to exhibit the deference of a subordinate.

One refugee, employed by a German agency, reported her experience:

> She said, 'You cannot be a refugee.' But I told her 'I am one.' It is because I can speak English. [This] changes the images of a refugee from ... the starving children of the posters, to real people who used to manage their own affairs and then became displaced. This image ... is so world-wide that I decided not to get angry [with her].... The fact that our status has changed does not mean that our abilities have gone down. (Harrell-Bond, 1986, p. 12)

Hyndman's (1996) work among the Somalians led her to conclude that their collective self-esteem has been undermined by decades of aid dependence. Quoting an aid worker, she notes:

> The humiliations of refugee life have further contributed to undermining self-confidence ... the traditional aid approach has generally encouraged its recipients to represent themselves as helpless victims of circumstances. Some Somalis have been representing themselves in this way for so long that, along with convincing the donors of its reality, they've also convinced themselves.

This, she observes, has led to a 'diminution' of their capacities 'as their energy and intelligence are increasingly directed towards manipulating donors for "freebies"' (1996, p. 107).

Steen's (1993) study of the Tamils compared the outcomes of Denmark's policy with the *laissez-faire* welfare approach of the UK. Because of their economic success, Steen describes the Tamils in the UK as 'Thatcher boys'. In contrast, she found that the Tamils in Denmark had been effectively deskilled by the extended orientation programme this government provides; even those who arrived with employable skills had been discouraged by their social worker from seeking employment until they learned Danish.

There is a great deal of evidence suggesting the iatrogenic effects of the welfare model which defines the roles that refugees are expected to play *vis-à-vis* their helpers (Harrell-Bond, 1986; Voutira and Harrell-Bond, 1995). For example, the Finnish approach to refugees has been described as treating them like

> other weak groups such as children, disabled people and alcoholics … [they are] often understood as persons who must undergo a kind of re-socialisation into Finnish society … treated in the same way as small children … there is a risk that the welfare system transforms active adults refugees into passive clients. (Wahlbeck, 1997, p. 101)

In this respect, perhaps the Hungarians were fortunate. Rather than being treated as persons in need of 'welfare', from the outset the responsibility for adapting to their new society was placed squarely on them.

The 'ideal' refugee

The stereotype of helplessness also informs refugees' perceptions concerning the role they are expected to play to gain the approval of the helper and be successful in obtaining aid. As most refugees are able to infer, ingratiating themselves with camp authorities and individual helpers is one of the most effective survival strategies in the context of fierce competition over scarce humanitarian aid resources. On the other hand, when given the opportunity, most people are willing and able to volunteer information concerning their grievances *vis-à-vis* the helpers.

When I first arrived in Sudan in 1982, I toured the camps in the east with the new commissioner who was introducing himself to the refugee committees. On each occasion, after introductions, the refugee leaders proceeded to list their complaints and demands. When I had an opportunity to meet some refugees, away from the official party, I began a discussion of family matters, and was busy learning from them how exile was affecting their practice of customary matrimonial law.

My guide suggested that I should also meet the committee. Once they had gathered, they immediately began listing the deficiencies of the assistance programme. I asked why they were telling *me* their problems, as I had *nothing to do with aid*. I proceeded to tell them about the 'good' Saharawi who lived under much worse conditions than they did, but who were reluctant to complain. The committee retorted angrily that they did not like their role any more than I did, but what else, other than recite their woes, were they supposed to do when a European visited them?

Letters which refugees write to organizations from which they hope to get assistance of one type or another are a rich source of evidence of what refugees believe is the necessary style to obtain it. Frequently their letters begin, 'I am a poor refugee', and one I received contained a photograph. Rather than signing his name on the back of this photo, the writer wrote 'A Poor Refugee' (Gilbert, 1995).

Refugees living in camps in southern Sudan composed praise songs to sing whenever a UNHCR representative appeared in the camp. These songs referred to the organization as their 'father and mother'. In Africa, as in many societies, the image of father is a metaphor for denoting roles of responsibility as well as of authority. By singing such songs, refugees were positioning themselves as totally dependent for their survival on the organization which had assumed authority over them.

During my research in southern Sudan, I found it most annoying to have grown men and women crouch at my feet while speaking with me, although no doubt such a gesture also reflects Ugandan values of respect for authority. It felt as if this particular expression of respect was going too far; possibly as a result of my own western cultural sensitivities, I saw it as a manifestation of servile behaviour. To avoid it, I carried an extra chair and would invite people to sit on it while we were talking. On one occasion a refugee refused to rise from his knees. The regional director of Oxfam had just been sitting in my extra chair. This Ugandan refugee asked me, 'How could I sit in a chair which Mr. Campbell has just sat in?' Evidently, interpreting people's behaviour is a complex matter. This refugee's response was perhaps an expression of his recognition of social hierarchies and a recognition of his own status *vis-à-vis* this representative of the aid system.

In 1982, James Appe, a Ugandan and a refugee himself, spent several weeks reading the files of the UNHCR Yei Field Office in southern Sudan. He was so disgusted by the letters of complaint from his co-nationals that he admonished UNHCR to stop treating refugees like 'patients in a hospital'. But very frequently the role of a patient is imposed on refugees by those responsible for their reception.

While there may be justification for ensuring that newcomers are not carriers of tuberculosis, a disease which has become a general health threat in the world, there is no justification for setting up a system which *conditions* refugees to think of themselves as ill or leads them to believe that the medical profession will be able to solve their life problems. In Ireland, for example, the 'programme' refugees (persons accepted to be resettled in the country through agreements with UNHCR) are taken to a special reception centre where they are subjected to complete medical examinations, including dental checks and psychological 'screening'. A similar approach is followed in the Netherlands. One researcher found that long after being found their own private housing, refugees in that country expected doctors to help them sort out housing and other matters, perhaps because in the reception centre the only trained professionals they met were doctors and nurses.

In short, the application of the welfare model, combined with the reality of refugees' initial relative powerlessness in the new environment, tends, as the Danish example so clearly illustrates, to attract and condition the behaviour of helpers whose interests are served by pathologizing, medicalizing and labelling the refugee as 'helpless and vulnerable' (Steen, 1993).

Stereotypes of the refugee

Perhaps the necessary alternative stereotype to the docile, 'grateful' refugee is that of a cheating, conniving, manipulative, dishonest person out to subvert the aid system. Neither image embodies the complexities of human personalities reacting in situations of extreme stress. In Dadaab, Hyndman observed that sometimes the agency staff would 'maintain that a refugee camp [population] can be treated as a trustworthy community', while at other times 'they treat [the same population of] refugees as institutional subjects who *cannot be trusted*' (Hyndman, 1996, p. 109; emphasis added).

It is quite true that refugees may likely exhibit anger and aggressiveness, normal feelings for anyone who has been placed in a position of powerlessness and lacks opportunity to take control of his or her own life. Although few humanitarian workers like to admit it in public, one of the hazards of working with refugees is dealing with their acts of 'aggression'.[27] So common are such incidents that UNHCR includes instructions to staff in its handbook on what to do when refugees riot or occupy its offices or compound (UNHCR, 1982). Many humanitarian agency offices are guarded by armed police. It is little wonder, however, when the treatment of refugees is so often inconsistent. 'One moment they are asked to become leaders and decision-makers in the camp; the next they are herded behind barricades at gun point in order to be counted for a UNHCR census' (Hyndman, 1996, p. 109).

The contradictions inherent in 'humanitarian' assistance are most graphically illustrated in the behaviour of the 'helpers' and the behaviour of refugees in the context of giving and receiving food rations. 'For the helpers, the ultimate "good" is the maintenance of their exercise of authority, for the refugees, it is the acquisition of material goods' (Voutira and Harrell-Bond, 1995, p. 216). Refugees resist all efforts to count them in order to control the rationing of food (Harrell-Bond *et al.*, 1992). This may involve shifting individual family members between camps, the false registration of household members, assuming another identity and, very frequently, the concealment of death:

> One family admitted to me after I got to know them very well, [that] the grandmother whom they had initially claimed as a result of Israeli action in 1948 had in fact died about eight months later while they were in a tent on the beaches of Khan Younis. Unable to survive without her ration card, the family concealed her death; they buried their mother in the sand under the tent. When they were rehoused, they were unable to bring the body with them. (Louise Weighill, personal communication)

Under the assumption that all refugees 'lie', extraordinary efforts to conduct 'accurate' censuses are taken. As Hyndman also observed, these involve herding refugees into enclosures and night swoops on camps. As one emergency manual advises:

> Spot checks involve an actual head count and are best carried out at unsocial hours like midnight or dawn when the majority of people will be in their houses. You will need a large number of staff to go round counting every person. (Mitchell and Slim, 1990)

In a particular 'messy' attempt to conduct a surprise nocturnal census in Somalia, 'retaliatory' violence broke out:

> At high speed and with ten people in one car they [the census-takers] drove into the camp and stopped just in front of a compound gate. Everybody had to run out of the car, burst into the compound, flashlights flashing around, run into the houses and other structures and count the number of people present.... As all this happened at night and without the people in Sigalow knowing that they would be visited, the whole procedure caused considerable disturbance.... After two of these runs the project manager was asked to stop. He however insisted on trying another one. Then a hail of stones was thrown at the car. The front wind-screen was smashed, glass flew inside the car and, at high speed, the driver taking considerable risks [of running over refugees] safety was finally reached. (as quoted by Harrell-Bond et al., 1992)[28]

Recognizing the serious challenge that ration fraud played in undermining its attempts at fairness, Oxfam commissioned the above-mentioned handbook for the 'organisation and operation of emergency registration of refugees'. The authors introduce categories of 'guards' and 'shepherd' to police the queues, and 'markers' who are responsible for daubing the registered refugee with gentian violet to prevent cheating. In an annex, entitled 'Cheaters', aid workers are warned to daub this gentian violet on a part of the body difficult to reach since a 'determined' cheater can wash it off within 24 hours (Mitchell and Slim, 1990).

More recently, UNHCR and the World Food Programme have introduced other techniques aimed to cut down on ration fraud. Structures called *corrals* have been built through which refugees must pass to get their ration.[29] Initially, the aisles were lined with wire netting, but the refugees learned that if they coated the wire with hot wax, it would snap. Consequently, the sides of the aisles had to be reinforced built with wood or bricks.

The power struggle between those who give aid and those who receive is not unlike that portrayed in the book *One Flew over the Cuckoo's Nest* (Kesey, 1973). Sheldon Gellar describes this as the 'Ratched–McMurphy model'; with agency staff taking Nurse Ratched's role:

> Nurse Ratched, who runs a ward in a mental hospital with an iron hand ... has the right to define the inmates' problems, and to assign prescriptions to resolve them. ... Nurse Ratched sets the agenda, controls the discussion, and resists any questioning of her approach. (Gellar, 1983, as quoted by Harrell-Bond, 1986, p. 19)

Those who talk back, like the martyr McMurphy, are likely to incur the wrath of Nurse Ratched, who feels obliged to domesticate or destroy him in order to re-establish her unquestioned authority and regain control of the ward. Like Nurse Ratched, agency personnel in the field stand at an epicentre of political and economic power, and their daily experiences continually confirm and reinforce their views – of themselves, and of the intransigence *and* the helplessness of refugees (Harrell-Bond, 1986).

The potential role of self-management of refugee camps

In the introduction to this chapter, I mentioned the role the Saharawi refugees played in sensitizing me to the importance of examining the relationships which develop between refugees and their helpers. When I returned from Algeria, I discussed with Oxfam staff just why they thought 'their' refugees were so different from the Saharawi. It was one response, 'We are so busy saving lives at the beginning that by the time we have time to think we have made too many mistakes', that raised my curiosity about just how the humanitarian 'regime' operated in an emergency. It was this statement that stimulated the question, 'Is one of worst problems faced by refugees their "helpers"?', and, in consequence, the inverse conclusion that self-management can be a key to reducing stress.

In Algeria I found nearly 200,000 people living in tented camps in the Saharan desert under extremely unfavourable environmental and material conditions. In the same way that India allowed Tibetan refugees to have their settlements administered by their own government-in-exile, Algeria,

a supporter of the Saharawi's war for self-determination and independence, also allowed the Saharawi autonomy in the region of Tindouf.

With the exception of a few goats and camels, they were totally
dependent for survival on aid – even water and fuel (bottled gas), which
had to be transported to them from outside the area. There were no
humanitarian agencies present. When asked why, the response was, 'We
do not want "experts" in our camps. It would diminish our sense of
responsibility for ourselves.' They actively used their time in exile to build
a twentieth-century democratic nation, women's equality being one of the
strongest features of their social organization.

Everyone over 16 is a member of a committee. One, the justice
committee, is responsible for ensuring that everyone who marries is aware
of the social responsibility they are undertaking and that neither of those
marrying has been coerced by relatives into taking a partner against their
will. A special school for women provides day care for the children and
elderly dependants. Women are enabled to improve their educational level
– whether they arrived illiterate or had come to the camps with some
higher education. Practical skills taught do include sewing, particularly
how to mend the tents which were torn by the wind and sand, but women
can also learn vehicle repair and how to shoot a rifle. It is the women who
are largely responsible for protecting the camps if the Moroccans attack.
Even this military instruction, originally done by men, is now in the hands
of women. As one man explained to me, 'Our women were never veiled
and they always worked, but the difference today is that women are
politicized and are at the base of our national culture.'

Because they had only one doctor and a handful of nurses on their
arrival in Algeria in 1975, a health programme was established which
began in the neighbourhood; each resident was seen by a member of the
health committee every day. At the time of my visit, the 'central hospital'
boasted little more than one microscope and an outdated US-made
delivery table as equipment, but the medical workers proudly displayed
the advances they had made in reintroducing effective traditional
medicines to treat some of the most recurrent health problems such as
diarrhoea during the soaring summer temperatures and flu and colds
during the bitter winters. Food is provided through the Algerian Red
Crescent to the Saharawi Red Crescent and is distributed through the food
committee to each household.

With sometimes four small bodies crowded onto a desk built for one,
the schools were called 'palaces' for children. Given the shortage of
trained teachers, the elderly, including the Imams, are responsible for
teaching the youngest children to read and write in Arabic. The Saharawis
devised a number of strategies to counteract the influence of the children's
preoccupation with the war their fathers, brothers, and even sisters are
fighting, which was manifested in the children's art work and the games

they played with the stones in the sand. Each year a few children are sent to Europe on 'holidays' from the camps. They return to teach their classmates how to draw flowers instead of guns. The only request I could prise out of my hosts was for sports equipment and toys.

Conclusions

As mentioned earlier, it is not only the Saharawi who have been granted self-government and autonomy from the host state; so have the Tibetans in India. There are other examples in Africa which are even less well documented because, like the Saharawi, the presence of outsiders in the camps is only 'by invitation' and researchers have not been invited (Lawless and Monahan, 1988; Wallace, 1994).[30] South African refugees in Tanzania and Zambia and Namibians in Angola who did live in self-managed camps are cases in point.[31]

In her thesis, Hyndman describes an initiative by one NGO, CARE, to democratize Dadaab camp and the resistance of UNHCR to this proposal. She analyses why she agrees that this would not work in the context of a camp. Her first point is that the populations which make up refugee camps are not 'communities', they are made up of groups of individuals which are 'hierarchically positioned and partitioned'. It is not, she notes, easy to transfer the principles of community development and organization to refugee camps. When the idea of elections was being considered by the refugees, the discussion revolved around 'who will represent whom?' and 'what will the relationship among committees be?' In her view, elections would simply 'reproduce and reinscribe' the power of those already in position of 'authority and relative privilege'.

> The majority of refugees, especially the women, do not generally attend ... consultations. Refugee men are more likely to have the time, the language skills necessary to converse with NGOs and participate in political process, and the social authority to attend. The community development structures of 'opportunity', 'participation', and access are distorted by the institutional setting of the camps and the gender relations of Somali culture within.... I attended one meeting between refugee agencies and camp elders where the latter group submitted a list of those refugees they unilaterally decided should be representatives.... Most ... were the same male elders. They also noted the remuneration expected. Although agency staff are paid for their work, this proposal had not considered paying refugees, expecting them to work for the welfare of their community as volunteers. (Hyndman, 1996, pp. 147–8)

If 'democracy' was to come to Dadaab, it would come on terms determined by the agency. This is the knockdown argument for why 'self-management' will not work in Dadaab. Political power, as Hyndman rightly notes, cannot be separated from economic resources. Citing Giddens's analysis of power (1981), she notes that

> responsibility for meaningful decision-making cannot be separated from the resources necessary to carry out decisions taken ... [if the agencies] are unwilling to relinquish any of the economic means which would enable refugee self-management to occur, they will defeat the proposed objectives of refugee self-governance and democratic process. (Hyndman, 1996, p. 109)

Is a major problem facing refugees their helpers? Obviously, like all of us, refugees need help of one kind or another, especially because, although they are ordinary people, they are in extraordinary conditions. 'Their problem lies in their circumstances, the society they live in, the reaction of people to their presence, and the inhumane laws and treatment they are subjected to' (Appe, as quoted by Beristain and Doná, 1997, p. 4). Even without scientific evidence that 'proves' that assistance which is based on the notion of the 'helpless' refugee whose problems can be 'fixed' by welfare services causes refugees distress, it would appear obvious that something is terribly wrong with current policies. How can refugees be helped without adding to their burdens, bearing in mind that any sort of intervention will have unintended consequences? It is the task of humanitarian workers to be aware of this. Perhaps the message of how the settlement of refugees could be more constructively approached is most eloquently expressed by a refugee himself:

> After the long and fearful journey ... only gradually should a refugee be made to feel that he has 'arrived'. He must be kept somehow 'on the run'. He should be assisted on a very small scale so that he can see himself creating his new home. He could feel then that it belongs to him and would care for it. This would help him rediscover himself. 'After such a trial, I'm able to achieve this. Perhaps I had not really died. No, I'm still my old self.' This alone will enable the refugee to set up a sound basis for his assistance, by his own efforts. [Programmes should] be designed only after on-the-spot interviews with refugees and careful assessment of their particular problems as individuals and as a group ... the solution is to give refugees greater responsibility for assisting themselves – they must be assisted marginally in order to assist themselves totally.
>
> What happens when a refugee is put into a situation where he is made to depend entirely on aid agencies to tell him what and how much to eat and when and where to sleep? In the end he will let agencies 'think' for him. This means he has no personality that he can respect.... The one fundamental problem: the reason why it is so often difficult to assist refugees, is that they are not recognised as having any responsibility for their affairs at the beginning – and this affects the whole subsequent programme and will last as long as the refugees remain where they are. *Refugees must not be settled, but must be allowed to try to settle themselves.* (as quoted by Harrell-Bond, 1986, p. 300)

Notes

1 'Empowering' is part of the *doxa* of 'humanitarian speak' as well as 'development speak'. Can one think of any example where power was *given* away? Information, of course, is a form of power. Is this why almost everything related to assistance programmes as managed by humanitarian organizations is 'highly confidential' and documents are classified in terms of the levels in the hierarchy in which they may be circulated? See Hyndman (1996).

2 Indra (1993), reporting on research by Fuhr, notes that 43 per cent of the sponsors viewed sponsorship as a moral obligation, 33 per cent saw it as an act of compassion and goodwill, and only 11 per cent viewed it pragmatically as a means of bringing more refugees to Canada.

3 Although the refugee camp has become almost synonymous with the experience of being a refugee, and this discussion concentrates on that particular environment, it should not be forgotten that unequal power relations between helpers and the beneficiaries may obtain elsewhere.

4 For example, Carlin (1990), Wilson (1988), Shisana and Celentano (1985), Muecke (1992), Ata *et al.* (1992), Klimidis *et al.* (1992), CIMADE (1981), Eisenbruch (1988), Ressler *et al.* (1988), Dawes (1990), Kulig (1990), Williams and Westermeyer (1986), Cole *et al.* (1992) and Neuwirth and Vincent (1997).

5 In UNHCR 'speak', there are three 'durable' solutions for refugees: repatriation, integration (in the country of first asylum) and 'resettlement', meaning finding a country other than that of first asylum where refugees can be 'resettled'. This latter 'solution' has, since the 1970s, been largely one of 'last resort'; that is, for persons who have severe health problems which could be treated better in the North, 'women at risk', and persons who cannot be protected. There have been new moves to get resettlement back on the agenda with equal status to the other two 'solutions'. UNHCR is currently preparing a handbook setting out the criteria which should be applied by its staff in considering applications for resettlement (see UNHCR, 1996).

6 Those who believe in reincarnation may understand painful life situations, even detention and torture, as a result of inherited karma.

7 For decades, refugees living in Nairobi have been subjected to arbitrary police harassment. At the time of writing, July 1997, the situation was particularly acute. Hit squads from Burundi and Rwanda were in Nairobi and killings took place. There was no security for persons prepared to testify as witnesses for persons being accused of war crimes in Arusha.

> I just spoke to one of the Rwandese academics who is hiding in the home of friends. The little group of Burundian, Rwandese and Zairean academics is now scattered around in town and they are terrorised. They had to pay for not being arrested, some of them were arrested, some of them are still missing ... and a bus is leaving to Kakuma [camp] today with some of the people who were in Nairobi. We were supposed to have meetings with the group of academics, but obviously everything is cancelled. (G. Verdirame, e-mail 30.7.1997)

8   Many comparisons of assisted refugees with those who are self-settled have already been made (e.g. Hansen, 1982, 1990; Harrell-Bond, 1986; Kibreab, 1983, 1989, 1991a, b; Malkki, 1990), but there is a lack of comparative work on the psychological impact of refugees' experiences of stress in these different contexts.

9   During the struggles against apartheid South Africa and for the independence of Namibia, both ANC and SWAPO refugees also enjoyed self-governance and autonomy in exile in Africa.

10   Hyndman (1996, p. 110) expresses her 'scepticism' about the willingness of the aid agencies to give away any meaningful decision-making power to refugees, and, even if they did, she asks what 'formal link of accountability to the refugees would exist to ensure that power is shared on an on-going basis?' As Waldron (1987, p. 5) pointed out, accountability in assistance programmes for refugees has quite another meaning: 'As long as the food and numbers balance, accountability is satisfied ... when the balance is disrupted, so is the security of the individual bureaucrat and the system as a whole.'

11   Indra found that a major complaint of sponsors was the *lack* of gratefulness among their beneficiaries. It appears to be a requirement, for although receiving requires the recipient to cede status or power to the giver, s/he must express gratefulness for being disempowered (Indra 1993, p. 243).

12   Hyndman quotes Edward Said's comments concerning outcast populations: 'their existence always counts, though their names and identities do not, they are profitable without fully being there', and Trinh Minh-ha: 'naming is part of the human rituals of incorporation, and the unnamed remains less than the inhuman or sub-human' (Hyndman, 1996, p. 96).

13   Indra (1993, p. 236) notes that sponsored refugees often complained that while the material help they received was of a better quality, the items concerned were used, while things given refugees under the government programme were new.

14   On one occasion in 1982–3, a Ugandan refugee was digging the UNHCR vehicle out of the mud. In this position, his 'bathrobe' did

not conceal his underwear. He was wearing a beautiful pair of antique Victorian women's cotton knickers elaborately decorated with handmade lace. I pointed out that these were valuable where I came from and that my daughter collected such clothes. If he wanted to sell them to me, I was prepared to buy. 'Madam,' he said, 'I have nothing else to put on.'

15   Interview, 13 July 1997. Indra, reporting on her and others' studies of resettlement in Canada, notes that refugees express much ambiguity about their relations with sponsors (1993, p. 239).

16   On the other hand, Malkki (1992) observed refugees sometimes who were clinging to these rights in the midst of situations where they could not claim them. They could recite international refugee law and she comments on how knowledgeable 'ordinary people in the camp were about these laws and conventions'. She quotes one agency staff member who said, 'in exasperation: "They are very clever, those Bahutu. They know their rights as refugees. They will cite to the UNHCR officials Article so-and-so of the Geneva Convention! *They* chase after the *UNHCR*." '

17   In the words of Minh-ha, 'The "needy" cannot always afford to refuse, so they persist in accepting ungratefully' (as quoted by Hyndman, 1996, p. 117).

18   Indra (1993) also notes that this was still a major motivation for Canada's acceptance of the Vietnamese in the 1970s.

19   One memorable case was that of a woman who escaped with her three children. Her 17-year-old son by her first marriage had participated in the fighting against the Russian occupation and had had to get out of Hungary. Her marriage to a famous football player with whom she had two younger children had suffered sufficient strain that she had decided to take the opportunity to leave. She gradually came to realize the dramatic change in lifestyle survival in the USA would entail. She explained that she could not possibly work; she had varicose veins and did not speak English, she would prefer to return to Hungary. I was instructed that before the US government would pay for her return, I would have to ascertain whether the husband was willing to receive her. To her relief, all was forgiven.

20   Indra also discusses the problems of refugees and their sponsors which emerged because of lack of understanding of the other's 'cultures' (1993, pp. 243–4).

21   How many aid workers make an effort to learn the language of the refugees with whom they work? In Zimbabwe, one of the first 'interventions' for Mozambicans was to start English classes so that the refugees could speak to agency staff (Robert Mazur, personal communication). In fairness, once this host government became more involved in the education of refugees, the syllabus was taught

in Portuguese and teaching materials were obtained from the Frelimo government.

22   For all previous interviews, I had been relying on a clergyman's wife who was Hungarian to translate over the telephone.

23   See Indra's work cited in this chapter and Chan and Indra (1987) for more comprehensive bibliographical sources of resettlement studies in North America.

24   Margaret Reeves, an Oxford medical student, who spent seven weeks in the infamous Benako camps, reports how in the first conversation she had with a refugee they discussed Camus and Sartre:

> My meeting with François was just the first to turn on its head my image of who is a refugee ... what had I expected? Like most of us, my image of refugees had been conditioned by the media which portray them as faceless peasants, hopeless, helpless, starving and dying, or passively waiting for the aid which is so generously donated by us in the West. (1997, p. 8)

25   I use the past tense because more often than not nowadays refugees are detained in camps where they are completely dependent on international assistance and unable to grow food for themselves. This level of aid is described as 'care and maintenance'.

26   From Harrell-Bond (1986, Introduction).

27   In the contexts of two attempts to count refugees in Kakuma camp, refugees actually 'tore apart the enclosures built for the exercise, and on the other, they kidnapped staff participating in the "head-count"'. To gain control over the situation, UNHCR finally had to 'consort with the leaders of the Sudanese People's Liberation Army (SPLA).... Meeting with political groups contravenes UNHCR official policy, but ... staff felt they had little choice' (Hyndman, 1996, p. 101).

28   Readers who have not visited a refugee camp may think this case is exceptional. It is not. Hyndman reports on a similar secret plan which was devised to avoid refugees subverting the count:

> At five in the morning approximately two hundred Kenyan police and army personnel surrounded the camp. Six counting centers had been set up. All refugees were awakened and instructed to move to the nearest center, each of which was fenced and guarded. UNHCR staff, many of whom had flown in from other locations to assist, communicated by walkie talkie between the centers. Refugees then filed through narrow corridors through which only one person at a time could pass. Here, they were counted – their hands marked with ink to signify this – and moved to the next area cordoned off within the fenced center.... The exercise was complete by early morning. (1996, p. 101)

29 Since most people in the world have seen cowboy films, the significance of this description is unlikely to have been lost on the refugees.
30 The Polisario Front is represented in a number of countries and some advocacy groups have been formed. In addition to political activities in support of the Saharawi's demand for self-determination, money and material assistance is sent through the Algerian Red Crescent to the Saharawi Red Crescent. There have been initiatives funded by NGOs such as an agricultural project to grow vegetables. However, unless an NGO is willing to work through the Polisario Front and the Saharawi Red Crescent, leaving control over the use and distribution of aid in their hands, their contributions are not welcomed.
31 It is interesting that despite the RSP's library's extensive holdings, with the exception of Shisana and Celentano (1985) I could find *no* literature on the life of refugees in either ANC or SWAPO camps! There is extensive literature on the repatriation of Namibia (see the RSP catalogue on the World Wide Web). This is reminiscent of the case of the Fula refugees from Guinea in Sierra Leone. They were allowed to live anywhere in the country and were not labelled refugees. However, when they also spontaneously repatriated, it was announced by UNHCR as being a successful repatriation.

References

Africa Rights (1997) *Human Rights Watch*. Africa Rights.

Aga Khan (1981) *Study on Human Rights and Massive Exoduses*, UN Economic and Social Council, Commission on Human Rights, 31 December.

Ager, A. (1993) Mental health issues in refugee populations: a review. Project on International Mental and Behavioral Health, Harvard Medical School, Department of Social Medicine.

Ager, A., Ager, W. and Long, L. (1995) The differential experience of Mozambican refugee women and men. *Journal of Refugee Studies*, 8 (3), 263–87.

Ake, C. (1996) *Democracy and Development in Africa*. Washington, DC: Brookings Institution.

Aron, A. (ed.) (1988) *Flight, Exile, and Return: Mental Health and the Refugee*. San Francisco, CA: Committee for Health Rights in Central America.

Ata, A.W., Klimidis, S. and Minas, I.H. (1992) Adolescent (Vietnamese) refugee migration and settlement issues in Australia. Presented at Migration and Health, Conference of the International Organization for Migration with WHO and UN Population Fund, June/July.

Baskauskas, L. (1981) The Lithuanian refugee experience and grief. *International Migration Review*, 15 (1), 276-91.

Beiser, M. (1987) Changing time perspective and mental health among south east Asian refugees. *Culture, Medicine and Psychiatry*, 11, 437–64.

Beiser, M. (1993) After the door has been opened: the mental health of immigrants and refugees in Canada. In V. Robinson (ed.), *The International Refugee Crisis: British and Canadian Responses*. London: Macmillan.

Beiser, M., Turner, R.J. and Ganesan, S. (1989) Catastrophic stress and factors affecting its consequences among southeast Asian refugees. *Social Science Medicine*, 28 (3), 183–95.

Berry, J. (1991) Refugee adaptation in settlement countries: an overview with an emphasis on primary prevention. In F.L. Ahearn and J.J. Athey (eds), *Refugee Children: Theory, Research and Services*. Baltimore: Johns Hopkins University Press.

Berry, J., Poortinga, Y.H., Segall, M.H. and Dasen, P. (1992) *Cross-cultural Psychology: Research and Applications*. Cambridge: Cambridge University Press.

Beristain, C. and Doná, G. (1997) *Psychology in Humanitarian Assistance*. Brussels: European Community Humanitarian Organisation.

Bracken, P.J., Giller, J.E. and Summerfield, D. (1995) Psychological responses to war and atrocity: the limitations of current concepts. *Social Science and Medicine*, 40 (8), 1073–83.

Carlin, J. (1990) Refugee and immigrant populations at special risk: women, children and the elderly. In W. Holtzman and T. Bornemann (eds), *Mental Health of Immigrants and Refugees*, pp. 224–33. Proceedings of conference sponsored by Hogg Foundation for Mental Health and the World Federation for Mental Health, Hogg Foundation for Mental Health.

Cernea, M. (1995) Understanding and preventing impoverishment from displacement: Reflections on the state of knowledge. *Journal of Refugee Studies*, 8 (3), 245–64.

Chan, K.B. and Indra, D.M. (eds) (1987) *Uprooting, Loss and Adaptation: The Resettlement of Indochinese Refugees in Canada*. Ottawa: Canadian Public Health Association.

CIMADE (1981) The influence of political repression and exile on children. *Mental Health and Exile*, 14–21.

Coles, E., Espin, O. and Rothblum, E. (1992) *Refugee Women and Their Mental Health: Shattered Lives*. New York: Harrington Park Press.

Dahoud, O. and Pelosi, A.J. (1989) The work of the Somali Counselling Programme in the UK. *Bulletin of the Royal College of Psychiatrists*, 13, 619–60.

Dahoud, O. and Pelosi, A.J. (1991) The Somali people: refugees in two worlds. In L. Appleby and R. Araya (eds), *Mental Health Services in the Global Village*. London: Gaskell.

Daley, P. (1989) Refugees and underdevelopment in Africa: the case of Barundi refugees in Tanzania. Unpublished DPhil thesis, Faculty of Anthropology and Geography, University of Oxford.

Dawes, A. (1990) The effects of political violence on children: a consideration of South Africa related studies. *International Journal of Psychology*, 25, 13–31.

de Voe, M. (1986) Framing refugees as clients. *International Migration Review*, 15 (1), 88–94.

Eisenbruch, M. (1984) Cross-cultural aspects of bereavement. I: A conceptual framework for comparative analysis. *Culture, Medicine and Psychiatry*, 8, 283–309.

Eisenbruch, M. (1988) The mental health of refugee children and their cultural development. *International Migration Review*, 22 (2), 282–300.

Eisenbruch, M. (1990) Cultural bereavement and homesickness. In S. Fisher and C.L. Cooper (eds), *On the Move: The Psychology of Change and Transition*. Chichester: Wiley.

Gellar, S. (1983) The Ratched–McMurphy model: a critique of participatory development models, strategies and projects. Paper presented to the African Studies Association Annual Meeting, Boston.

Giddens, A.A. (1981) *A Contemporary Critique of Historical Materialism*. London: Macmillan.

Gilbert, R. (1995) Letters from refugees: an insight into the refugee experience. RSP Student Paper, RSP Library.

Goffman, I. (1961) *Asylums: Essays on the Social Situation of Mental Patients and Other Inmates*. New York: Doubleday Anchor.

Hannan, L. (1997) Police round up refugees 'spies': hundreds are being sent to camps in an operation denounced as illegal by lawyers. *Guardian*, 31 July.

Hansen, A. (1982) Self-settled rural refugees in Africa: the case of Angolans in Zambian villages. In A. Hansen and O. Smith (eds), *Involuntary Migration and Resettlement: The Problems and Responses of Dislocated People*, pp. 13–25. Boulder, CO: Westview Press.

Hansen, A. (1990) *Refugee Self-Settlement versus Settlement on Government Schemes: The Long-Term Consequences for Security, Integration and Economic Development of Angolan Refugees (1966–1989) in Zambia*. Geneva: UNRISD.

Harrell-Bond, B.E. (1981) The struggle for the Western Sahara: a three part series. Part I: The background, No. 27, 1981; Part II: The legal/political milieu, No. 38, 1981; Part III: The people, No. 39, 1981. Hanover, NH: The American Universities Field Staff.

Harrell-Bond, B.E. (1985) Humanitarianism in a strait-jacket. *African Affairs*, 334, 3–13.

Harrell-Bond, B.E. (1986) *Imposing Aid: Emergency Assistance to Refugees*. Oxford: Oxford University Press.

Harrell-Bond, B., Voutira, E. and Leopold, M. (1992) Counting the refugees: gifts, givers, patrons and clients. *Journal of Refugee Studies*, 5 (3/4), 205–25.

Hyndman, M.J. (1996) Geographies of displacement: gender, culture and power in UNHCR refugee camps, Kenya. Unpublished PhD thesis, Faculty of Graduate Studies, Department of Geography, University of British Columbia, September.

Hyndman, M.J. (1997) Refugee self-management and the question of governance. *Refuge*, 16 (2), 16–22.

Indra, D. (1988) An analysis of the Canadian private sponsorship programme for Southeast Asian refugees. *Ethnic Groups*, 7, 153–72.

Indra, D. (1993) The spirit of the gift and the politics of resettlement: the Canadian private sponsorship of South East Asians. In V. Robinson (ed.), *The International Refugee Crisis: British and Canadian Responses*. London: Macmillan.

Kay, D. (1987) *Chileans in Exile: Private Struggle, Public Lives*. London: Macmillan.

Kesey, K. (1962) *One Flew Over the Cuckoo's Nest*. London: Methuen.

Kibreab, G. (1983) *Reflections on the African Refugee Problem: A Critical Analysis of Some Basic Assumptions*. Uppsala: Scandinavian Institute of African Studies.

Kibreab, G. (1989) Local settlements in Africa: a misconceived option? *Journal of Refugee Studies*, 2 (4), 486–90.

Kibreab, G. (1991a) Integration of African refugees in first countries of asylum: past experiences and prospects for the 1990s. Paper commissioned by the Program on International and US Refugee Policy, Tufts University, Department of Economic History and Uppsala University, Sweden. Research report no. 26.

Kibreab, G. (1991b) The state of the art review of refugee studies in Africa. Uppsala, Paper in Economic History.

Klimidis, S., Ata, A. and Minas, I.H. (1992) I. Adolescent self-concept and psychopathology: comparisons of immigrant, refugee and native born samples. Paper presented at a course on mental health of children exposed to violent environments, Oxford, RSP Library.

Kulig, J.C. (1990) A review of the health status of southeast Asian refugee women. *Health Care for Women International*, 11, 49–63.

Lawless, R., and Monahan, L. (eds) (1988) *War and Refugees: The Western Sahara Conflict*. London: Pinter.

Malkki, L. (1990) Context and consciousness: Local conditions for the production of historical and national thought among Hutu refugees in

Tanzania. In R.G. Fox (ed.), *National Ideologies and the Production of National Cultures*. American Ethnological Society Monograph Series, No. 2.

Malkki, L. (1992) Citizens of humanity: images of international community and trusteeship. Paper presented at the UNU/WIDER Workshop, 'Trust and the Refugee Experience', University of Bergen, Norway, June.

Mandani, M. (1973) *From Citizen to Refugee: Ugandan Asians Come to Britain*. London: Pinter.

Marris, P. (1986) *Loss and Change*. London: Routledge & Kegan Paul.

Marx, E. (1990) The social work of refugees: a conceptual framework. Elizabeth Colson Lecture. *Journal of Refugee Studies*, 3 (3), 189–203.

Mauss, M. (1925) *The Gift*, tr. I. Cunnison. New York: Free Press.

Mitchell, J. and Slim, H. (1990) *Registration in Emergencies: Oxfam Practical Health Guide*. Oxford: Oxfam.

Muecke, M. (1992) Anxiety among Cambodian refugee adolescents in transit and in resettlement. *Western Journal of Nursing Research*, 14 (3), 267–91.

Needham, R. (1994) Refugee participation. *Refugee Participation Network (RPN)*, pp. 17–19. Oxford: Refugee Studies Programme.

Neuwirth, G. and Vincent, C. (eds) (1997) *Women Refugees in International Perspectives 1980–1990: An Annotated Bibliography*. Ottawa: Research Resources Division for Refugees.

Proudfoot, M.J. (1957) *European Refugees 1939–1952: A Study of Forced Population Movement*. London: Faber & Faber.

Reeves, M. (1997) Could Oxford dons survive? *Oxford Magazine*, Nought Week, Hilary Term, Oxford University, pp. 8–9.

Ressler, E., Boothby, N. and Steinbock, D. (1988) *Unaccompanied Children: Care and Protection in Wars, Natural Disasters and Refugee Movements*. Oxford: Oxford University Press.

Ritchie, J.M. (1992) Exile in Oxford. *Oxford Magazine*, Fourth Week, Trinity Term, Oxford University, pp. 3–5.

Shisana, O. and Celentano, D.D. (1985) Depressive symptomalogy among Namibian adolescent refugees. *Social Science and Medicine*, 21 (11), 1251–7.

Skran, C. (1995) *Refugees in Inter-war Europe: The Emergence of a Regime*. Oxford: Clarendon Press.

Spitzer, L. (1989) *Lives in Between: Assimilation and Marginality in Austria, Brazil, West Africa 1780–1945*. Cambridge: Cambridge University Press.

Steen, A.B. (1993) Refugee resettlement: Denmark and Britain compared. *Refugee Participation Newsletter*, no. 14. Oxford: Refugee Studies Programme.

Subba, T.B. (1990) *Flight and Adaptation: Tibetan Refugees in the*

Darjeeling–Sikkim Himalaya. Dharamsala, India: Library of Tibetan Works and Archives.

Summerfield, D. (1991) The rise of post-traumatic stress disorders [letter]. *British Medical Journal*, 303, 1271.

Summerfield, D. (1997) The legacy of war: beyond trauma to the social fabric. *Lancet*, 349, 1568.

Summerfield, D. and Hume, F. (1993) War and post-traumatic stress disorder: the question of social context. *Journal of Nervous and Mental Disease*, 181, 522.

UNHCR (1982) *Handbook for Emergencies: Management, Administration and Procedures*. Geneva: UNHCR.

UNHCR (1996) Excerpts from the *Resettlement Handbook*, 1996 version. Division of International Protection, Geneva.

UNHCR (1997) Refugee voices from exile. *Refugees*, 107, 3–30.

Uthman ibn Fudi (1978) *Bayan wujub al-hujra 'ala 'l-'ibadd*. Translated by F.H. El Marsi; edited by J.O. Hunwick. Khartoum University Press/Oxford University Press.

Voutira, E. and Harrell-Bond, B.E. (1995) In search of the locus of trust: the social world of the refugee camp. In E.V. Daniel and J.C. Knudsen (eds), *Mistrusting Refugees*. Berkeley: University of California Press.

Voutira, E., Mahmud, N., Oestergaard-Nielsen, E., Urquiola, A., Whishaw-Brown, S. and Yu, H. (1995) *Improving Social and Gender Planning in Emergency Operations*. Report submitted to the World Food Programme, Refugee Studies Programme, July.

Wahlbeck, O.R. (1997) Kurdish refugee communities: the diaspora in Finland and England. Unpublished DPhil thesis, University of Warwick.

Waldron, S. (1987) Blaming the refugees. *Refugee Issues*, 3 (3).

Waldron, S. (1992) Food for thought: refugee survival strategies and administrative control in organised settlements. Paper presented at International Meeting of Population Movements, Food Crises and Community Responses, Centre for the Study of the Administration of Relief, New Delhi, India, January.

Wallace, T (1994) Saharawi women: 'between ambition and suffering'. In B. Walker (ed.), *Women and Emergencies*, pp. 50–3. Oxford: Oxfam.

Williams, C. and Westermeyer, J. (eds) (1986) *Refugee Mental Health in Resettlement Countries*. Washington, DC: Hemisphere.

Wilson, R. (ed.) (1988) *Age in Exile: A Report on Elderly Exiles in the United Kingdom*. Prepared for the Age in Exile conference, November, Noordwijkehout, The Netherlands. London: British Refugee Council.

7

Refugee acculturation and re-acculturation

Giorgia Doná and John W. Berry

Introduction

Since 1945, there have been 160 wars and armed conflicts in the developing world with at least 50 currently ongoing (Zwi and Ugalde, 1989). The number of civilian casualties has increased dramatically (see Chapter 5). Whereas 5 per cent of the victims of conflict in World War I were civilians, in World War II the proportion increased to 50 per cent, and in current conflicts about 90 per cent of casualties are civilians (UNICEF, 1986). Civil wars and counter-insurgency have become the most significant push factors in refugee migration (Aga Khan and bin Talal, 1986). As a consequence of the changing nature of conflicts, entire nations are confronted with what Martin-Baró (1989) calls social and psychosocial trauma, and forced migration of almost 20 million people has become a feature of twentieth-century history.

An examination of how refugees adjust to their new contexts must take into consideration the current characteristics of forced migration. The flight of individuals to the West constitutes a minor feature of forced migration compared to the mass movements of refugees (e.g. Rwandans, Kurds, Guatemalans, etc.) within the developing world (Muecke, 1992; Stein, 1986). Yet most research on forced migration is being conducted in industrialized nations (Ager, 1994; Marsella *et al.*, 1994; Williams and Westermeyer, 1986). There is a clear need for research on forced migration in the developing world (Ager, 1994; Muecke, 1992). Reflecting on a quarter-century of international migration research, the editors of the journal *International Migration Review* reported

> an enormous gap between what is known about international migration in industrial democracies as opposed to other settings.... Therefore, expanded research on international migration in Asia, Africa, South America, the Arab region and other non industrial areas was seen as a top priority for international migration studies in the future. (*International Migration Review*, 1989, p. 399)

Within the developing world, forced migration is characterized by integration to the country of first asylum, life in refugee settlements, and repatriation (see Chapters 2 and 3). In Africa, refugees generally see settlement to the country of first asylum and repatriation as preferred durable solutions (Moore, 1988). However, in recent years even African countries, which have always shown hospitality to neighbouring refugees, are beginning to be reluctant to accept new refugees and to question the cost of their hospitality (Chambers, 1986; Stein, 1986). This has resulted in an increasing number of refugees living in camps, a phase of the refugee experience not sufficiently researched (Chan and Loveridge, 1987; Stein, 1986).

Whereas in the past refugees spent a short period of time in camps, from the 1980s an increasing number of refugees have not been able to repatriate, have not been given the opportunity to integrate in the host country and have no prospects for resettlement (Fagen, 1990). Life in refugee camps has become the norm (Vernez, 1991). Guatemalans who fled in 1981 lived in settlements for about twelve years; Cambodians and Vietnamese spent almost twenty years in Hong Kong.

Since the UN declared the 1990s as the decade of repatriation, refugees have been strongly encouraged to return voluntarily to their countries of origin. Recent years have witnessed the mass return of refugees in Africa (e.g. Rwandans from neighbouring countries in 1994 and again from Zaire in 1996), Central America (e.g. Guatemalans from Mexico in 1993) and Asia (e.g. Vietnamese from Hong Kong camps in 1989).

The aim of this chapter is to review the literature on acculturation and to analyse its relevance for refugee migration and settlement in the developed and, particularly, the developing world. In such a review, there are four emerging issues in the analysis of acculturation that are to be addressed. The first is the need to 'unpack' culture in the context of cultural proximity. While refugee migration to developed countries has been characterized by differences as regards individualism and collectivism, gender equality or parent–child relationships (Liebkind, 1996) between the refugee group and members of the host country, research on forced migration in developing countries needs to analyse in greater detail cultural variations in value orientations, family relations, gender relations, etc., as differences are less obvious.

The second is the need to consider acculturation processes in situations of relative segregation from the host society, such as refugee settlements. The third is the challenge to develop and test theories for understanding the reversal of acculturation, namely 're-acculturation' following repatriation. Finally, the fourth is the need to move away from using mainly psychometric scales and towards the utilization of more qualitative methods.

The analysis of acculturation

The increasing numbers of individuals moving across national boundaries has during the course of the twentieth century prompted an interest in the process by which migrant groups adjust to being in contact with different cultures, a phenomenon called acculturation. Although anthropologists first became interested in the general process of different cultures entering into contact with one another (Redfield *et al.*, 1936), the amount of anthropological study of acculturation fell significantly in the 1960s (Murphy, 1964, cited in Palinkas and Pickwell, 1995). The decline of interest on the part of anthropologists was, however, replaced by an increasing attention on the part of other social scientists, notably sociologists (e.g. Gordon, 1964) and psychologists (e.g. Graves, 1967).

Whereas Redfield *et al.* (1936) were mainly interested in group phenomena such as cultural norms and patterns, psychologists focused their attention on individual changes. The different emphasis is reflected in their definitions. Redfield *et al.* (1936) defined acculturation as 'those phenomena which result when groups of individuals having different cultures come into continuous first-hand contact with subsequent changes in the original cultural patterns of either or both groups' (p. 149). Graves (1967) was more interested in individual psychological outcomes such as changes in attitudes and behaviours resulting from culture contact.

Variations in conceptualizations and terms emerged (such as assimilation, biculturalism, integration, interculturation and negotiation). However, researchers agree that acculturation is multidimensional (Berry, 1980; Padilla, 1980; Phinney, 1996; Rogler *et al.*, 1991), in terms of both its content and its process. This viewpoint has generated a shift from thinking of the content of acculturation in demographic terms (country of origin, length of residence, etc.) or single topics (such as language usage) to conceptualizing acculturation as involving different dimensions assessed through psychometric scales (Rogler *et al.*, 1991). Several reviews of these scales are available (Berry *et al.*, 1986; Phinney, 1996; Rogler *et al.*, 1991).

The use of psychometric scales has allowed the redefinition of acculturation theory and methods. However, research conducted by relying only on psychometric scales has limitations. Psychometric scales generally give equal weight to different items and rely on mean scores. But different dimensions of one's acculturative experience may vary in importance and strength among groups and individuals, as is the case with ethnic identity (Keefe and Padilla, 1987). Also, the use of psychometric scales to assess acculturation does not address the issue of inconsistency. Acculturating individuals may frequently develop inconsistencies between attitudes and behaviours. Acculturation then becomes a process of negotiation between two systems of belief and behaviour (Palinkas and Pickwell, 1995).

While there are various assumptions about the process of acculturation (Basic Behavioral Task Force, 1996; Berry *et al.*, 1986; Feagan,
1984), it is currently understood that acculturation is not a linear
process, with individuals ranging from unacculturated to biased in
favour of the dominant culture. The term 'assimilation', however
neutral it may seem, is associated with the predominant ideology that
the 'good groups' are those that assimilate to the dominant culture
(Feagan, 1984). The ideology of assimilation does not reflect what
happens in reality, when migrants preserve their cultural and ethnic
identity over time (Gordon, 1981) and, in some instances, even
reconstruct their native environment in the new country (Wickher and
Schoch, 1987). Furthermore, discussions about acculturation as a linear
process are limited as they extrapolate the 'process' from studies
conducted at one point in time from cross-sectional studies, while it is
only through longitudinal studies that the dynamics of acculturation can
be properly assessed (Palinkas and Pickwell, 1995).

Acculturation is now seen as a multidimensional phenomenon that
includes one's orientation towards one's ethnic group, towards the larger
society and possibly towards other ethnic cultures (Phinney, 1996; Rogler
et al., 1991).

Berry (1980) has developed a model that describes different strategies
for acculturation. Individuals and groups living together are confronted
with two issues: 'Is my cultural identity of value and to be retained?' and
'Are positive relations with the larger (dominant) society to be sought?'
Even though these issues can be responded to on a continuous scale, from
negative to positive, for conceptual purposes they can be presented as
dichotomous yes/no options (see Figure 7.1). When individuals answer
negatively on the first issue and positively on the second one, an
assimilation strategy is favoured, namely the relinquishment of their
cultural identity and the acceptance of the one held by the host country. It
implies a cultural and behavioural assimilation, in which behaviours of
the individual becomes more similar to those of the dominant society.
Also, it implies a structural assimilation, in which the acculturating group
chooses to take part in the social and economic life of the larger social
system. When the answer to both the issues is positive, an *integration*
strategy is present, where the individual wants to maintain his or her
heritage identity and at the same time become part of the larger societal
framework. When the answer to the first issue is 'yes' and to the second
one is 'no' a *separation* strategy is present. Individuals have no desire to
relate to the larger society, but they want to maintain their traditions and
culture. Finally, the negative answer to both issues gives rise to
marginalization, which is characterized by a loss of contact with both
the dominant group and the traditional one.

Researchers on acculturation view acculturation as occurring at

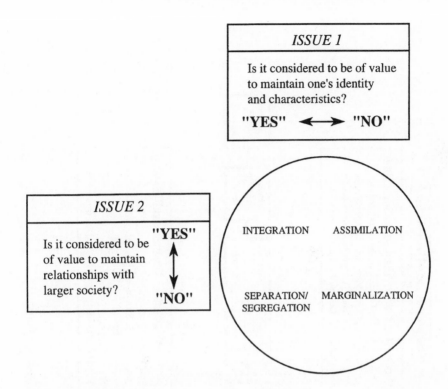

Figure 7.1 Different strategies for acculturation
Source: Berry (1980)

both individual and group levels. These levels may be viewed as different phenomena rooted in different disciplines (anthropology and psychology) which require separate concepts and measures (Williams and Berry, 1991). However, these two levels are intertwined, and individual acculturation is best understood within the framework of group acculturation. The process of individual acculturation is influenced by characteristics of the acculturating group and characteristics of the host society (Berry and Kim, 1988).

A framework for the study of acculturation

Berry (1997) has proposed a framework for the study of acculturation that takes into account the multidimensionality of acculturation and the link between individual and group acculturation (see Figure 7.2). The framework describes psychological acculturation within the context of the group and the dominant society. It also presents a series of moderating factors that affect individuals' adaptation to the new society.

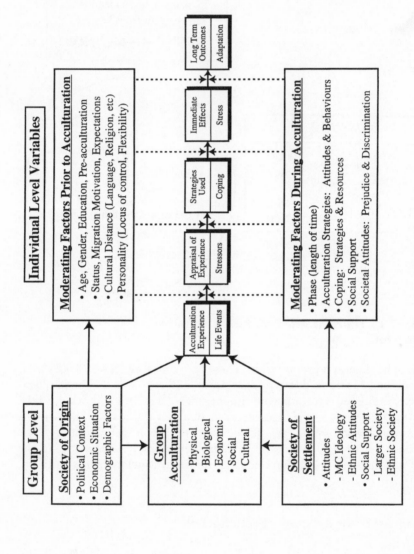

Figure 7.2 Framework for the study of acculturation *Source:* Berry (1997)

At the group level, social, cultural and psychological changes may occur for both the dominant and the non-dominant groups; however, it is this latter category that experiences the greatest pressure to change (Berry and Kim, 1988). Group-level acculturation refers to changes common to the whole group. Migration may expose the community to physical changes (new housing), biological changes (new diseases), political changes (loss of autonomy), economic changes (new forms of employment), cultural changes (new norms) and social changes (new patterns of dominance).

Psychological acculturation refers to changes in both overt behaviour and covert traits that occur at the individual level while the group is collectively experiencing acculturation (Graves, 1967). Changes in values, abilities, motives and identity may occur during psychological acculturation (Berry, 1991).

The process of group and psychological acculturation leads eventually to some form of adaptation. Adaptation may mean increased stress because of language problems, unfamiliar tasks and foreign norms, or it may mean enhancement of one's life by providing new economic opportunities, political freedom and new knowledge. The end result depends on a number of factors moderating the relationship between the process of acculturation and its long-term adaptation. Among such factors are the nature of the host society, the type of acculturating group, and characteristics of the acculturating individuals such as their acculturation strategies, coping resources, social support and societal attitudes.

Acculturation of refugees in the developed world

Berry and Kim (1988) categorize acculturating groups into five types: immigrants, refugees, ethnic groups, Native Peoples and sojourners. This categorization is made according to the presence or absence of migration, the extent to which the decision to migrate is voluntary and the degree of permanence of contact.

Among acculturating groups, refugees face the greatest risks owing to the involuntary, migratory and potentially temporary nature of their experience (Berry and Sam, 1997). Berry *et al.* (1987) found that refugees and Native Peoples have higher psychosomatic stress than migrants, sojourners and ethnic groups. Young and Evans (1997) compared Salvadorean refugees in Canada and Anglo-Canadians with regard to psychological distress, quality of life and satisfaction with life. While Salvadorean refugees did not differ with respect to psychological distress compared to the Anglo-Canadian sample, the refugee sample manifested lower quality of life and life satisfaction than Anglo-Canadians. The domains most affected by the acculturation experience were marital relations, parent–child relations, material well-being and job satisfaction.

Marital problems may arise owing to the more egalitarian nature of gender relations in the West, and with changes in family power relations due to women entering the labour force (Young and Evans, 1997), while loss of occupational status was identified as an important problem for Central American refugees in Canada (Allodi *et al.*, 1986).

However, forced migration does not lead necessarily to negative outcomes (Beiser *et al.*, 1988; Berry, 1997). Beiser *et al.* (1988) noted that while migration may be a risk factor for mental health problems, 'differences in personality characteristics or in the social conditions in which migrants find themselves are more powerful predictors of mental health outcomes than migration *per se*' (p. 3).

The nature and course of individual acculturation depends on a number of factors. Experiences prior to migration are clearly a potential influence. For instance, early traumatization (taking place before the age of 12) was associated with higher levels of antisocial behaviours among Cambodian refugee adolescents resettled in the United States (Kinzie and Sack, 1991). Anticipatory refugees, who left their homeland in an orderly way and with preparation, are more likely to acculturate more satisfactorily than acute refugees, who left their homeland quickly and without preparation (Kunz, 1973, 1981).

However, experiences occurring after arrival to a country of resettlement are also important. Liebkind (1996) found that predeparture traumatic experiences of Vietnamese refugees had a lower impact on stress symptoms than postmigration acculturation conditions.

The most commonly cited mediating factors that influence acculturation are adopted acculturation strategies and social support. In a study with Indochinese refugees, both adults and children, Rumbaut (1991a) found that men were more likely than women to adopt a bicultural (integration) strategy, while there were no significant gender differences in preferences for assimilation or traditionalism (separation). A comparison between Vietnamese and Korean adolescents and parents in Canada (Kwak and Berry, 1997) showed that parents in both groups endorsed separation more strongly than their children. Among adolescents, the Vietnamese children endorsed assimilation more strongly than the Korean sample, with their involuntary migration due to particularly difficult conditions in their home country a likely explanation for the difference. Different acculturation strategies emerged for different dimensions of the acculturation experience. Parents and children in both groups tended to adopt an integration strategy with regard to language and cultural traditions (of the home and host country), but separation with regard to marriage (Kwak and Berry, 1997).

Adopting an integration strategy, as opposed to a separation one, was found to predict lower acculturative stress among Central American refugees in Canada (Doná and Berry, 1994) and Southeast Asian refugees in the United States (Rumbaut, 1991b). In her study with Vietnamese refugees in Finland, Liebkind (1996) found that the more members of the younger generation endorsed an assimilation strategy and adopted Western values, the more they reported symptoms of anxiety and depression.

Social support is another strong predictor of successful adaptation (Berry *et al.*, 1987), as it helps to buffer the acculturative experience. For instance, Berry and Blondel (1982) found that Vietnamese refugees settling in Canada who could speak Chinese generally had better mental health status than those who could not speak Chinese. Speaking Chinese improved the likelihood of receiving employment and advice through the well-established Chinese communities in the country.

Refugee acculturation changes over time, leading to an overall improvement in mental health. A longitudinal study of Vietnamese refugees in Canada conducted in 1981, 1983 and 1992 showed that after they had spent ten years in Canada, unemployment rates were below the national average and education achievement was at or above the national norms, and health indicators (anxiety, psychosomatic symptoms, depression) did not reveal heightened problems (Beiser, 1994). Rumbaut (1991b) also found that levels of distress among Southeast Asian refugees decreased over time and that biculturalism (integration) emerged as a significant negative predictor of distress over time.

In conclusion, research on refugee acculturation to developed countries shows that while refugees may be at risk of experiencing mental health difficulties, a number of intervening variables occurring prior to and during acculturation mitigate this risk.

Acculturation of refugees in the developing world

As already indicated in the Introduction to this chapter, there is a need to know more about refugees in the developing world, especially about refugees who live in camps, and about those who return home. The following sections describe research conducted with Guatemalan refugees living in settlements in Mexico and Guatemalans who have returned to their home country. Berry's framework of acculturation is used in the context of forced migration and repatriation, where issues of cultural contact in neighbouring countries and of re-acculturation arise. The framework is useful because it takes into account the ecological, social, political and cultural components of group acculturation, and proposes their influence on psychological individual acculturation.

Forced migration of Guatemalans to Quintana Roo, Mexico

In 1978, the Guatemalan army initiated a counter-insurgency campaign to combat the growing popular demands for changes in the economic and sociopolitical *status quo*. At the end of 1981, an eighteen-month campaign of mass terror began in order to weaken popular resistance and to decrease the guerrillas' base of support. Both guerrilla units and the civilian population were attacked. No distinctions were made between civilians and combatants, no rules of war were followed, and no prisoners of war were taken (Manz, 1988). A 'scorched earth' policy led to burned crops, levelled homes and some four hundred destroyed communities.

Entire communities of indigenous peasants living in the northern highlands of Guatemala fled to Mexico. The first groups of Guatemalan refugees crossed the border in the state of Chiapas (in the southeastern part of Mexico) at the beginning of 1981 (Comisión Mexicana de Ayuda a Refugiados, 1985). At first, these refugees were hosted by the Mexican communities in the area. Later, 92 small camps were formed, the majority of them near the border with Guatemala.

The refugee influx continued until 1984. By then 46,000 Guatemalan refugees had crossed Mexico's southern border. Because of economic and political problems, in 1984 the Mexican government decided to resettle the refugees in Campeche and Quintana Roo.

In the state of Quintana Roo, four settlements were established. In late 1986 and early 1987 the United Nations High Commissioner for Refugees and the Mexican Commission for the Help of Refugees carried out a socioeconomic study of the situation in these four settlements, and concluded that the main obstacle for self-sustainment was lack of land (UNHCR, 1991). With the acquisition of new land in 1988, a multi-year plan began. The main purpose of the plan was for Guatemalan refugees settled in Quintana Roo to become self-sufficient and gradually integrate into Mexican society.

By the end of 1990 the basic infrastructure (shelter, access roads, urban streets, electricity, drinking water, schools and clinics) was completed. Each settlement has a clinic, a school, some electricity, a technician and/or a medical doctor. Since 1988 the State Health Ministry has been responsible for primary health care in all four refugee settlements in Quintana Roo. Since the 1989–90 school year, the settlements' schools have been incorporated into the national educational system. Mexican teachers are hired as school directors to supervise Guatemalan educators. In spite of climatic obstacles, the refugees now produce all their basic food needs, and even sell excess quantities on the local and regulation market. As of July 1992, the total population in the four settlements was 8181 people, in 1490 families. There were 4194 men and 3987 women (UNHCR, 1991).

Salient acculturation dimensions for Guatemalans in refugee settlements

With acculturation being a multidimensional phenomenon, it is generally appropriate to investigate the dimensions which are particularly salient for the group under study. In the case of Guatemalans living in refugee settlements in Mexico, three areas consistently emerged as relevant. These were areas frequently mentioned by the refugees, which also had a historical and practical basis. These three dimensions were cultural maintenance and cultural involvement (or acculturation attitudes), attitudes towards community leaders (Guatemalans or outsiders) and intention to return.

From a practical point of view, attitudes towards cultural maintenance and cultural involvement, and attitudes towards community figures are important because they evaluate the refugees' opinions towards recent policies that favour integration and sufficiency in the settlements in Mexico. As a reflection of these policies, UNHCR, in collaboration with the Mexican government, implemented programmes to help the approximately 43,000 refugees living in the settlements in Mexico to integrate and become self-sufficient (*Refugees*, 1990). These programmes were based on a combination of subsistence farming, casual wage labour within the province and income-generating projects in the settlements themselves (Stepputat, 1990). They emphasized the preservation of the refugees' ethnic and cultural values, the participation of women, the physical and intellectual development of children, and the promotion of the environment.

Intention to return is important because refugees living in the settlements in Mexico at the time of the study were discussing with the Guatemalan government the possibility of an organized and collective repatriation. Informal conversations with Guatemalan refugees in Mexico during two preliminary field visits revealed that repatriation was a major concern of the community.

These three dimensions are also meaningful concepts from a theoretical perspective. Acculturation attitudes (integration, separation, assimilation and marginalization) are an important element for the understanding of acculturation (Berry *et al.*, 1989; Doná, 1990). Consultations with members of the community, observations conducted during preliminary fieldwork and a literature review revealed issues relevant to the Guatemalan community in Mexico (i.e. *hacerce mexicano* (to become Mexican), mixed marriages, rural versus urban subsistence, etc.).

Attitudes towards community leaders are an index of sufficiency and acculturation. They are particularly important with regard to refugees in camps (Chan and Loveridge, 1987; Fagen, 1990; Murphy, 1955). An analysis of the policies implemented in the camps in Mexico and observations and discussions with members of the refugee community, of the Mexican government and UNHCR revealed issues of concern with regard to leadership. These included health, education, religion, women's organizations, management of the camp, enforcement of regulations and organization support.

Return is a central feature of the refugee experience. It is part of the definition of being a refugee, and of the involuntary nature of refugee migration. In a study with Central American refugees in Canada (Doná, 1990), 30 per cent of the respondents said that if an opportunity arose, they would return to the country of origin, 39 per cent expressed uncertainty and 24 per cent replied negatively. While refugees who move to the West may see repatriation as more distant, for refugees living in camps near the border with the home country the possibility of returning home is a dominant feature of their life as forced migrants. Informal interviews with the refugees showed diversified aspects of attitudes to return. Refugees differentiated between the importance of living in Guatemala, fears of returning and happiness about returning. They also distinguished a generalized wish to return as different from planning to return to Guatemala, and between planning to return with the first group of returnees or later.

The following analysis is based upon a three-phase study conducted between August 1991 and July 1992 involving 205 survey interviews with participants recruited through a range of social groupings.

Acculturation attitudes

In line with the need to assess the relevance of different dimensions of acculturation, items suggested by respondents were analysed with regard to their degree of endorsement. Almost 90 per cent of a subsample composed of 56 women said that they desired to marry among Guatemalans, to wear the *huipil* (traditional indigenous Guatemalan dress), to live as a Guatemalan, to have the children learn the history of Guatemala, to maintain their Mayan language, to be informed as to current happenings in Guatemala, to keep their customs, and essentially to live as Guatemalans.

While attitudes towards the issues of concern were generally positive, enjoying the marimba (traditional Guatemalan music), travelling to Guatemala, going to Guatemalan stores and working the land were met with a slightly lesser degree of endorsement.

Attitudes towards the Mexican culture were slightly less favourable but still positive. Respondents liked Mexicans because they felt that they are like themselves – *indios* (indigenous peoples) – and that Mexicans are good and honourable people. The similarity between Guatemalans and Mexicans disappears, however, when discussing more intimate interactions, such as marriage. While some women agreed with Guatemalans marrying Mexicans if the couple get along, most of them thought that Mexicans are not like Guatemalans. They had negative comments such as 'Mexicans do not keep their word', or 'they get Guatemalan women pregnant and then leave them'. A few of them reported that they felt discriminated against, or were treated as 'second-class' individuals.

In general, despite a few negative feelings of discrimination, the women felt grateful to the Mexicans for having given them *posada*, a place to rest. Furthermore, they had friendly relations with the Mexicans living in the neighbouring villages. They were invited to participate in parties organized by Mexicans and they invited the Mexicans to their own parties. The exchange of products also occurred between the refugees and the Mexicans. Refugees went to the market in the Mexican town of Chetumal to buy and sell products. Mexicans came to the settlements to sell fabric, fruit and other products and to buy pigs or chickens. Furthermore, work opportunities were offered to the refugees outside the settlements. Refugees worked in the Mexican tourist town of Cancún, five hours away. Men worked mainly in construction, girls worked in houses as cleaning-women. The reciprocal benefits of these interactions support integration.

Acculturation strategies

The study considered refugees' views regarding the acculturation strategies (Figure 7.1) of integration, separation, assimilation, and marginalization (Doná, 1990, 1993a, b). Following the categorization, 89 respondents endorsed the integration strategy and 76 the separation one. No respondent endorsed assimilation or marginalization. (A study on the process of acculturation of Central American refugees in Canada found a similar distribution, with the majority of Central American refugees endorsing an integrationist strategy (72), followed by separation (17), four respondents endorsing assimilation and none marginalization (Doná, 1990). The number of Guatemalan refugees preferring an integrationist strategy indicates a high level of support for the policies of integration being implemented by the Mexican government.

The endorsement of integration and separation can be explained by the nature of the refugees' attitudes towards Guatemalan culture. While differing in their attitudes towards the Mexican culture, respondents in the integration and separation modes share positive attitudes towards the Guatemalan culture (see Figure 7.1). Owing to the involuntary nature of their migration, Guatemalan refugees have little reason to dislike or relinquish the customs of their culture of origin (Berry and Kim, 1988). Furthermore, living in refugee settlements with other individuals from Guatemala serves to keep alive the legacy of their culture of origin. While

Guatemalan refugees in Mexico City may conceal their origin for fear of being expelled, by changing their clothing, pronunciation and hairstyle, refugees in the settlements can wear their traditional clothes and speak their Mayan language without fear of recrimination. The absence of endorsement of either assimilation or marginalization as modes of acculturation emphasizes the positive value accorded to the Guatemalan culture by the refugees.

Attitudes towards community figures

While the literature on acculturation describes culture contact in terms of cultural maintenance and relations with the dominant society (Berry, 1992; Phinney, 1996), relations with other groups have generally not been examined. In refugee camps, exposure to outsiders involved in humanitarian assistance is common, for instance, with potential implications for processes of acculturation and adjustment.

Guatemalan refugees indicated varied preferences for the cultural background of those active in the community, dependent upon the nature of the role concerned. Respondents preferred to have Guatemalan people leading activities in the areas of education, religion, women's organizations and settlement management. However, they favoured outsiders, namely representatives of UNHCR, in the area of organizational support. They preferred Mexicans to take leadership in the area of health.

Lack of strong support for exclusively Guatemalan community figures may be due to the fact that refugees are more concerned with the type of work accomplished by community figures than their nationality. For instance, some women commented that they do not care whether the teachers are Guatemalans or outsiders as long as they teach well. Others said that they welcome either Guatemalan or outside community figures depending on the ideas and teachings they communicate.

Furthermore, the women interviewed noted that Guatemalans and outsiders had much in common. For instance, some women commented that it is the same to have Guatemalan or outside catechists because they bring the message of the same God. They also liked to have both Guatemalans and outsiders as representatives of women's groups because it demonstrated the common issues faced by women.

The women interviewed who had positive attitudes towards Guatemalan teachers, supervisors and representatives of women's groups indicated as a reason for their preference the fact that these individuals can speak the Mayan language, teach the customs of Guatemala and continue the work after repatriation. They trust Guatemalans implementing rules because they have experience from working in co-operatives in Guatemala, and because they develop rules suitable for Guatemalans.

In the area of organizational support, preference was generally given to outsiders, namely the representatives of UNHCR. Women commented that these representatives were helping them by providing them with economic aid and good advice. The women commented that, since they live outside their country of origin and they are refugees, the help of UNHCR is important as a source of support. Women also manifested stronger preference for outsiders in the area of health. They commented that they favour Mexican technicians over health promoters because technicians can prescribe medicines and are more knowledgeable, especially about serious illness.

Intentions to return

Discussions among refugees regarding return were taking place at the time of the fieldwork. Comments about return were frequently linked to cultural maintenance and involvement with the Mexican society and other groups.

Respondents valued living in Guatemala, expressing a clear desire to return. There were various reasons for wanting to return. These were economic (owning land in Guatemala), social (having family members in Guatemala) and political (wanting to return to improve the conditions in the home country). Thoughts about return generally reflected a direct comparison of life in the settlements with life in Guatemala (e.g. being better off in Guatemala than in the settlements) or on an attachment to the country (e.g. elderly women wanting to return to die in the homeland).

An interesting finding is that the point of reference for wanting to return or wanting to settle in Mexico was generally Guatemala, and not Mexico. While refugees who intended to return stressed the positive aspects of life back home, those who intended to settle explained their decision not by emphasizing the positive aspects of life in Mexico but by emphasizing the negative aspects of life in Guatemala. Lack of peace, the possibility of being killed, the presence of danger and the level of repression were the most common reasons for not wanting to return. Refugees feared that the circumstances that forced them to leave Guatemala had not changed, and they worried that the government would not respect their rights if they repatriated.

Indecision about returning or settling in Mexico was based upon uncertainty regarding certain conditions being met. Refugees were generally willing to return if their repression ceased, if they were given land, if the government accepted the conditions for a collective and organized repatriation, and if they were accompanied by outsiders who would ensure their safety and protection.

Again, refugees who intended to return did not generally do so because they held negative attitudes towards Mexican culture but rather because they held positive attitudes towards their culture of origin. Their intention to repatriate was related to a general liking of the good life they had had in Guatemala, and its positive features such as having good land, being close to relatives and family members and living in peace before the attacks.

Acculturation of refugees in settlements

The study presented above highlights some conceptual and methodological issues for acculturation research in the developing world, especially in the case of refugees living in settlements. In such a context, it could be argued that acculturation is not an issue. Within the developing world, national boundaries are colonial impositions that separate ethnic and tribal groups, and movements across borders occur easily. Guatemalan refugees in Mexico, for instance, were hosted at first by the local population, who were familiar with seasonal migrant workers in their farms. Cultural distance is reduced, cultural diffusion is present, and differences in values (e.g. individualism and collectivism) are not prominent.

In settlements, contact with the host society may generally not be as frequent as with refugees settling in the West. Miller (1996) distinguishes between permanent resettlement and life in camps according to the lesser degree of adaptation and integration required of the latter, where refugees see their life in exile as temporary. The closed community of a refugee camp may preclude any significant interaction with the host country.

However, the study reported above makes it clear that temporarily settled refugees are very aware of being in a different country and of the differences between themselves and the host community. Interactions do occur and in some instances result in mixed marriages. The Mexican government itself recognized the usefulness of integrating refugees and the local population. Although born in refugee settlements, children of Guatemalan refugees born in Mexico are given Mexican citizenship, and with it the right to own land. *Hacerce mexicano* (to become Mexican) was an issue of concern for the refugees. Issues of integration emerged, for instance, in the area of education, where adoption of the Mexican educational system in the settlements was modified to include the teaching of Guatemalan history (Miller, 1996).

Forced migration within the developing world differs from migration to the West because it frequently involves mass migration as opposed to individual flight. The fact of refugees fleeing together for the same reasons and living together in settlements creates conditions for a rediscovery and an articulation of cultural issues not highlighted in the home country. As

Cohen (1985, p. 69) writes, 'people become aware of their culture when they stand at its boundaries: when they encounter other cultures, or when they become aware of other ways of doing things, or merely of contractions to their own culture'. Refugees in Mexico talked about being Mayan, indigenous and not Ladino. They also used culture as a political tool to reassert their rights, for example, in education.

In analysing acculturation as a multidimensional phenomenon, concepts presented in Berry's framework, such as group and individual changes, and the role of moderating variables such as acculturation attitudes for adaptation, have proved useful. However, in the context of forced migration, developing countries and refugee settlements, new issues (return, attitudes towards other groups) not generally considered in acculturation research emerge as highly salient for refugee acculturation. Methodologically, the use of participant observation and unstructured interviews was important in revealing such salient and context-specific features of acculturation.

The fact that the majority of refugees in the settlements endorsed integration as their preferred strategy suggests that cultural contact through being interspersed with members of the host country is not a necessary condition for psychological involvement in the host society. Informal links between Guatemalans and Mexicans soon after the refugees' flight gave rise to positive attitudes, which, combined with a policy of integration adopted by the host country, resulted in adoption of an integration strategy. This occurred despite the fact that refugees lived in settlements and that they were planning to return to Guatemala.

Indeed, at the time of fieldwork, members of the Permanent Commissions, the political representatives of the refugees in the settlements, were holding meetings with representatives of the Guatemalan government, the Mexican government and other international organizations to discuss the terms of a collective and organized return. Refugees, then, perceived their stay in the settlements as temporary. They were grateful to the Mexicans for having given them *posada*, a place to rest for a while. Despite the perceived temporariness of their residence in Mexico, they endorsed integration. This shows that permanent settlement in the host country is not necessary for the adoption of integration strategies.

Discussions among members of the refugees' representatives and the Guatemalan government resulted in the signing of a formal agreement for repatriation. In the following section, the experience of Guatemalan refugees' repatriation is used as a case study to highlight a challenge for acculturation research, namely whether it is relevant to study repatriation as a re-acculturation phenomenon or whether there is a need to develop new concepts.

The return

The UN declared the 1990s to be the 'decade of repatriation'. The current repatriation movements in Latin America (Guatemalans, Salvadoreans), Africa (Rwandans) and Asia (Cambodians and Vietnamese from Hong Kong) render of acute interest the study of how refugees who have returned after years abroad (e.g. Rwandan refugees who fled in 1959 and returned to Rwanda in 1994) and young people who were born abroad (Miller, 1996) adjust once they return to their country of origin.

The research literature on repatriation is mainly concerned with performance and readjustment of expatriates who return home after assignments abroad (Black, 1992; Briody and Baba, 1991; Gregersen, 1992). Some studies of migrants who have returned home are available (Gmelch and Gmelch, 1995; Stringham, 1993). Few publications deal directly with refugees' repatriation (Kovalskys, 1987), highlighting the alienation, isolation and marginalization suffered by repatriating individuals who find themselves in an environment that has become unfamiliar, and the practical difficulties in achieving professional, educational, social and political reinstatement into the current mainstream society (Kovalskys, 1987).

Can the process of returning home be understood as a process of re-acculturation or do new concepts and theories have to be developed? Do changes in cultural norms, beliefs and behaviours occurring as a result of migration lead to a degree of cultural differentiation that justifies talking of 'culture contact' on return? We will proceed to describe the return of Guatemalan refugees and subsequently analyse their experience in relation to the above questions.

Guatemalans return home

After ten years in exile, on 20 October 1992, the representatives of the Guatemalan refugees in Mexico signed an agreement with the government of Guatemala stipulating the terms for the conditions for their return to Guatemala. Return is seen by the refugees as a collective and organized movement distinct from repatriation, carried out by single individuals or families.

Since January 1993, about 4800 Guatemalans have returned in organized and collective fashion to Ixcàn, northwest Guatemala, an area from where most of them originally fled. A total of some 15,000 have signed up to return, even though some small-scale returns have been cancelled owing to the problematic political climate in Guatemala. In 1993, those internally displaced also signed an agreement with the government for their 'coming into the open' and subsequent return to the area from which they had fled. The area in which returnees from Mexico set up their settlements is interspersed with settlements to which the internally displaced have returned and where 'model villages' were established in the 1980s.

In order to consider whether returnees' readjustment is best conceptualized as re-acculturation, we must first analyse whether cultural changes occurred during the years in which the refugees were abroad and the internally displaced moved into the jungle, and whether these changes culturally differentiate the refugees from those who stayed behind.

The *refugees* who fled to Mexico and lived in settlements were exposed to Mexican lifestyle and interacted with Mexicans and international aid workers. Life in the settlements was conducive to the development of a political identity as indigenous populations and refugees. They formed committees and elected political leaders to represent them and their needs to the Mexican government, the Guatemalan government and the international community. Refugees travelled outside the settlements for training and meetings. The terms of the agreement for their return and the arrangement of a collective and organized return are a sign of the development of a community which shared not only a geographical location but also common goals. The refugees in Mexico fit Cohen's (1985) notion of both aggregational and relational community. The former refers to an aggregation of people who have something in common which distinguishes them in a significant way from members of other groups. The latter expresses the opposition of one community to others. Its tenet is that individuals become aware of their culture when they stand at its boundaries. Being in Mexico made the Guatemalan refugees aware not only that they had their own needs but also that they were different from the Mexicans.

While the refugees were in Mexico, contacts with the Mexicans and international aid workers contributed to improving their economic conditions. In Quintana Roo, for instance, refugees had access to water from wells beside their houses and to electric light in the central area of the settlements; they were exposed to new crafts such as making hammocks or baking bread in the oven; they engaged in urban jobs such as construction and housework as maids; and they were introduced to new tools such as a mill to grind corn. Politically, they elected their representatives and formed many committees (health promoters, sector representatives, women's groups, etc.).

In Guatemala, as a result of the repression, the *internally displaced* moved deeper and deeper into the jungle, where they lived separated from the rest of the country for years. In a similar manner to the refugees, they also became aware of being a distinct entity, and called themselves 'Communities of Populations in Resistance'. They elected their own political representatives to discuss their conditions for 'coming into the open'. Geographically, internal displacement was characterized by isolation and constant movement. One refugee reported that his family and group moved at least seventy times during those years. Economically, agriculture continued to be the main source of survival. Issues of security altered social and economic relations. Because of the need for constant *vigilancia* (alertness), young people and men took turns in guarding their group. As a consequence they could not participate in the cultivation of their land or the teaching of their children.

Because of isolation and a limited exchange of goods, the internally displaced were not much affected by contact with other cultures and changes. They lived in very harsh conditions. Women would wash the clothes in a river only at sunset and sundown, and fire was kept low to avoid being detected by the army. The internally displaced developed a strong sense of belonging as a result.

When refugees and the internally displaced fled, the area they left came increasingly under army control. Individuals who stayed behind, and other peasants relocated from other parts of Guatemala, were settled in 'model villages'. In these villages army control was high, and so was social pressure. Each family had to provide services as 'vigilantes' and report to the nearby army base any unusual movement by fellow villagers (Manz, 1988). As a result conformity, fear and social pressure increased.

The different experiences undergone by refugees, the internally displaced and model villagers thus resulted in different types of communities, which are distinctive politically, socially and culturally. Group-level changes occurred in geographical terms (living in different locations), in economic terms (collective cultivation of the land was strong among internally displaced but not among refugees; rural subsistence was the main source of survival for the internally displaced with reduced exchange of goods, while it was less important for 'model villages', and in the case of refugees it was integrated with urban subsistence), technologically (the internally displaced lived for years without electricity and running water, while model villagers had access to them and refugees had access to services), politically (different representatives were elected with different goals), socially (given the need for interdependence in survival, the internally displaced developed strong ties among themselves; refugees also developed a sense of identity but not as strong as that of the internally displaced) and culturally (appearance and lifestyles were different, with refugees in Quintana Roo replacing traditional ways of dressing with Mexican ones, while the internally displaced generally maintained them).

What happens when refugees go home?

Return to Guatemala confronts refugees, the internally displaced and model villagers with the task of developing new ways of living together. Perceptions of in- and out-group memberships were present and changed over time. In 1995 returnees held very positive attitudes towards the internally displaced. They called them *hermanos* (brothers) and sympathized with the difficult life they had led while in the jungle. In 1996, however, political leaders of the returnees changed their attribution of the characteristics of the internally displaced and referred to them as guerrillas or guerrilla supporters. Mistrust of model villagers was present in 1995 and 1996, as they were perceived as spies and supporters of the army. Some returnees expressed unwillingness to stay long in model villages for fear of being harassed.

The returnees also expressed their belief that cultural differences were present between themselves and the internally displaced. They considered themselves as *mas desarroyados* (more developed) than the internally displaced and model villagers.

Tensions among the returnees and the other groups emerged after return and deteriorated over time. The main source of tension was land, a key issue that reflects different cultural changes and values. One of the conditions for the refugee return was the acquisition of the land previously owned in Guatemala or the purchase of new land for the sons born in Mexico. This problem had not been solved and between 1995 and 1996 considerable tensions arose.

Different experiences and exposure to different influences also create tensions. While in Mexico, the refugees in the settlements received international aid and education and service support from UNHCR, the Mexican government and international organizations. Those who stayed in Guatemala under army control received some help through the government, while the internally displaced (because of their isolation) received only limited support (mainly through non-governmental organizations). As a consequence, differences in attitudes towards humanitarian assistance and dependency have evolved. The returnees have learned to ask for and receive assistance. They see assistance as one of their rights. The internally displaced have relied mainly on themselves and on a few outsiders to survive. They are more self-sufficient. The model villagers under surveillance and army control accepted the situation as it was. As a consequence of different relations with outsiders involved in humanitarian assistance, returnees tend to have developed a more dependent attitude than the internally displaced.

Despite changes in values and behaviours, a number of factors offer potential to facilitate readjustment. The most important of these is the presence of neighbours, relatives and family members across the three communities. The shared history of repression and discrimination that all have endured as indigenous populations may also be a powerful factor. This was demonstrated in the participation of individuals from the various types of community in the commemoration of a massacre which occurred in one of the villages. The sharing of health and education services and resources also offers the potential for bringing together these now disparate strands of the Guatemalan community.

The above description of the return home of the Guatemalan refugees and their attitudes towards, and interactions with, the internally displaced and model villagers indicate that it is feasible to look at return as re-acculturation. Cultures are evolving and changing (Vega, 1992). Group-level changes have occurred in the three groups described. Individuals belonging to the three groups perceive themselves differently from members of the other groups, and tensions arise over issues that reflect changing values and attitudes.

Individuals returning home, especially after years in exile, are confronted with varying degrees of readjustment difficulty. Challenges vary according to cultural distance (migration to the West or to a neighbouring country), length of stay abroad, type of migration (individual or group), as well as individual circumstances.

Conclusion

This chapter has addressed issues of refugee acculturation with a particular focus on refugee settlement and repatriation within the developing world. It has summarized established work on refugee acculturation and attempted to extend such analysis to the acculturative challenges of refugee settlement and return in the developing world.

While current theories on acculturation agree on its multidimensionality, research with Guatemalans in Mexico has shown that different dimensions are salient in different contexts. Research on acculturation strategies in the West indicates that an integration strategy is generally the preferred one (Berry *et al.*, 1987; Doná, 1990). Research in the settlements discussed here shows that integration may be preferred even in settings of forced migration, relative isolation from the host country, and temporary settlement.

The general finding, obtained with different acculturating groups in different host countries, is that integration is commonly the preferred strategy. However, differences among individuals who choose integration have emerged (Doná and Berry, 1994). Future research would advance theory by looking in more depth at integration itself.

Methodologically, the study of acculturation has moved from the assessment of acculturation through group comparison and demographic variables, to single items and lately psychometric scales. However, reliance on psychometric scales for cross-cultural research may result in construct, method or item bias (van de Vijver and Leung, 1997). Construct bias refers to the fact that in cross-cultural settings, psychometric scales may not represent the behaviours of interest. Method bias refers, for instance, to different levels of familiarity with the instruments, such as the use of paper-and-pencil methods as opposed to interviews. Item bias may refer to differences in the appropriateness of the content, the formulation of items or the translation of items. Psychometric scales may also be culturally insensitive to the oral tradition of refugee populations within the developing world, who may be more familiar with telling stories than answering close-ended questions. It is possible that the development within acculturation research of a greater interest in the developing world calls for a return towards more anthropologically oriented qualitative methods. Ager (1994) also recommends the use of refugees' narrative as a unifying tool for research with refugees. This does not mean that qualitative methods should be used exclusively. It is the convergence of different methods – such as participant observation, questionnaires and interviews – which has the potential to provide richer information. By such means it is to be hoped that work on acculturation within the developing world will usefully inform research on refugee acculturation within developed societies.

References

Aga Khan, S. and bin Talal, H. (1986) *Refugees: The Dynamics of Displacement*. London: Zed Books.

Ager, A. (1994) *Mental Health Issues in Refugee Populations: A Review*. Working Paper for the Harvard Center for the Study of Culture and Medicine. Harvard Medical School, Department of Social Medicine.

Allodi, F., Berger, P., Beyersbergen, J. and Fantini, N. (1986) Community consultation on refugee integration: Central American refugees and survivors of torture in Ontario. *Canada's Mental Health*, 34, 10–12.

Basic Behavioral Science Task Force of the National Advisory Mental Health Council (1996). Basic behavioural science research for mental health: sociocultural and environmental processes. *American Psychologist*, 51 (7), 722–31.

Beiser, M. (1994) *Longitudinal Study of Vietnamese Refugee Adaptation*. Toronto: Clarke Institute of Psychiatry.

Beiser, M., Barwick, C., Berry, J.W., da Costa, G., Fantino, A.M., Ganesan, S., Lee, C., Milne, W., Naidoo, J., Prince, R., Tousignant, M. and Vela, E. (1988) *After the Door Has Been Opened: Mental Health*

Issues Affecting Immigrants and Refugees. Ottawa: Ministries of Multiculturalism and Citizenship, and Health and Welfare.

Berry, J.W. (1980) Acculturation as varieties of adaptation. In A. Padilla (ed.), *Acculturation: Theory, Models and Some New Findings*, pp. 9–25. Boulder, CO: Westview.

Berry, J.W. (1991) Managing the process of acculturation for problem prevention. In J. Westermeyer, C.L. Williams and A. N. Nguyen (eds), *Mental Health Services for Refugees*, pp. 189–204. Washington, DC: Government Printing Office.

Berry, J.W. (1992) Acculturation and adaptation in a new society. *International Migration*, 30, 69–83.

Berry, J.W. (1997) Immigration, acculturation, and adaptation. *Applied Psychology: An International Review*, 46 (1), 5–34.

Berry, J.W. and Blondel, T. (1982) Psychological adaptation of Vietnamese refugees to Canada. *Canadian Journal of Community Mental Health*, 1, 81–8.

Berry, J.W. and Kim, U. (1988) Acculturation and mental health. In P. Dasen, J.W. Berry and N. Sartorious (eds), *Health and Cross-cultural Psychology: Towards Applications*, pp. 207–36. London: Sage.

Berry, J.W. and Sam, D. (1997) Acculturation and adaptation. In J.W. Berry, M.S. Segall and C. Kagitcibasi (eds), *Handbook of Cross-cultural Psychology*, 2nd edition, vol. 3, pp. 291–326. Boston: Allyn and Bacon.

Berry, J.W., Trimble, J.E. and Olmedo, E.L. (1986) Assessment of acculturation. In W.J. Lonner and J.W. Berry (eds), *Field Methods in Cross-cultural Research*. London: Sage.

Berry, J.W., Kim, U., Minde, T. and Mok, D. (1987) Comparative studies of acculturative stress. *International Migration Review*, 21, 491–511.

Berry, J.W., Kim, U., Power, S., Young, M. and Bujaki, M. (1989) Acculturation attitudes in plural societies. *Applied Psychology: An International Review*, 38 (2), 185–206.

Black, J.S. (1992) Coming home: the relationship of expatriate expectations with repatriation adjustment and work performance. *Human Relations*, 45 (2), 177–92.

Briody, E.K. and Baba, M.L. (1991) Explaining differences in repatriation experiences: the discovery of coupled and decoupled systems. *American Anthropologist*, 93 (2), 322–44.

Chambers, R. (1986) Hidden losers? The impact of rural refugees and refugee programs on poorer hosts. *International Migration Review*, 20, 245–63.

Chan, K.B. and Loveridge, D. (1987) Refugees in transit: Vietnamese in a refugee camp in Hong Kong. *International Migration Review*, 18 (2), 237–57.

Cohen, A.P. (1985) *The Symbolic Construction of Community*. London: Routledge.

Comisión Mexicana de Ayuda a Refugiados (1985) *Refugiados guatemaltecos* [The Mexican Commission for the Help of Refugees. Guatemalan refugees]. Mexico City: COMAR.

Doná, G. (1990) Acculturation and mental health of Central American refugees in Canada. Unpublished master's thesis, Queen's University, Kingston, Ontario.

Doná, G. (1993a) Acculturation and mental health of Guatemalan refugees living in settlements in Mexico. Unpublished doctoral thesis, Queen's University, Kingston, Ontario.

Doná, G. (1993b) Guatemalan refugee women: cultural issues in repatriation and settlement. Paper presented at the conference Gender Issues and Refugees: Development Implications, Toronto, May.

Doná, G. and Berry, J.W. (1994) Acculturation attitudes and acculturative stress of Central American refugees. *International Journal of Psychology*, 29, 57–70.

Fagen, P.W. (1990) Worldwide refugees: problems of disruption, fear, and poverty. In W.H. Holtzman and T.H. Bornemann (eds), *Mental Health of Immigrants and Refugees*, pp. 7–15. Austin: University of Texas.

Feagan, J.R. (1984) *Racial and Ethnic Relations*, 2nd edition. Englewood Cliffs, NJ: Prentice Hall.

Gmelch, G. and Gmelch, S. (1995) The readjustment of women migrants in Barbados, Ireland, and Newfoundland. *Human Organization*, 54 (4), 470–3.

Gong-Guy, E., Cravens, R.B. and Patterson, T.E. (1991) Clinical issues in mental health service delivery to refugees. *American Psychologist*, 46 (6), 642–8.

Gordon, M. (1964) *Assimilation in American Life*. New York: Oxford University Press.

Gordon, M. (1981) Models of pluralism: the new American dilemma. In R. Lambert and A.W. Heston (eds), *Annals of the American Academy of Political and Social Science*, vol. 454: America as a multicultural society, pp. 178–88. Philadelphia: American Academy of Political and Social Science.

Graves, T. (1967) Psychological acculturation in a tri-ethnic community. *Southwestern Journal of Anthropology*, 23, 337–50.

Gregersen, H.B. (1992) Commitments to a parent company and a local work unit during repatriation. *Personnel Psychology*, 45 (1), 29–54.

International Migration Review (1989) Foreword: IMR at 25: reflections on a quarter century of international migration research and orientations for future research. *International Migration Review*, 23 (3), 393–402.

Keefe, S. and Padilla, A. (1987) *Chigano Ethnicity*. Albuquerque: University of New Mexico Press.

Kinzie, J.D. and Sack, W. (1991) Severely traumatized Cambodian children: research findings and clinical implications. In F.L. Ahearn, Jr and J.L. Athey (eds), *Refugee Children: Theory, Research, and Services*, pp. 92–105. Baltimore: Johns Hopkins University Press.

Kovalskys, S.J. (1987) Exilio and desexili [Exile and repatriation]. *Revista Chilena de Psicología*, 9 (2), 51–4.

Kunz, E. (1973) The refugees in flight, kinetic models and forms of displacement. *International Migration Review*, 7, 125–46.

Kunz, E. (1981) Exile and resettlement: the refugee experience. *International Migration Review*, 15, 42–51.

Kwak, K. and Berry, J.W. (1997) Generation differences on acculturation attitudes and values among Vietnamese and Korean families in Toronto. Paper presented at the 14th Biennial Conference of the Canadian Ethnic Studies Association, Montreal, November.

Liebkind, K. (1996) Acculturation and stress: Vietnamese refugees in Finland. *Journal of Cross-cultural Psychology*, 27 (2), 161–70.

Manz, B. (1988) *Refugees of a Hidden War: The Aftermath of the Counterinsurgency in Guatemala*. Albany: State University of New York Press.

Marsella, A.J., Bornemann, T., Eklad, S. and Orley, J. (eds) (1994) *Amidst Peril and Pain: The Mental Health and Well-Being of the World's Refugees*. Washington, DC: American Psychological Association.

Martin-Baró, I. (1989) Political violence and war as causes of psychosocial trauma in El Salvador. *International Journal of Mental Health*, 18 (1), 3–20.

Miller, K. (1996) The effects of state terrorism and exile on indigenous Guatemalan refugee children: a mental health assessment and an analysis of children's narratives. *Child Development*, 67, 89–106.

Moore, J. (1988) The refugee problem in Southern Africa. In L. Tomasi (ed.), *In Defence of the Alien*, vol. 10, pp. 120–6. Proceedings of the 1987 Annual Legal Conference on Immigration and Refugee Policy. New York: Center for Migration Studies.

Muecke, M.A. (1992) New paradigms for refugee health problems. *Social Science and Medicine*, 35, 515–23.

Murphy, H.B.M. (1955) *Flight and Resettlement*. Paris: UNESCO.

Padilla, A.M. (1980) The role of cultural awareness and ethnic loyalty in acculturation. In A.M. Padilla (ed.), *Acculturation: Theory, Models and Some New Findings*. Boulder, CO: Westview Press.

Palinkas, L.A. and Pickwell, S.M. (1995) Acculturation as a risk factor for chronic disease among Cambodian refugees in the United States. *Social Science and Medicine*, 40 (12), 1643–53.

Phinney, J.S. (1996) When we talk about the American ethnic groups, what do we mean? *American Psychologist*, 51 (9), 918–27.

Redfield, R., Linton, R. and Herskovits, M. (1936) Memorandum on the study of acculturation. *American Anthropologist*, 38, 149–52.

Refugees (1990) *Refugees*, 81, 33–5.

Rogler, L.H., Cortes, D.E. and Malgady, R.G. (1991) Acculturation and mental health status among Hispanics: convergence and new directions for research. *American Psychologist*, 46 (6), 585–97.

Rumbaut, R.G. (1991a) The agony of exile: a study of the migration and adaptation of Indochinese refugee adults and children. In F.L. Ahearn, Jr and J.L. Athey (eds), *Refugee Children: Theory, Research, and Services*, pp. 53–91. Baltimore: Johns Hopkins University Press.

Rumbaut, G. (1991b) Migration, adaptation and mental health. In H. Adelman (ed.), *Refugee Policy, Canada and the United States*, pp. 381–424. Toronto, CA: York Lanes Press.

Stein, B.N. (1986) The experience of being a refugee: insights from the research literature. In C.L. Williams and J. Westermeyer (eds), *Refugee Mental Health in Resettlement Countries*, pp. 5–23. Washington, DC: Hemisphere.

Stepputat, F. (1990) The hard road to self-sufficiency. *Refugees*, 80, 31–3.

Stringham, E.M. (1993) The reacculturation of missionary families: a dynamic theory. *Journal of Psychology and Theology*, 21 (1), 66–73.

UNHCR (1991) Self-sufficiency and integration of Guatemalan refugees in Quintana Roo. Unpublished manuscript.

UNICEF (1986) *Children in Situations of Armed Conflict*. New York: UNICEF: E/ICEF.CRP.2.

van de Vijver, F. and Leung, K. (1997) *Methods and Data Analysis for Cross-cultural Research*. London: Sage.

Vega, W. (1992) Theoretical and pragmatic implications of cultural diversity for community research. *American Journal of Community Psychology*, 23, 375–91.

Vernez, G. (1991) Current global refugee situation and international public policy. *American Psychologist*, 46 (6), 627–31.

Wickher, H. and Schoch, H. (1987) Refugees and mental health: South East Asian refugees in Switzerland. In D. Miserez (ed.), *Refugees: The Trauma of Exile*, pp. 153–78. Dordrecht: Martinus Nijhoff.

Williams, C.L. and Berry, J.W. (1991) Primary prevention of acculturative stress among refugees: application of psychological theory and practice. *American Psychologist*, 46 (6), 632–41.

Williams, C.L. and Westermeyer, J. (eds) (1986) *Refugee Mental Health in Resettlement Countries*. Washington, DC: Hemisphere.

Young, M.Y. and Evans, D.R. (1997) The well-being of Salvadorean refugees. *International Journal of Psychology*, 32 (5), 289–300.

Zwi, A. and Ugalde, A. (1989) Towards an epidemiology of political violence in the Third World. *Social Science and Medicine*, 28, 633–42.

8

Refugee women: a gendered and political analysis of the refugee experience

Agnès Callamard

Introduction

The focus on refugee women as mandating specific policies and as a distinct topic of inquiry may be traced back to the mid-1970s. This was a time of a growing awareness of women's rights, as well as on the role of women in general (and refugee women in particular) in the development process. The following twenty years was marked by the proclamation of the UN decade for women, the 1985 Nairobi conference and the 1995 Beijing Conference on Women, which highlighted the situation of refugee women as an area of special concern and gave a new impetus to international and local efforts. Yet the incorporation of women within the field of refugee policies and refugee studies has been slow, marginal and contradicted by broader structural constraints. Although marked by important steps towards ending the marginalization of the issue, including the creation of the position of the UNHCR refugee women's co-ordinator and the Beijing Platform for Action, these past twenty years have also been characterized by an ever-growing number of refugees and displaced populations, the impact and legacy of superpower rivalry, and the multiplication of internal conflicts, and national(istic) politics. UNHCR, in its never-ending quest for durable solutions, has embarked on worldwide repatriation policies which largely undermine, if not outrightly contradict, the organization protection mandate in general and the protection of refugee women in particular. The discrepancy between the public relations statement 'women and children represent 80 per cent of the world refugee population' repeated *ad nauseam* and the 'voluntary' return (at the barrel of a gun) of a number of these same refugee women and children painfully demonstrates the limits of the rights and protection framework put forward in Beijing, and the obstacles faced in its translation into practice.

As a field of action research, the focus on refugee women has remained the prerogative of refugee women themselves, some policy-makers and a few social scientists and legal scholars calling attention to the issue in the context of refugee camps and the refugee determination process. An important step towards ending the marginalization of the issue and breaking 'artificial boundaries created by professional, institutional and regional divisions' (Giles *et al.*, 1996, p. 12) was initiated in 1993 with a world conference on 'Gender Issues and Development' held in Toronto. The conference generated a dialogue between activists, NGOs and students and allowed for exchange across disciplines and activism. Two approaches emerged in terms of conceptualizing and acting upon the situation of refugee women – one emphasizing development, and the other human rights. Since then, the latter approach has generally taken precedence over the former, an evolution sanctioned during the Fourth UN World Conference on Women.

But, as this chapter demonstrates, the interconnection between development and human rights for refugee women has seldom been fully realized. This state of affairs may be traced back to an incomplete gendered understanding of the refugee experience resulting from the creation of 'the refugee' as a 'generic and essentialized figure' (Malkki, 1992), a political and legal artefact meant to exclude certain aspects pertaining to one's identity or to one's experience of persecution (Tuitt, 1996; Hathaway, 1988, 1991; Goodwin-Gill, 1983). This artefact or generic figure is intended to be ungendered and desexualized, although 'the persecution standard adopted within ... the definition under the Geneva Convention ensures, however, that the few identified within these definitions are adult and male' (Tuitt, 1996, p. 33). In the past ten years or so, efforts have been made towards 'engendering' the refugee definition through a focus on women's rights. But, as this chapter argues, whereas this approach has influenced the fairly legalistic discourse (albeit not the practice) over individual women asylum-seekers who manage to reach one of the more progressive Western countries (Canada, the USA, Australia and New Zealand in particular), it has not yet permeated the analysis of the situation of refugee women self-settled or in refugee camps. This chapter seeks to highlight the gendered and sexual nature of the refugee experiences through a review of existing evidence on the discrimination faced by refugee women in terms of access to international assistance, income and physical protection. It argues that discrimination and violence against refugee women are politically determined and politically sanctioned, under the actions or influence of international, national and local actors, and therefore that the situation of many refugee women in camps amounts to persecution under the accepted definition. The chapter further suggests that such persecution has been heightened by the recent mechanisms devised by nation-states to control refugee movements, reduce their political and economic costs and transform human and political tragedies into humanitarian (meaning technical) and security crises. If the militarization and criminalization of refugee camps constitute major obstacles to the protection of refugee women, current answers to this militarization, including forced repatriation to unsafe areas, are no less threatening.

The gendered experience of refugees in camps: refugee women, power and social change

As noted above, the focus on the role of refugee women in the settlement and development process emerged in the mid-1970s with the UN Decade for Women. Two factors had prompted the international community to notice the existence and functions of refugee women. The first was the emergence, following the publication of Esther Boserup's (1970) seminal work *Women's Role in Economic Development*, of a new field of research and policy labelled Women in Development. The second was a widespread disenchantment with both development and refugee assistance, and the shift of emphasis from national to community development and the provision of basic needs and self-sufficiency (as highlighted, for instance, by the 1974 Cocoyoc Declaration). Although, as Deniz Kandiyoti (1990) had noted, the effects of gender inequality did not initially receive separate attention above and beyond those of class membership, concerns with greater equity, grassroots participation and self-sufficiency paved the way for policy proposals and reforms related to women, eventually resulting, among other end-products, in the production of *UNHCR Guidelines on the Protection of Refugee Women*, released in 1991. As explored elsewhere (Callamard, 1993), these and other policy papers make claims for refugee women on two bases: the needs or vulnerability of refugee women, and their central role and contribution to the welfare of the refugee community. The assumption here is that projects of refugee assistance that focus on women refugees will be more likely to translate into an amelioration of the welfare of the community. Drafted for UNHCR and other relief agencies staff, the 1991 UNHCR guidelines recognize and highlight the serious shortcomings of existing (gender-biased) relief programmes and their implications for the lives of the refugee women and the community as a whole. As such, they certainly constituted a milestone in the organization's interpretation and handling of its mandate, but one that has been subsequently undermined by the broader policies of the organization.

Empirical research focusing on refugee camps has, on the whole, preceded or corroborated the not-so-covert self-critique that the authors of the guidelines had made, although the picture drawn by researchers has attributed more weight to one main factor – ignored or underestimated by the UNHCR guidelines – namely, the political and power structures within the camp.

The entry point towards addressing and confronting the political nature of refugee women's 'vulnerability' within the camp context has been through a focus on the economic strategies within the camp and/or an evaluation of refugee assistance projects. What have been termed refugees' survival strategies include a variety of activities ranging from farming and wage labour to hunting, gathering and the trade of food relief (Mazur, 1991; Refugee Studies Programme, 1989; Weaver, 1988), all of which are heavily determined by the local economic structures (Refugee Studies Programme, 1989). Some of these activities may be defined as 'diet supplementation strategies' in that they are aimed solely at diversifying and increasing the (insufficient) food ration allocated to the refugees. Others have a broader objective, namely to enhance the prospects of economic integration within their country of asylum (Daley, 1991; Callamard, 1995).

Not surprisingly, research also shows that the nature, scope and objective of these economic activities differ sharply among men and women refugees and that individual refugees' adjustment to their new circumstances and the process of social changes within the refugee community as a whole entails a transformation of the gender division of labour. Christensen's (1983) study of three Ethiopian refugee camps in Somalia and Spring's research (1979) among Angolan refugees demonstrate the gender-differentiated survival strategies. In Zambia, Anita Spring noted different assimilation processes among refugee men and women who had self-settled within Zambian villages. Her research especially highlights the importance of marriage as a vehicle of economic wealth and social integration for refugee women. Among Ethiopians, the income-generating activities devised by refugees were divided into female and male spheres, with men less frequently money-earners than the women. Johnson's research in Wad el Hilayew camp for Eritrean refugees in Sudan revealed as well the transformation of the gender division of labour, although in this case change occurred at the expense of women:

> People who had brought draught animals with them such as donkeys or camels set themselves up as transporters of water, firewood and fodder in the camp. This activity had previously been regarded as women's work within the family and as a result of its appropriation by men as a commercial venture many women became even more marginalised in refugee society than they had been in Eritrea (Johnson, 1981, p. 420)

Evidence gathered among Mozambican refugees in Malawi highlights similar patterns. Ager *et al.*'s survey (1995) of some 200 refugee households demonstrated that while women were more likely to work than men, they were also less likely to generate any income from their work, as the latter was principally domestic in nature. Research conducted in Lisongwe refugee camp in Malawi (Callamard, 1996) highlighted similar circumstances, with Mozambican women having been expelled from the allocation and trade of food.

Analysis of the factors or forces contributing to the rapid changes of the gender division of labour, in many cases at the expense of refugee women, highlights the interrelationships between structure and human agency as well as among various actors. Christensen (1983) attributes both gender differentiation in terms of economic activities and the emergence of a women's consciousness to structural factors, including the unequal sex ratio in the adult population (about two-thirds of the households covered by her study were headed by a woman) and the fact that refugees belonged to nomadic societies. She does not elaborate on the possible role of the camp management and of the local cultural environment in fostering 'new' gender roles within the camp setting, although she does hint at it when she concludes that women's committees, set up by the camp commandant, functioned as a channel in the introduction of community development programmes. Other writers have brought to light the role of both pre-flight patterns and relief programme. For instance, Daley (1991) attributes gender differentiation between Burundian refugees' economic activities to the patriarchal tendencies of Burundian society and male bias of the settlement programme. Ager *et al.* (1995) recognize the pre-existing gender inequalities within Mozambican society, but nevertheless suggest that relief projects and structures for refugee representation had exacerbated existing gender inequality. Projects had

> addressed their attention to increasing skills and increasing participation on the assumption that these would foster increases in power and financial status.... The evidence from this study ... is that these strategies were generally unsuccessful in achieving the hypothesised gains in such key outcome areas. (1995, p. 284)

As for the structures for representation, they were clearly male-dominated and

> generally insensitive to representing the needs of women. Many women reported block chairmen for instance, being unsympathetic regarding the resolution of domestic disputes. Women who had complained through these structures regarding favouritism in distribution of food had generally not received a sympathetic hearing either. (Ager *et al.*, 1995, p. 283)

Callamard, studying a different camp in Malawi, reaches a conclusion very similar to that of Ager *et al.* (1995), although shifting the explanatory emphasis from the relief programme *per se* to the role of international and local actors as agents of change. Hence:

> The refugee camp had fostered a culture of its own, constructed by both international, Malawian and Mozambican agents which pictured Mozambican women as essentially backward individuals. Refugee men themselves participated in this ideological construction through fostering a set of ideas that came to justify the male domination of economic structures. (1996, p. 191)

Supporting Schroeder and Watts's conclusion (1991), my own research points to the need to recognize that local agents are not passive subjects of social change imposed by outsiders and 'external' forces, but that they are able to transform supra-local influences and forces into local forms:

> The initial gender bias and gender-blindness of the international mechanisms of assistance and relief have been consolidated locally to displace refugee women from their usual sphere of work and power, and justified locally on the basis of women's biological characteristics, physical weaknesses and social backwardness. (Callamard, 1996, p. 192)

What these and other studies underscore is that refugee assistance programmes have failed to recognize that the forces and mechanisms of subordination, domination and exclusion of refugee women are located in both the reproductive sphere of the household (Callamard, 1993, 1994; Ager *et al.*, 1995; Forbes Martin, 1992) and the political and power structures of the camp which, in all cases, reinforce and strengthen the patriarchal tendency of the community (Callamard, 1996; Ager *et al.*, 1995). The first factor has been well documented in the feminist literature (Beneria, 1979) and suggests that projects should aim, first and foremost, at facilitating refugee women's household tasks and increasing time availability (Callamard, 1993, 1996; Ager *et al.*, 1995). As far as the second is concerned, UNHCR (1991) itself has acknowledged the shortcomings of its programmes and the lack of gender awareness of its staff, although both have been mainly analysed from the perspective of women's lack of access to resources. Taken together, the evidence provided by the research surveyed above places emphasis on the interaction of a number of actors (the refugees themselves and their leaders, national and international actors) and the relief programme itself in fostering gender inequality.

The above analysis is not meant to deny that refugee women and men do mediate the effects of the camp as a device of power and control. In fact, the above analysis may be said to be *about* mediation, although clearly these are not the only examples or the sole meaning (usually) associated with the concept. A number of researchers have demonstrated that mediation, or resisting, may encompass the transformation of consciousness of oneself as an individual and as a refugee. Hence, refugees may struggle against the meanings – of refugeeness, repatriation and places of return – imposed by the outside world and the camp management (Stepputat, 1994; Mandani, 1973). The process of resisting what Wood (1985) defined as 'authoritarian designation' may result in the emergence and development of nation-ness (Malkki, 1990) or in a redefinition of 'refugee' with an explicitly politicized meaning used to extract benefits from international and national authorities (Zetter, 1991). Refugee women's experiences before becoming refugees, in flight and during asylum can lead to empowerment through a process of politicization and self-awareness (Moussa, 1991; Bennett *et al.*, 1995; Christensen, 1983):

> [S]ome of the women have realised that they can manage very well on their own in the camp, or that the husbands in the camp are of little practical help.... The male role-set is most affected in the camp situation. The men have lost their previous major function as providers and decision-makers in the household.... Camp life therefore has made the males idle and redundant to a large extent. (Christensen, 1993, p. 15)

At its 'best', mediation may move from an individual's sense of empowerment to a form of collective movement:

> My name is Maria Guadelupe Garcia.... I am a member of the Organization of Guatemalan Refugee Women, Mama Maquin. Our women's organization began in 1990 in three different states in Mexico among the various refugee camps. In that year, I met many women who had suffered from similar kinds of discrimination. Since that time, we have learned many things about indigenous rights, the rights of women and the importance of our participation in the decision-making process. (Hernandez and Garcia, 1996, p. 265)

These examples also tend to show that the extent and nature of mediation are bounded and determined by individuals' positions *vis-à-vis* the political and social structures of the refugee community, their own sense of worth and the political and economic circumstances. But examples of mediation, at least as reported in the literature, remain few and isolated. And personal testimonies or life-stories are often the ones of 'survivors'. In fact, as Moussa (1991) herself contends, refugee women's experiences may also lead to disempowerment as a result of brutality and violence, a process well demonstrated by McLellan (1996) with reference to Cambodian women refugees. The experiences of Afghan refugee women in Pakistan, as a collective, leaves little doubt as to the extent of oppression, persecution and disempowerment that refugee life may result in, given a certain set of political and ideological conditions (Amnesty International, 1995; Forbes Martin and Copeland, 1988). If mediation entails challenging internationally imposed identities and codes of behaviours, it also means reshaping or reconstructing structures of power in ways that are rarely going to benefit the most disadvantaged individuals, including many women. The unequal allocation of food relief may be linked to existing shortcomings at the international and national level. But ultimately these shortcomings are given a local form through a collusion of interest between refugee leaders and local actors responsible for its distribution (Rizvi, 1990; Callamard, 1995).

The reality and scope of mediation and resistance should be neither denied nor romanticized. To insist on the political nature of refugee women's vulnerability, on the fact that they are victimized rather than victims (Moussa, 1991), is also to acknowledge that, within the context and setting of a 'controlling institution' (Hitchcox, 1990) that does not offer much in terms of protection, the 'weapons of the weak' may be quite ruthless in their effects against the weakest members of a given community. This point will be further elaborated in the following section, on sexual violence.

The gendered nature of refugee experience: sexual violence

A thread that runs throughout the literature on refugee experiences, be it through personal accounts and life-stories (Mandani, 1973; Moussa, 1991; Bennett *et al.*, 1995) or through other forms of research (Hansen, 1981; Hitchcox, 1990; Malkki, 1992; Jok, 1995), is the profound loss of individuality, self-esteem and independence endured by refugees and fostered by the dynamics of relief assistance. This is a thread that transcends historical and national barriers to characterize the essence of the refugee camp and the life of refugee populations as a whole. In her ground-breaking 1990 work on Southeast Asian camps, Linda Hitchcox embraces Goffman's study of mental asylum and Foucault's work on prisons to conceptualize the refugee camp as a 'controlling institution' with control working in two ways:

> First of all, all individuals are constrained to behave as if they were dependent and helpless, which assists the perpetuation of an institution largely composed of workers whose role is to respond to people who have problems and are in need.... Secondly, the majority of Vietnamese, within their role as refugees are consenting participants in the process of control.... Complete control and corresponding dependence is achieved when the person can no longer differentiate between the identity of refugee as it is constructed in the camp and the understanding he has of himself as an individual who is Vietnamese. (1990, p. 174)

Hitchcox's representation echoes Mandani's personal account: '[T]hey had successfully turned the camp into a total institution, like a prison or an insane asylum.... The Kensington camp gradually became a nightmare in totally controlled living' (Mandani, 1973, p. 96), and Malkki's (1990) description of camps for Hutu refugees in Tanzania as a systematized and generalizable 'technology of power' with the refugees subjected to techniques of control, investigation and intervention. These are the techniques which also elicited demeaning attitudes and behaviours among the Dinka displaced population: portraying oneself as poor and needy, resorting to begging, doing odd jobs or lying about one's conditions, and harsh attitudes and violence against women:

> The result of these conditions is an increasing loss of self-determination by the people of Southern Sudan through dependency on relief, and a gradual loss of cultural patterns.... *As the whole society becomes affected, women are constantly pushed to the bottom* .... When disaster strikes this economy, women suffer most. (Jok, 1995, p. 32; emphasis added)

Sexual violence against refugee women

One most common, yet little-researched, form of suffering imposed on refugee women is violence. Empirical evidence on the violence suffered by refugee women is at best sketchy, save for the research conducted in Kenya and Southeast Asia, and the increasing number of life-stories and testimonies. But the (incomplete) picture drawn by these works is harrowing, and the certainty that what is known by outsiders is just the tip of an iceberg of violence makes this picture of even greater concern. In a recent ground-breaking psychosocial exploration of trauma among forty refugee women, former political activists in their respective countries of origin, Inger Agger (1994) emphasizes the role of sexuality in political persecution. Similarly, the painful picture drawn by refugees, relief workers or researchers centres on the role of sexuality in the oppression of refugee women in particular and the functioning of refugee structures in general. For sexual violence does not end with the war, the flight and the attacks at sea, but becomes entangled within the making and functioning of the refugee camp.

The controlling institutions created for refugees have a clear gendered and sexual dimension, and one that must be first understood in contradistinction with the creation of an ungendered and desexualized generic figure. The collective basis of refugee status in situations of mass movement has no specific provision for women: the generic figure of the refugee is, here, a generic community that, as with the individual-based definition of the Geneva Convention, provides for no distinction among its members (unless they have engaged in certain types of crimes). The obligations of the country of asylum are, at best, gender-neutral, an approach which, in practice, translates into gender discrimination and violence against women.

Sexual violence within the camp must also be understood in relation to the sexual and political power structures within the societies of origin and countries of asylum. A large number of Somali refugee women who experienced rape in Kenyan camps had fled similar experiences, or fear of such experiences, in war-torn Somalia (African Rights, 1993; Africa Watch, 1993). Testimonies also showed that sexual violence perpetrated against them within the confines of the camp, or on the outskirts, by 'bandits' was often linked to clan politics and clan membership. At best, the Kenyan police ignored their plight and request for protection; at worst, they themselves were involved in the criminal acts; in both cases, they were active participants in the politics of rape. The role of officials from the country of asylum was especially blatant in Djibouti, where Ethiopian and Eritrean refugee women have been raped with a frightening frequency and impunity by border guards, policemen or soldiers (Nyakabwa and Lavoie, 1995; Moussa, 1993; Aitchinson, 1984). In many situations, however, rape and sexual violence are widely unreported. Even in the case of the refugee camps in Goma, Zaire, which had attracted international attention because of the constant climate of insecurity, killings and the presence of perpetrators of the 1994 genocide in Rwanda, attempts to look into allegations of rape were unsuccessful and met with resistance (Halvorsten, 1995).

The role of sexuality and sexual violence within refugee camps is further demonstrated by the prevalence of prostitution, sexual favours and domestic violence, all of which are common characteristics of the functioning of the institutions. Anecdotal evidence underlines the prevalence of these forms of violence among Mozambican refugee women in Malawi (Lawyers Committee for Human Rights, 1995), Ethiopians in Sudan (Rogge, 1989), refugee women in Thailand (NGO Working Group on Refugee Women, 1989). All studies, and indeed the 1991 and 1994 UNHCR guidelines, argue that the institutionalization of prostitution and sexual favours within a camp emerges and develops as a result of the shortcomings and inadequacies of relief programmes, including the lack of physical protection afforded to women. The marginalization of women within the formal political and economic structures of the camp (as well as within the household) contributes to subject refugee women to gender-specific abuses that are, often enough, interrelated: 'Victims of repeated sexual assault, and responsible for the survival of their children, many of the most destitute women refugees decide to make a profit out of their situation and ... resort to prostitution as a living' (Nyakabwa and Lavoie, 1995, p. 28). With the exception of the few examples cited above, such abuses remain unreported and unnoticed or, even worse, are considered by some relief staff as regrettable yet 'essentially inevitable incidents in refugee life', according to a 1993 in-house evaluation of UNHCR's policy on refugee women (cited in Berthiaume, 1995, p. 12).

At a policy level, the approach embraced by the UNHCR and other relief organizations (UNHCR, 1991, 1994; NGO Working Group on Refugee Women, 1989) has been to tackle those factors and conditions that foster gender-based vulnerability, such as the physical planning of camps, the design and implementation of food relief, health assistance, etc. Experience indeed shows that being forced to walk long distances along dark or isolated paths to collect food, water and fuel, the lack of adequate lighting at night, and the lack of lockable sleeping and washing areas are all factors which erode the security of women. In Côte d'Ivoire, women refugees were attacked when they left the camp because they could not bring themselves to use camp latrines that were next to those for men (Marshall, 1995). In the worst-case scenarios presented by Somali camps in Kenya, UNHCR put into place the Women Victims of Violence project which provides for counselling, medical treatment, relocation of the victims, etc. (Berthiaume, 1995; Nyakabwa and Lavoie, 1995). The Canadian Council for Refugees and UNHCR have also implemented the 'Women At Risk Refugee Sponsorship' project to assist in the resettlement of women refugees identified by UNHCR as being at risk. All these attempts appear to have had some success (Marshall, 1995), and they do go quite some way towards addressing aspects of the problems and enhancing protection. But they also face a number of shortcomings, beginning with the fact that they are too few in number and insufficiently funded to cope with the needs, which are under-reported and little investigated. Additionally, as argued below, the links between sexual violence and women's rights remain to be established at both a conceptual and a policy level.

Gender, sexuality and persecution

As mentioned in the Introduction to this chapter, the invisibility of gender and sexual violence characterizes the codification and intervention throughout refugee experiences, including the process of determination of refugee status. A number of legal scholars, along with UNHCR, have highlighted the gender biases of the refugee definition and/or of its interpretation by immigration officials. Some (Castel, 1992; Indra, 1987; MacKinnon, 1986) have called for the inclusion of gender within the attributes of persecution, implying a redrafting of the refugee Convention of 1951. Indra, for instance, cites the omission of gender from the enumerated grounds of persecution as an illustration of the depth of gender delegitimation in refugee contexts and she calls for a redefinition of persecution to give credibility to women's 'private sphere' experiences:

> the key criteria for being a refugee are drawn primarily from the realm of public sphere activities dominated by men. With regard to private sphere activities where women's presence is more strongly felt, there is primarily silence – silence compounded by an unconscious calculus that assigns the critical quality 'political' to many public activities but few private ones. Thus state oppression of a religious minority is political, while gender oppression at home is not. (Indra, 1987, p. 3)

Other scholars and policy-makers (UNHCR, 1991; Greatbatch, 1989; Spijkerboer, 1994; Macklin, 1995) have called for a broader interpretation of the definition of persecution as per the refugee Convention, especially underlining the gendered nature of both the 'social groups' and the 'political opinions' elements of the 1951 definition. Underlying this approach is the view that the problem lies first and foremost in the interpretation of the Convention by policy-makers and legislative bodies, rather than within the legal norms themselves.

The debate over engendering the refugee definition is not an academic one: gender-specific guidelines have been adopted by the Canadian Immigration and Refugee Board, the USA, Australia and New Zealand. The 1991 UNHCR guidelines put forward an interpretation of the refugee Convention that suggests that sexual violence, persecution or severe discrimination on the basis of gender, and failure of state protection, may constitute a basis for granting refugee status to women. The Beijing Platform for Action (paragraph 137) recognizes that 80 per cent of the world's refugees and displaced people, including the internally displaced, are women and children, and calls for particular attention to be paid to sexual violence against such women. It especially refers to 'sexual violence or other gender-related persecution' as constituting a well-founded fear of persecution under the UN Refugee Convention and its 1967 Protocol. Further, a number of ground-breaking cases in the USA, Canada and Europe have demonstrated the possibilities of providing refugee status to women fleeing persecution characterized by both its gender specificity (such as domestic violence, female genital mutilation or failure to conform to certain discriminatory social norms) and the lack of state protection. For instance, in March 1993 the Canadian government granted refugee status to a Trinidadian-born woman victim of domestic violence. Some women fleeing female genital mutilations have also been granted refugee status in the USA and Canada. These are no small victories, with regard both to the lives of the women concerned, and to the rethinking of a broader, and gendered, refugee identity.

Yet one cannot but be struck by two dichotomies. The first contrasts legal discourse and debate in the West over the issue, with the practice: few refugee women's claims, be they gender-specific or not, are ever granted. The UK especially has a dismal record in the area (*Marie Claire*, 1997). Most European states do not even feel obliged to provide gender-disaggregated data on asylum claims, a state of affairs demonstrating deeply entrenched gender insensitivity and/or sexism among national immigration bureaucracies. One can only wonder how resettlement policies, under these conditions, successfully target the refugee populations.

The second dichotomy contrasts the vibrancy of the debate at national and international level with its quasi-disappearance as far as the millions of refugee women in camps are concerned. The gendered approach to human rights and the refugee definition has yet to cross the gates (real or invisible) of the refugee camp. The protection of refugee women who do reach the refugee determination process in Ottawa, New York or Paris is thought of, debated and argued in court as a women's rights question, whereas protection of refugee women within the compound of the camps is a matter of good physical planning, well-planned assistance programmes and the maintenance of security.

The aforementioned dichotomy reaches an ironic proportion, albeit sadly so, when one imagines Somali, Ethiopian or Cambodian refugee women requesting individual-based refugee status on the basis of the persecution they had to endure in their respective camps and the lack of protection afforded to them by the state of asylum, the UNHCR and, more generally, the international community.

As well demonstrated by Spijkerboer (1993), international human rights and humanitarian and refugee law are unanimous in describing rape as persecution. In all the cases surveyed above, the state of asylum and/or the UNHCR have failed to protect the refugee women from such persecution. The responsibility of the state is especially blatant when its agents (be they policemen, border guards or soldiers) engage, *with total impunity*, in acts of violence against refugee women. Such a responsibility is no less acute when perpetrators are private individuals, but the state is unwilling to prosecute them and fails to offer protection and remedies to the victims. Furthermore, a case may also be made against the UNHCR on the basis of its failure to offer non-discriminatory or equal protection for refugee women and ensure their right to physical safety within the camp.

Do these claims have a persecution ground? A large number of scholars, including this writer, will argue that sexual violence is a form of power and control over women. When sexual violence is organized or condoned by the authorities, or indeed when these latter turn a 'blind eye' to incidents of rape, such incidents should be considered as part of the political structures and, as such, persecution on account of political opinion. But even if one were to take Hathaway's approach (1991) that the harm (or threat of harm) a claimant faces must be linked to her sociopolitical situation and resultant marginalization, evidence does give ground for claims on the basis of membership of a 'social group' (for instance, single Eritrean or Somali refugee women living in a Djibouti or Kenyan refugee camp without the protection of a male relative) or of clan membership. Four main arguments may be developed to demonstrate the validity of such claims.

First, the harm tends to be gender specific: refugee women and girls, rather than men, are victims of rape in camps, and as noted above, rape, or the threat of rape, may constitute persecution (Spijkerboer, 1993).

Second, the victims tend to be the members of specific social groupings which may be gender-based or otherwise. Existing evidence indicates that many rape victims are, often enough, without the protection of male relatives (UNHCR, 1991), or are targeted because of their age and the specific domestic activities (such as fetching firewood outside the camp) that are traditionally attributed to this age group (Nowrojee, 1996). Testimonies of Somali women underline also that women and girls have been singled out for rape because of their membership of a particular Somali clan.

Third, as demonstrated above, the situation of refugee women in camps is characterized by severe gender discrimination, in violation of the general principle of non-discrimination which governs the allocation of all legal rights, including those set by the refugee Convention. As a matter of fact, the United Nations' Charter, the 1948 Universal Declaration of Human Rights, the International Covenant on Economic, Social and Cultural Rights and the International Covenant on Civil and Political Rights are expressly stated to be of universal application, and include prohibitions of discrimination on the basis of sex. As noted above, UNHCR and NGOs have attempted to remedy the situation by developing gender-specific projects and programmes. But despite repeated calls from the NGOs and the Executive Committee of UNHCR, such projects are rarely or insufficiently implemented. Hence, the former UNHCR women's co-ordinator summarized five years of UNHCR policy towards women as follows: '[W]e could have done more and we could have done better. We have achieved some things. But we've still got a long way to go' (in Berthiaume, 1995, p. 10).

Fourth, the huge majority of refugee women have not had access to effective protection, save for the few who have managed to be resettled through such programmes as the Women At Risk Sponsorship. The authorities of the state of asylum (be it Kenya, Djibouti or Malawi) have consistently failed to prosecute perpetrators of rape, including policemen, soldiers, refugee men or 'outsiders'. Furthermore, UNHCR itself appears reluctant to bring the complaints of refugee women before the relevant authorities, as the case of Somali women in Kenya underlines (Lawyers Committee for Human Rights, 1995; Nowrojee, 1996). It can be contended that, although the writers of the 1991 and 1994 UNHCR Guidelines for Refugee Women have clearly understood the political nature of refugee women's victimization, UNHCR as an institution has so far been unable effectively to address the issue of discrimination against refugee women and abuses of their rights.

Conclusion

There is little doubt that many refugee women's experiences in refugee camps amount to persecution according to the accepted definition. Sadly enough, supposing that some of them could make it to the European or North American fortress, their claims might be undermined by the sheer number of victims. Clearly, the existing conventions and agreements which regulate the definition of refugees and the ensuing obligations of the international community and the state of asylum are neither sufficient to ensure the protection of refugee women nor, in any case, being enforced by any of the parties to the refugee crisis, be they the donor countries, the countries of asylum, refugees themselves or UNHCR. Furthermore, the achievements that *have* been made on this front, including the afore-mentioned guidelines and a number of specific gender-specific policies and projects for refugee women, have suffered major setbacks in recent years. Some of these have taken the form of broader policies or doctrines, such as the artefact of the 'Safe Zone', the Internal Flight 'Alternative' or, more recently, 'voluntary' repatriation following the shelling of refugee camps or the presence of armed forces. Other setbacks, however, not so recent (Zolberg *et al.*, 1989), have included the militarization or criminalization of refugee camps: Goma, as described by outsiders and refugees themselves, appears to bear many more resemblances to Hobbes's description of the state of nature (1985) than to a UNHCR-run camp for displaced persons. But if Hobbes, writing in the seventeenth century, could see in the all-powerful and frightening figure of the Leviathan the solution to the horrors generated by the state of nature, one would expect from the actors involved in the refugee crisis at the end of the twentieth century a different approach to solving problems in refugee camps. Recent experiences with militarized camps and the long-term presence of refugees have reflected a rather reductionist and short-term understanding of 'security'. They have also sharply altered the meaning and scope of refugee protection: refugee women were, in the past, denied protection as women; they are now denied protection as women *and* as refugees. At a time when the human rights framework appears to dominate international debates and initiatives (at the UN level, for instance, through the recent reform proposed by the Secretary-General), one should strive to define 'insecurity' and 'security' on the basis of existing internationally accepted standards and principles: mass expulsion at the barrel of a gun constitutes insecurity. And so do lack of food and sexual violence. All are also human rights concerns. Notwithstanding the fact that, together with children, women constitute the vast majority of displaced populations, they are also the ones whose rights and protection are most likely to be undermined by a generic, ungendered and ultimately militarized approach to security, refugee protection and assistance.

Note

The views expressed in this article are those of the author alone and should not be attributed to Amnesty International.

References

Africa Watch Women's Right Project (1993) *Seeking Refuge, Finding Terror*, vol. 15, no. 13. New York: Human Rights Watch.

African Rights (1993) *The Nightmare Continues*. London: African Rights.

Ager, A., Ager, W. and Long, L. (1995) The differential experience of Mozambican refugee women and men. *Journal of Refugee Studies*, 8 (3), 263–87.

Agger, I. (1994) *The Blue Room*. London: Zed Books.

Aitchinson, R. (1984) Reluctant witnesses: the sexual abuse of refugee women in Djibouti. *Cultural Survival Quarterly*, 8 (2), 26–7.

Amnesty International (1995) *Women in Afghanistan: A Human Rights Catastrophe*. ASA 11/03/95.

Beneria, L. (1979) Reproduction, production and the sexual division of labour. *Cambridge Journal of Economics*, 3, 203–25.

Bennett, O., Bexley, J. and Warnock, K. (1995) *Arms to Fight, Arms to Protect*. London: Panos.

Berthiaume, C. (1995) Do we really care? *Refugees*, 100, 10–13.

Boserup, E. (1970) *Women's Role in Economic Development*. London: George Allen & Unwin.

Callamard, A. (1993) African refugee women and changing international priorities. *Refuge*, 12 (8), 18–22.

Callamard, A. (1994) Refugees and local hosts: a study of the trading interactions between Mozambican refugees and Malawian villagers in the district of Mwanza. *Journal of Refugee Studies*, 7 (1), 39–62.

Callamard, A. (1995) Populations under fire, populations under stress.

Unpublished PhD dissertation, New School for Social Research, New York.

Callamard, A. (1996) Flour is power. In W. Giles, H. Moussa, and P. Van Esterik (eds), *Development and Diaspora: Gender and the Refugee Experience*, pp. 176–98. Dundas: Artemis.

Castel, J. (1992) Rape, sexual assault and the meaning of persecution. *International Journal of Refugee Law*, 4, 39–56.

Christensen, H. (1983) Survival strategies for and by camp refugees in Somalia. *Horn of Africa*, 5 (4), 3–20.

Daley, P. (1991) Gender, displacement and social reproduction: settling Burundi Refugees in Western Tanzania. *Journal of Refugee Studies*, 4 (3), 248–66.

Forbes Martin, S. and Copeland, E. (1988) *Making Ends Meet? Refugee Women and Income Generation*. Washington, DC: Refugee Policy Group.

Giles, W., Moussa, H. and Van Esterik, P. (1996) Introduction. In W. Giles, H. Moussa and P. Van Esterik (eds), *Development and Diaspora: Gender and the Refugee Experience*. Dundas: Artemis.

Goodwin-Gill, G. (1983) *The Refugee in International Law*. Oxford: Clarendon Press.

Greatbatch, J. (1989) The gender difference: feminist critiques of refugee discourse. *International Journal of Refugee Law*, 1 (4), 518–27.

Halvorsten, K. (1995) *Refugee Camps in Zaire: Security and Humanitarian Issues*. Report prepared for the Joint Evaluation of Emergency Assistance to Rwanda, Copenhagen.

Hansen, A. (1981) Refugee dynamics: Angolans in Zambia, 1966 to 1972. *International Migration Review*, 15, 175–95.

Hathaway, J. (1988) International refugee law: humanitarian standard or protectionist ploy? In A. Nash (ed.), *Human Rights and the Protection of Refugees under International Law*. Montreal: Canadian Human Rights Foundation.

Hathaway, J. (1991) *The Law of Refugee Status*. Toronto: Butterworths.

Hernandez, G. and Garcia, N. (1996) Mama Maquin refugee women: participation and organisation. In W. Giles, H. Moussa and P. Van Esterik (eds), *Diaspora and Development*. Dundas: Artemis.

Hitchcox, L. (1990) *Vietnamese Refugees in Southeast Asian Camps*. Basingstoke: St Anthony's/Macmillan.

Hobbes, T. (1985) *Leviathan*. London: Penguin Books. (First published in 1651.)

Indra, D. (1987) Gender: a key dimension of the refugee experience. *Refuge*, 6, 3–4.

Johnson, T. (1981) Eritrean refugees in Sudan. *Disasters*, 3 (4), 418–24.

Jok Madut Jok (1995) Dinka women and the future of Dinka society. *Refugee Participation Network*, 20, 31–2.

Kandiyoti, D. (1990) Women and rural development policies. *Development and Change*, 21, 5–22.

Lawyers Committee for Human Rights (1995) *African Exodus: Refugee
Crisis, Human Rights and the 1969 OAU Convention*. New York:
LCHR.

MacKinnon, C. (1993) Theory is not a luxury. In D. Dallmeyer (ed.),
Reconceiving Reality: Women and International Law, pp. 83–92.
Washington, DC: American Society of International Law.

Macklin, A. (1995) Refugee women and the imperative of categories.
Human Rights Quarterly, 17, 214–77.

McLellan, J. (1996) Silent screams and hidden pain. In W. Giles, H.
Moussa and P. Van Esterik (eds), *Development and Diaspora*, pp. 238–
57. Dundas: Artemis.

Malkki, L. (1990) Context and consciousness: local conditions for the
production of historical and national thought among Hutu refugees in
Tanzania. In R. Fox (ed.), *Nationalist Ideologies and the Production of
National Cultures*, pp. 33–62. Washington, DC: American Anthropological Association.

Malkki, L. (1992) National geographic: the rooting of peoples and the
territorialization of national identity among scholars and refugees.
Cultural Anthropology, 7 (1), 24–44.

Mandani, M. (1973) *From Citizen to Refugee*. London: Pinter.

Marie Claire (1997) Persecuted for being a woman. *Marie Claire*,
February, pp. 52–6.

Marshall, R. (1995) Refugees, feminine plural. *Refugees*, 100, 3–9.

Mazur, R. (1991) Self-reliance and future orientation among refugees in
Southern Africa: alternative conceptions and interests. Paper presented
at the 1991 Carter Lecture Series Conference, University of Florida,
Gainesville.

Moussa, H. (1991) Women refugees: empowerment and vulnerability.
Refuge, 10 (4), 12–14.

Moussa, H. (1993) *Storm and Sanctuary: The Journey of Ethiopian and
Eritrean Women Refugees*. Toronto: Artemis.

NGO Working Group on Refugee Women (1989) *Working with Refugee
Women: A Practical Guide*. Geneva.

Nowrojee, B. (1996) Sexual violence against refugee and displaced
women. In C. Mulei, L. Dinasse and M. Garling *et al.* (eds), *Legal
Status of Refugee and Internally Displaced Women in Africa*, pp. 273–
94. Nairobi: UNIFEM/AFWIC.

Nyakabwa, K. and Lavoie, C. (1995) Sexual violence against women
refugees in the Horn of Africa. *African Women*, 10, 26–31.

Refugee Studies Programme (1989) *Food Provisioning amongst Mozambican Refugees in Malawi: A Study of Aid, Livelihood and Development*. Report prepared for the World Food Programme, Malawi.

Rizvi, G. (1990) The Afghan refugees: hostages in the struggle for power. *Journal for Refugee Studies*, 3 (3), 244–61.

Rogge, J. (1989) *Too Many Too Long: Sudan's Twenty Year Refugee Dilemma*. Toronto: Rowman & Allanheld.

Schroeder, R. and Watts, M. (1991) Struggling over strategies, fighting over food: adjusting to food commercialisation among Mandika peasants. *Research in Rural Sociology and Development*, 5, 45–72.

Spijkerboer, T. (1994) *Women and Refugee Status*. The Hague: Emancipation Council.

Spring, A. (1979) Women and men as refugees: differential assimilation of Angolan refugees in Zambia. *Disasters*, 3 (4), 423–8.

Stepputat, F. (1994) Deterritorialization and community in refugee studies: the case of Maya diaspora and return movement. Paper presented at the Fourth IRAP Conference, Refugee Studies Programme, Oxford.

Tuitt, P. (1996) *False Images: The Law's Construction of the Refugee*. London: Pluto Press.

UNHCR (1991) *Guidelines on the Protection of Refugee Women*. Geneva: UNCHR.

UNHCR (1994) *Prevention of and Response to Sexual Violence against Refugees*. Geneva: UNHCR.

Weaver, J. (1988) Searching for survival: urban Ethiopian refugees in Sudan. *Journal of Developing Areas*, 22, 457–76.

Wood, G. (1985) The politics of development policy labelling. In G. Wood (ed.), *Labelling in Development Policy: Essays in Honour of Bernard Schaffer*, pp. 5–32. London: Sage.

Zetter, R. (1991) Labelling refugees: forming and transforming a bureaucratic identity. *Journal of Refugee Studies*, 4 (1), 39–62.

Zolberg, A., Suhrke, A. and Aguayo, S. (1989) *Escape from Violence*. New York: Oxford University Press.

9

The experience of refugee children

Fred Ahearn, Maryanne Loughry and Alastair Ager

Approximately one-half of the global refugee population comprises children under the age of 16 (UN, 1996). As established earlier (see Chapter 5), it is generally inappropriate to entertain a view of such children as having been unintentionally caught up in political conflicts. Typically, they are members of civilian populations that have been targeted by military actions seeking to create fear and social instability. On occasions, children are themselves an explicit target of violence: 'Remember to kill the little rats' as well as the big rats (broadcast on Radio Mille Collines, Rwanda, April 1994 to the forces of the Interahamwe engaged in genocide against the Tutsis, cited by Levine, 1997).

Children often play a crucial role in household survival strategies in times of war and forced displacement, and their experience is therefore very much intertwined with that of adults. However, there are issues which make it valid – and, indeed, important – to consider the particularities of the experience of refugee children (as reflected, for example, in the development by UNHCR of specific guidelines for work with children; see Tolfree, 1991; UNHCR, 1994; Crisp, 1996). It is the purpose of this chapter to explore these issues.

The challenges of displacement

Children who flee their homes as refugees face a broad range of challenges to their development and, indeed, survival. The areas of challenge considered here are among the most common and salient, but are not intended as exhaustive categories of childhood experience.

Malnutrition, disease and disability

The deprivations and exertions of flight – and often of the pre-flight period also – render significant numbers of refugee children of poor nutritional status on arrival in the country of first asylum. Targeted feeding programmes (using height-for-weight indices, age priorities and other criteria) are thus frequently a major component of emergency assistance efforts in refugee-impacted areas (Chowdhury and Mears, 1994; UNHCR, 1994). With mass population movements, close proximity and strained (or non-existent) sanitation facilities create the conditions for transmission of infectious disease (notably cholera). Vaccination and oral rehydration programmes – increasingly linked to public health education activities – are thus frequently another major priority in refugee assistance efforts.

In countries of first asylum – particularly in emergency situations and where reception is in the context of a refugee camp structure – children's experience of assistance in the early stages of settlement is thus likely to be heavily determined by their health status. An emphasis on 'child survival' inevitably prioritizes health screening, feeding programmes and immunization over other activities – and areas of need. Awareness of the broader agenda of 'child survival and development', however, has led agencies increasingly to consider more social and psychological domains of the experience of the refugee child. While this does raise the issue of competing priorities for support of refugee children, recent work has suggested the potential for mutually reinforcing benefits from health programmes and social interventions. Eunson (1997), for instance, demonstrated the impact on cholera transmission of the building up of social networks among unaccompanied minors in Goma at the height of the refugee influx from Rwanda.

Such broader awareness of children's needs has also spread to consideration of such issues as physical disability. With the anti-personnel mine a common weapon with contemporary warfare, and children at increased risk of both exposure (through play) and injury (through stature), settings such as Angola, Cambodia and Rwanda see very high rates of physical disability characterizing the population of refugee and internally displaced children (UN, 1996).

Separation and loss

Circumstances around the time of flight render separation of family members a common occurrence. This is a problem faced by refugees of all ages, but the capacities of younger children for tracing other family members are clearly limited. The problem of unaccompanied minors as a consequence of military action and/or mass population movements has become a major issue in assistance efforts for refugee populations (Ressler *et al.*, 1988). Superimposed upon all other aspects of loss associated with leaving one's home and familiar surroundings is the fact that children may increasingly find themselves separated from family and/or other close relatives. While many refugee communities have evidenced willingness for foster-care (especially, but not exclusively, involving care by distant kin), for many children displacement involves major disorientation and disruption of familial relationships, with potential threats to social and emotional development (Tolfree, 1996).

Disruption of socialization

Forced migration typically disrupts not only familial bases of socialization, but also socialization through such structures as schools and places of worship (Ager, 1996). Figure 9.1 is a schematic representation of the manner in which a child's developing understanding of the world is not only shaped by direct experience, but mediated through familial and societal structures. Experience mediated through these channels guides a child's socialization into the world. Accordingly, disruption of family and societal systems impairs a child's capability to develop understandings to guide adaptive behaviour.

Thus disruption to schooling (e.g. Miller, 1996) or religious worship (e.g. Ressler *et al.*, 1988) may diminish a child's capacity to give structure and meaning to his or her experience. Attacks on clinics, schools, churches, mosques, etc. undermine those very structures within a society which – by providing rhythm, routine and meaning in children's lives – may serve to protect them from the direct experience of violence or threat.

Traumatic experience

Refugee children are – especially during the pre-flight and flight phases – demonstrably vulnerable to violent or threatening experiences which cannot be 'readily assimilated or integrated into the basic assumptive world of the child' (Raundalen and Dyregov, 1991). This definition of trauma avoids the term's rather lax use in describing both events and a child's potential reaction to them. The crucial factor for children is not the extent to which events are extreme or demanding; rather it is the extent to which such events disrupt subsequent interaction with, and interpretation of, the experienced world. In the terms of Figure 9.1, the child's conceptual understandings are incapable of assimilating – making sense of or, more broadly, 'coming to terms with' – an experienced event. A child's response to such a situation may be the development of symptomology suggestive of the recurrent failure to process the experienced event (e.g. 'flashbacks', nightmares, etc.), or the abandonment of previous understandings of the world in favour of concepts coherent with a more brutalized conception of the world (Ager, 1996). The latter is a particular

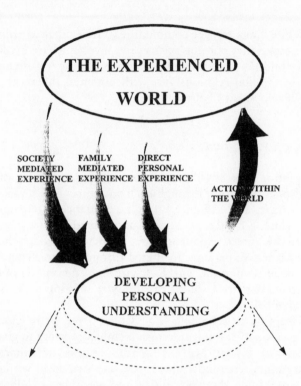

Figure 9.1   The shaping of the child's understanding of the world

concern for those who have been socialized into the role of 'child soldiers', generally following abduction (see Dodge and Raundalen, 1991; Boothby, 1994; Chapter 1, this volume).

Such a 'constructivist' approach as outlined above has been used increasingly to gain insight into the experience of war-affected and refugee children. The child is seen not as a mere 'recipient' of challenging experiences, but as an active 'constructor' of events and responses to them. Such approaches – which include Garbarino's (1996) conceptualization of children's 'social maps' – acknowledge the child as actively seeking to impose meaning on experience. Constructivist models may be seen as particularly interesting to the extent that they provide a means of integrating psychological, social and broader cultural dimensions of refugee children's experience.

Bases of childhood vulnerability and resilience

While critiqued as denoting too passive a notion of children's actions in the face of war and displacement (Dawes and Donald, 1994; Punamäki,

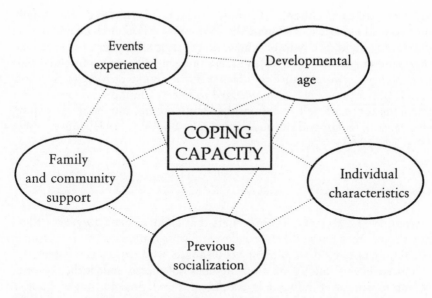

Figure 9.2 Influences on children's coping capacity

1996), 'coping capacity' remains a potentially valuable concept in considering those factors – personal, social, cultural, etc. – mediating between experience of demanding events and level of general well-being. McCallin (1996) and Laor *et al.* (1997) have sought to identify factors which provide – using the term of the latter – a 'protective matrix' determining coping capacity for a given child. Figure 9.2 presents a further scheme for categorizing such factors. Developed as a potential model for guiding programme support for refugee and other war-affected children, it provides an appropriate structure with which to review evidence supporting the influence and interaction of such factors in the experience of refugee children.

Events experienced

It is well established that there is no simple linear relationship between exposure to war experiences and symptoms of anxiety, insecurity and depression (Punamäki, 1996). However, a number of characteristics of experience have been shown to predict higher rates of psychological disturbance in children. Separation from parents, direct experience of violent acts and death of a family member were seen to have greatest developmental consequences in Macksoud and Aber's (1996) study of Lebanese children, while Kuterovac *et al.* (1994) identified destruction of the family home as the event with the greatest impact in a study of war-affected Croatian children. Chronic stressors (Terr, 1991) and totally unpredicted experiences (Punamäki, 1996) pose different challenges to the developing child, for both of which, however, greater impact is predicted than with single, anticipated (and therefore generally well-contextualized) events. Prolonged exposure to violence in the course of socialization as a 'child soldier' is widely acknowledged to have enduring consequences on understandings of self, relationships with others and adopted coping strategies (Dodge and Raundalen, 1991; Boothby, 1994; Ager, 1996; UNICEF, 1996)

Developmental age

Garbarino and Kostelny (1996) report that children aged 10 years or less are three times more likely to develop post-traumatic stress disorder (PTSD) symptoms than adolescents or adults who experience potentially traumatic events. Such a relationship does not merely reflect the personal coping resources of individuals at different developmental stages. Laor *et al.* (1997), for instance, demonstrated a close association between mothers' levels of symptomology and the adjustment of children under (but not those over) 5 years of age. For younger children the capacity of the mother (or equivalent figure) to buffer stressful stimuli may be a particularly important part of the protective matrix. For older children, with potentially broader access to structures of support and meaning (including peers), the role of maternal adjustment is less influential.

Individual characteristics

Children with higher levels of sociability and an active – goal-oriented – coping style generally prove more resilient in the face of difficult circumstances (Dawes and Donald 1994; Garbarino, 1996). Gender differences in vulnerability and resilience may be related in a complex manner to both differing cultural expectations and – in many contexts – their differential exposure to violence and other events. Kuterovac *et al.* (1994) found higher reported distress in girls, but note the potential for such differential reportage to reflect expectations on boys not to express such emotions. Macksoud and Aber (1996) noted Lebanese boys to have been more exposed to war and violence than girls. During the *Intifada* in Palestine, the increased role and status of women was seen to strengthen the resilience of girls, while social disruption and the loss of male role models increased boys' vulnerability (Garbarino and Kostelny, 1996).

Previous socialization

It has been proposed that children who live in societies that have a greater traditional and religious heritage have broader resources to give meaning to events than children living in societies without such shared structures of belief (Tolfree, 1996). The work of both Punamäki (1996) and Dawes and Donald (1994) demonstrates the potential protective influence of ideological commitment with respect to anxiety and insecurity, although the former emphasizes the potential costs of political allegiance for adolescents in situations of political violence. Earlier socialization may also be of relevance. Straker *et al.* (1992) note the potential of early supportive childhood to predict resilience in township youths in the course of political struggle.

Family and community support

Current supports – in addition to prior resources from an individual's history of socialization – clearly play a role in determining a child's capacity to cope with extreme circumstances. The influence of mothers' coping capacity on the resilience of younger children was noted previously (Laor *et al.*, 1997), a conclusion which – with respect to the broad influence of primary carers – is well supported by many analyses (Tolfree, 1996; Garbarino, 1996; McCallin, 1996). Zivic (1993, p. 711) notes, for example:

> Trusting a close adult is a very important source of support for a child. Being aware that parents were not able to protect him or her reinforces the traumatic experience of a child exposed to the terror of war. For that reason, it is important that a close adult shows an example of competent coping and demonstrates self-control ... the best predictor of positive outcomes for the child who survives an intensive stress is the ability of the important adults around him [or her], primarily parents, to cope with the traumatic event.

Dawes and Donald (1994) find from their work in South Africa that the key requirement is not necessarily that of a parent but – within the community – a person who both provides emotional support and sensitively interprets the events which have occurred.

The following sections examine the interplay of the above factors in the experience of refugee children within refugee camps and, subsequently, of the small minority involved – after such temporary refuge – resettling in a third country.

Children in refugee camps

Children generally constitute the largest age group in refugee camp populations. It is a challenge to host governments, UN organizations and non-governmental organizations (NGOs) to support the physical and social needs of such children appropriately, generally through the provision of direct assistance to the children's families and communities (cf. Figure 9.2). This section considers the bases of such interventions, and provides a number of illustrative examples of such work.

In most social settings children, because of their age and position in society, have very little input into the programmes and policies designed to meet their needs. Policies and programmes in refugee camps also generally reflect this practice. Thus, how a child in a refugee camp experiences the impact of conflict and forced migration is influenced not only by that child's developmental phase and personality, the functioning of his or her family and the child's experience of conflict but also, significantly so, by the sensitivity of camp practices and culture to the needs of children, particularly with regards to the need for social and emotional security.

In the past, refugee camps were characterized as providing temporary protection from conflict and possible persecution. In recent years, however, there has been an increasing trend for these temporary havens to become long-term settings. Three-quarters of refugees are in asylum for more than five years (Muecke, 1992). Conditions have become harsher, with some camps becoming detention centres with prison-type conditions. In the Great Lakes region of Rwanda, Burundi and Congo, the camps have become militarized centres of violence and conflict. Within these settings, whether the children's developmental needs are met or unmet is particularly dependent upon the sensitivity of programmes to children's needs and those of their families.

Little is known of the long-term effects of children in chronic asylum (Muecke, 1992), although a large survey conducted to investigate the psychosocial well-being of children living in the detention centres of Hong Kong provided some indication of potential impacts (McCallin, 1992). These detention centres were known to be harsh environments and were often the scene of rioting and mass protest. McCallin (1992) found that, irrespective of the children's caregiving arrangements, the well-being of the children was deteriorating over time. Unaccompanied children and those with relatives other than parents appeared to show more signs of depression and anxiety than those children who were with their parents, but all showed signs of being affected by detention.

In such contexts, training programmes such as People Oriented Planning (POP) may usefully assist UN agencies and NGOs to consider the composition of the refugee population, the various roles played by the refugee population in the camp, the resources available to refugees and those that need to be provided by external agencies. Such programme planning facilitates the meeting of children's needs by maximizing the likelihood of appropriate response by assistance agencies. The following sections illustrate – particularly with respect to the field experience of the second author – some of the practical issues that arise in provision of support to refugee children in the context of camps.

Unaccompanied children

In many camps, the circumstances of children separated from family during the course of flight ('unaccompanied' or 'separated' children) is a particular concern (Ressler *et al.*, 1988). It has generally been found that it is most helpful to separated children if they can live as normal a family life as the camp permits. In many settings, separated children join up with the families of distant relatives or neighbours (Blomqvist, 1997). In some instances children group together and live under the watchful eye of the neighbouring community. In these instances their well-being may appropriately be monitored by a responsible NGO.

In Hong Kong and Southeast Asia under the Comprehensive Plan of Action thousands of unaccompanied children were placed in the care of caregiving families who looked to the well-being of the children while they awaited their refugee status determination. The children's care was monitored by trained paraprofessionals who supported both the children and the caregivers. These paraprofessionals were trained and supervised by a social work agency. This programme was a shift from the establishment of special centres for the collective care of unaccompanied children. The belief that children benefit from living in a family-type environment has increasingly been incorporated within assistance policy (UN, 1996).

Some children arrive in the camps attached, but can become separated through death and other events. Early in the post-genocide exodus from Rwanda thousands of refugees arrived in the camps each day. UNHCR and Save the Children worked with the NGO community to prevent the setting up of centres for separated children. They had found that such centres had a significant 'pull' effect, with parents and relatives leaving children at them in the hope that the children would receive better material support than they themselves were able to provide.

Family reunification needs to be set in motion as soon as possible in emergency settings as it enables the rebuilding of key supports for children's resilience (see Figure 9.2). In consequence, it may need to be given priority over other activities. It is important to begin documentation of the refugee children as soon as possible. The tracing of parents also needs to take place as soon as possible before time and distance put up further barriers (Blomqvist, 1997).

During the complex 1997 repatriations and evacuations from the Democratic Republic of the Congo many children became separated from families because of the difficult logistics surrounding the transport. Rapid documentation ensured that the majority of them were reunited with their family in a short period of time. In contrast, when children left Bosnia in the early 1990s it was anticipated that they would easily be able to contact their parents by phone or mail, and few formal records were kept. The subsequent deterioration in communications led to separation and loss of contact on a major scale. It is still not known how many separated children there are in Europe as a consequence of the conflict in former Yugoslavia.

Education

Children frequently have unequal access to schooling in refugee camps. This is because some children are expected to play additional roles in the family. Girls are especially affected, as often they are expected to assume a childminding role or additional family support roles such as queuing for water and other supplies (Ager *et al.*, 1995). Often it is possible to free the children from these roles by planning school timetables and food distributions in a comprehensive manner.

For instance, in Kakuma camp in Kenya it had been found that few girls progressed to higher grades in the camp's refugee schools. Many of the girls dropped out to help with the daily living chores. To help address this issue, an experienced and articulate refugee woman was employed to speak with the community about the importance of education for girls as well as boys.

The detention centres in Sri Lanka permit children to join in education at the local schools. In some towns such as Vavuniya this has resulted in a huge increase in student numbers. In addition, the schools have been overloaded because a number of the school buildings have been commandeered for refugee accommodation.

Post-primary education has been linked to the search for durable solutions and the standards of education available to the local children. In the Hong Kong detention centres the secondary school was closed because it was seen as an incentive for people to stay in the detention centres rather than voluntarily repatriate themselves. In Tanzania it was only possible to establish post-secondary schooling informally because of the host government policy. A large number of young Rwandan refugees continually petitioned NGOs in Tanzania for post-secondary education. Their needs were partly met by the establishment of community libraries in the camps as well as language classes.

Repatriation

Little is known about repatriated refugee communities, and children in particular, after they leave the camps. This is often because of the lack of access of the research community to the children. It is also a reflection on the scale of movement of people at times of repatriation. In a recent study in Rwanda (van Haren, 1997) it was reported that there were two major constraints in addressing the needs of adolescents and youth in the country programme for repatriation: (1) the necessity to link the needs of the repatriated children with the Rwandese government's overall strategy for youth, and (2) the sheer volume of the task facing international staff in Rwanda in assisting vast numbers of people with basic shelter needs.

Van Haren (1997) urged UNHCR, because of its protection mandate, to begin by addressing the needs of the most vulnerable of the youth, who were considered to include very young single mothers, older teenagers in female-headed households, older teenagers in centres for unaccompanied minors, very young returnee married couples and substance-addicted adolescents.

Case notes from programmes where the repatriation of children had been carefully monitored by NGOs provide valuable insights into the situation faced by such children. For instance, in Vietnam in 1992 a Scandinavian consortium of NGOs formed the agency NARV, Nordic Assistance to Repatriated Vietnamese. This programme was established to work in co-operation with the Vietnamese Ministry of Labour, War Invalids and Social Affairs and UNHCR in assisting the repatriation of unaccompanied minors from the Hong Kong and Southeast Asian camps. From 1992 to 1994 NARV monitored the return of approximately 2050 children, assisting them in education and vocational training and with personal – as well as practical – support. NARV reported that few of the children showed signs of poor psychological functioning upon their return. A follow-up study in 1996 found that there was no significant difference in measures of psychological and social well-being between the children who had returned to Vietnam and a comparable group who never left (Loughry and Nguyen, 1997).

The effects on children of living in camps will be known only when there has been more systematic follow-up of the children after they have left the camps. In the meantime, the challenge remains to establish programmes and policies for children who are in camps that ensure that their key supports are maintained while their future is being determined.

Implications

Guidelines on the support of children in refugee camp settings increasingly reflect the concerns and issues identified above. A working paper compiled by Save the Children Alliance professionals (International Save the Children Alliance, 1996) identifies the following seven principles in the promotion of well-being among children affected by armed conflict and displacement:

- Apply a long-term perspective that incorporates the psychological well-being of children.
- Adopt a community-based approach that encourages self-help and builds on local culture, realities and perceptions of child development.
- Promote normal family and everyday life so as to reinforce a child's natural resilience.
- Focus on primary care and prevention of further harm in the healing of children's psychological wounds.
- Provide support as well as training for personnel who care for children.
- Ensure clarity on ethical issues in order to protect children.
- Advocate children's rights.

The UNHCR response to the UN study on the Impact of Armed Conflict on Children (UN, 1996) identifies three phases of activity: emergency, post-emergency and repatriation–reintegration (Boothby *et al.*, 1997). Again, objectives within each of these phases demonstrate coherence with the preceding analysis. Thus, during the emergency stage priorities include identification of critical health, nutrition and sanitation problems; prevention of child–family separations; making recreation programmes available; and placing separated minors with foster families or in group care. In the post-emergency stage tracing and reunification, availability of basic education, and promotion of 'child-watch' networks and other community-managed programmes are prioritized. The repatriation–reintegration stage is then characterized by such priorities as needs assessment, landmine awareness campaigns, and a range of actions in support of legal, social and economic aspects of return.

Refugee children in resettlement

Although the UN emphasizes a range of 'durable solutions' for refugee displacement, relocation to a third country is currently the least favoured. Nevertheless, each year about a million refugees gain approval to resettle in third countries. The bulk of these are received by the USA, Australia, Sweden, Canada, Denmark and Norway.

It has become increasingly difficult for refugees to find places of safety in third countries. They are not always welcome and in some instances are attacked and driven out. The increasing numbers of displaced persons and the decline in refugees, those who have actually crossed a national border, attest to this problem. Poor and rich nations alike are closing their doors to refugees, arguing that it is better to return them to their countries of origin, even those countries still in conflict. Asylum claims to Europe have dropped by 60 per cent in the past five years, while in 1997 3.3 million refugees returned to their countries of origin.

Nonetheless, a few hundred thousand refugee children are resettled each year in countries where they usually do not speak the language, may or may not have family, and may face racism and xenophobia. What happens to these children once they arrive and how do they adjust? In this section, we review the literature on the key factors that influence the quality of adjustment for resettled refugee children.

Pre-migration factors

As suggested by the preceding analysis, the adjustment of a refugee child in resettlement may critically depend upon the child's experience before arrival. Investigators have pointed out the impact and pernicious effects of trauma, loss, separation and deprivation. They argue that these factors, often interrelated, strongly influence a refugee child's adjustment in resettlement.

TRAUMA

Trauma from violence, abuse and war is associated with depression, anxiety, and post-traumatic stress disorder. A review of twelve research studies (Fox *et al.*, 1994) revealed that pre-migration violence played a significant role in a child's health status and adaptation. Studies of children who resettled in the USA demonstrate similar results. For example, Sack *et al.* (1994) noted that roughly one-fifth of the adolescent survivors of the Pol Pot regime in Cambodia qualified for a current diagnosis of post-traumatic stress disorder (PTSD). Although there was a strong relationship between trauma and depression, other forms of psychopathology were much less evident.

In Canada, a study of Latin American refugee children aged from 8 to 12 revealed that the effects of armed conflict and trauma depended upon the trauma's intensity, its length of duration and the child's age when exposed to armed conflict and trauma. Central American children exposed to the effects of political violence demonstrated symptoms of PTSD, mediated by maternal mental health and the specific associated risk of having lost a father to violent death (McClosky *et al.*, 1995). An earlier study in Canada had similar findings among resettled Latin American children, namely that psychological symptoms in resettlement were associated with exposure to war (Rousseau *et al.*, 1989; cf. Figure 9.2).

Several Swedish studies of children and violence also confirm emotional difficulties in resettlement. One researcher particularly documented the link between organized violence and trauma in Iranian children (Almquist and Brandell-Frosberg, 1994).

SEPARATION AND LOSS

Another factor that has been shown to be related to serious emotional problems is the separation of a child from his or her mother or principal caregiver. A most-cited example of the negative effects of separation is the study of Freud and Burlingham (1943) that found that children evacuated from London during the bombing blitz of World War II experienced greater emotional stress than children who stayed in the city with their parents. In a study of refugee children in Norway (Hauff and Vaglum, 1993), family separation was found to be a clear predictor of psychopathology.

Other studies of refugee children have reinforced the connection of separation and psychopathology. Masser (1992) noted the relationship between post-traumatic stress symptoms and separation from primary caregiver for Central American refugee children in the USA. In the study of Iranian children cited above, the source of trauma was separation of children from their families (Almquist and Brandell-Frosberg, 1995).

While separation is a significant loss for a refugee child, Eisenbruch (1991) found that the emotional distress of resettled Cambodian adolescents living in Australia was interrelated with the loss of their culture, a phenomenon referred to as 'cultural bereavement'. Lipson and her colleagues (1991) found that the health and mental health of Afghan refugee families and their children were affected by the trauma and loss that they had experienced. Likewise, Castex (1992) found that Soviet refugee children in the USA grieved for lost companions, their friends that they had left behind.

DEPRIVATION

Severe deprivation in the form of insufficient food, water, medical care and shelter is also a factor in the experience of many resettled refugee children. Flight from their homes, the search for safety and displacement in refugee camps often are accompanied by severe deprivation. Carlin and Sokoloff (1985) reported that Korean children malnourished because of the civil war suffered both physical and mental delays in development. The effects of deprivation on physical and mental development are well known and, in many cases, are significant factors in the adjustment of resettled refugee children. The degree of deprivation and how long it continues obviously affect the severity of physical, developmental and emotional damage that one would encounter in resettled refugee children.

Resettlement: assets and problems

A number of factors arise to influence, positively and negatively, a refugee child's adjustment in a new environment. As suggested earlier, adaptation depends not only on past experiences, but also on the supports and limitations, the assets and problems that a refugee child and his or her family encounter. These emanate from a variety of sources, especially the community, the family, and the child him- or herself (see Figure 9.1).

THE COMMUNITY

Social and economic supports comprise key community assets. Research findings have confirmed that the degree of acceptance by members of the community, types of financial assistance for relocation expenses, including housing, food and clothing, and job opportunities, training and education aid or hinder refugees in their adjustment in a new country. Employment was a significant element in the adjustment of Polish and Czech refugees (Baker, 1988), while unemployment was associated with poor health among East German refugees (Schwarzer *et al.*, 1994). Family income is important to a refugee's psychological well-being (Tran, 1986). Moss *et al.* (1992) noted that the health of Central American refugee children resettled in Belize was correlated with policies that decrease socioeconomic marginalization by integrating their parents into the local labour market.

DeMonchy (1990) highlights the importance of community supports in the lives of refugee children and their families. She addresses the importance of connecting the resettled family and their children with the resources they need to meet their needs and to become independent. Among these assets are (1) the availability of culturally appropriate social, health, and mental health services; (2) effective and accessible service delivery programmes that employ trained bilingual and bicultural staff; and (3) links with the refugee community through social, religious and cultural organizations.

The lack of employment opportunities and social supports is linked with problems in resettlement, poor adjustment, and health and mental health difficulties. Very often, community resources are not utilized because of discomfort with services that are culturally unfamiliar, as in the case of Cambodian families and their children living in the USA (Strober, 1994).

Racism is often encountered by refugee families and children (Beiser *et al.*, 1995), manifesting itself through lack of acceptance, xenophobia and, in some cases, violence. A Vietnamese refugee girl in the Washington, DC, area spoke about her feelings of discrimination:

To tell you the truth, all I want is for people to accept me as I am and not as some Oriental. The best is that they ignore me. The worst is that they call me names. In either case, they don't like me and don't accept me.

THE FAMILY

The refugee family is another source of strength for the refugee child. Several studies substantiate this claim. For instance, it has been reported that the adjustment of Hmong children in the USA depended upon the strength and resilience of their family (McInnis, 1991) and in Canada upon the 'protective factor' of the family of refugee children (Hicks *et al.*, 1993). In addition, Edwards and Beiser (1994) speak of family environment and familial support as 'protective factors of mental health' for Southeast Asian refugee children who resettled in Canada. 'Families shield children from adversity' (Beiser *et al.*, 1995, p. 69). The stresses of change, acculturation, bereavement and trauma are mediated by the family. Refugee children cope better with these stresses when their families are stable, have adjusted well to a new country, and provide their children with support, encouragement and love. The importance of family and support systems seems to pervade the successful adaptation of refugee children who have survived extreme violence and trauma (Fox *et al.*, 1994).

Problems do arise and cause serious difficulties in resettlement. Children tend to adapt and assimilate faster than their parents. They master a new language and usually orient themselves to and adopt new values, customs and lifestyles more quickly than their parents. This often places children in the role of managing and mediating the new culture for parents, an action that can rob the parents of their traditional roles and control. This role reversal and the differential acculturation may be sources of intergenerational conflict. Parent–child problems among refugees have been found to centre around (1) communication difficulties, (2) school performance, and (3) antisocial behaviour (Boehnlein *et al.*, 1995).

THE REFUGEE CHILD

The adjustment of a refugee child living in a new country relies too on the abilities and characteristics of the child. His or her intelligence, dedication, language ability and persistence enable the refugee child to be successful at school; his or her relationship skill fosters the making of friends and interaction with others, especially those in the community; and his or her sense of personal identity contributes to confidence and security in what is done.

Personal identity is a factor that influences and interacts with refugee children's adjustment to a new environment and their health and mental health. Bromley (1988) demonstrated that the poor personal identity of Southeast Asian refugee adolescents in the USA is associated with tension-producing situations, value conflicts, interpersonal difficulties and trouble with coping. A similar study of Laotian adolescents revealed that their positive identity was intertwined with positive family relationships, school performance, social acceptance and peer relationships (Schapiro, 1988).

Another factor in successful adjustment is a refugee child's self-esteem. A Canadian study notes that 'self-esteem is an essential component of well-being and a predictor of achievement, including school success' (Beiser *et al.*, 1995). A lack of self-esteem is interrelated with post-traumatic stress, peer stress, and depression (DuongTran, 1995), and with health and mental health status among Vietnamese resettled in the USA (Lin *et al.*, 1979).

Implications

The research findings on refugee children demonstrate that their social and emotional adjustment is greatly influenced by pre-migration, migration and post-migration factors. A refugee child's experience with the traumas of war, violence, loss, separation and deprivation interacts with and markedly affects resettlement in a new country. Resettlement means adapting to a new language, customs, values, structures, institutions and lifestyles that present a host of change, challenges, difficulties and stresses. Positive adjustment of refugee children in resettlement is facilitated by the assets and strengths of their community and family, as well as their personal abilities and resources.

Most refugee children adapt to their new environments and have productive and satisfying lives, although some may have difficulties along the way. What can receiving countries and communities do to provide support for arriving refugee children? There are four key recommendations.

First, it is important to recognize that the refugee family, including the children, are generally ordinary people who have experienced extraordinary events. Culturally sensitive social, health and mental health services will allow them to deal with past traumas as well as connect with the resources that they need to become independent.

Second, refugee families need to remain together. Separation of children from their parents results in severe emotional problems. Resettlement policies should focus on (1) keeping the family intact, (2) tracing families' members to reunite families, and (3) as a last resort, placing unaccompanied children for adoption or long-term foster care. A refugee child has a better chance to blossom with a loving family that has the resources to be independent in their new country. It is preferable for that family to be the child's own family, but it may also be an adoptive or foster family.

Third, host countries should financially support the development of refugee self-help, civic, social and religious structures as a means of strengthening the resettled community. Indigenous groups, organizations and institutions are assets and positive supports for refugees' families and their children. Refugee mutual assistance agencies (MAA) may assume a role similar to the social settlements of the past, providing language classes, job training, day care, recreation programmes and co-operative services such as banking. MAAs can be the nerve-centre of the refugee community, a meeting-place for newcomers and a protective shield from the harsh realities of the new life.

Finally, countries everywhere, but especially in the developed world, must address the global rise of xenophobia and isolationism with policies that offer refugee families and children protection from oppression and persecution. We are living in an era of great economic and political uncertainty and change, where policies – without such active consideration – all too readily exclude those with such needs.

Note

The assistance of Silke-Andrea Mallmann in the preparation of this chapter is gratefully acknowledged.

References

Ager, A. (1996) Children, war and psychological intervention. In S.C. Carr and J. Schumaker (eds), *Psychology and the Developing World*. New York: Praeger.

Ager, A., Ager, W. and Long, L. (1995) The differential experience of Mozambican refugee women and men. *Journal of Refugee Studies*, 8 (3), 263–87.

Almquist, K. and Brandell-Frosberg, M. (1994) Iranian refugee children in Sweden: effects of organized violence and forced migration on preschool children. *American Journal of Orthopsychiatry*, 6 (2), 225–37.

Baker, R. (1988) Refugee assimilation: A study of Polish and Czech refugees. *Humboldt Journal of Social Relations*, 15 (2), 157–83.

Beiser, M., Dion, R., Gotowiec, A., and Hyman, I. (1995) Immigrant and refugee children in Canada. *Canadian Journal of Psychiatry*, 40 (2), 67–72.

Blomqvist, U. (1997) The protection of unaccompanied children in large-scale refugee and repatriation emergencies: Tanzania and Rwanda. *Refugee Participation Network*, 24, 16–19.

Boehnlein, J.K., Tran, H.D., Riley, C., Vu, K.-C., Tan, S. and Leung, P.K. (1995) A comparative study of family functioning among Vietnamese and Cambodian refugees. *Journal of Nervous and Mental Disease*, **183** (12), 768–73.

Boothby, N. (1994) Trauma and violence among refugee children. In A. Marsella, T. Bornemann, S. Ekblad and J. Orley (eds), *Amidst Peril and Pain: The Mental Health and Well-Being of the World's Refugees*, pp. 239–59. Washington, DC: American Psychological Association.

Boothby, N., Ameratunga, M. and Abramson, B. (1997) The UNHCR response to the Machel study. *Refugee Participation Network*, 24, 14–15.

Bromley, M.A. (1988) Identity as a central adjustment issue for the Southeast Asian unaccompanied refugee minor. *Child and Youth Care Quarterly*, **17** (2), 104–14.

Carlin, J.E. and Sokoloff, B.Z. (1985) Mental health treatment issues for Southeast Asian refugee children. In T.K. Owan (ed.), *Southeast Asian Mental Health: Treatment, Prevention, Services, Training, and Research*, pp. 91–112. Rockville, MD: National Institute of Mental Health.

Castex, G.M. (1992) Soviet refugee children: the dynamic of migration and school practice. *Social Work in Education*, **14** (3), 141–52.

Chowdhury, S. and Mears, C. (1994) *Healthcare for Refugees and Displaced People*. Oxfam Practical Health Guide no. 9. Oxford: Oxfam.

Crisp, J. (1996) Meeting the needs and realizing the rights of refugee children and adolescents: from policy to practice. *Refugee Survey Quarterly*, **15** (3), 1–24.

Dawes, A. and Donald, D. (1994) *Childhood and Adversity: Psychological Perspectives from South African Research*. Cape Town: David Roberts.

DeMonchy, M.L. (1990) Recovery and rebuilding: the challenge for refugee children and service providers. In F.L. Ahearn and J.L. Athey (eds), *Refugee Children: Theory, Research, and Services*, pp. 163–80. Baltimore, MD: Johns Hopkins University Press.

DuongTran, Q. (1995) Psychosocial correlates of depression in Vietnamese adolescents. *Child and Adolescent Social Work Journal*, 13 (1), 41–50.

Edwards, R.G. and Beiser, M. (1994) Southeast Asian refugee youth in Canada: the determinants of competence and successful coping. *Canada's Mental Health*, **42** (1), 1–5.

Eisenbruch, M. (1991) From post-traumatic stress disorder to cultural bereavement: diagnosis of Southeast Asian refugees. *Social Science and Medicine*, **33** (6), 673–780.

Eunson, P. (1997) Zaire: unaccompanied children as refugees: protecting their right to normal development. In P. Harman and C. Scotchmer (eds), *Rebuilding Young Lives: Using the Child-to-Child Approach with Children in Difficult Circumstances*, pp. 61–71. London: Child-to-Child Trust.

Fox, P.G., Cowell, J.M. and Montgomery, A.C. (1994) The effects of violence on health and adjustment of Southeast Asian refugee children: an integrative review. *Public Health Nursing*, 11 (3), 195–201.

Freud, A. and Burlingham, D.T. (1943) *War and Children*. New York: Ernst Willard.

Garbarino, J. (1996) Developmental consequences of living in dangerous and unstable environments: the situation of refugee children. In M. McCallin (ed.), *The Psychological Well-Being of Refugee Children: Research, Practice and Policy Issues*, 2nd edition. Geneva: International Catholic Child Bureau.

Garbarino, J. and Kostelny, K. (1996) The effects of political violence on Palestinian children's behavior problems: a risk accumulation model. *Child Development*, 67, 33-45.

Hauff, E. and Vaglum, P. (1993) Vietnamese boat refugees: the influence of war and flight traumas on mental health on arrival in the country of resettlement: a community cohort study of Vietnamese refugees in Norway. Vietnamese boat refugees. *Acta Psychiatrica Scandinavica*, 88 (3), 162–8.

Hicks, R., Lalonde, N. and Pepler, D. (1993) Psychosocial considerations in the mental health of immigrant and refugee children. Special issue: Cultural Diversity: Voice, Access, and Involvement. *Canadian Journal of Community Mental Health*, 12 (2), 71–87.

International Save the Children Alliance (1996) *Promoting Psychosocial Well-Being among Children Affected by Armed Conflict and Displacement: Principles and Approaches*. Geneva: ISCA.

Kuterovac, G., Dyregrov, A. and Stuvland, R. (1994) Children in war: a silent majority under stress. *British Journal of Medical Psychology*, 67, 363–75.

Laor, N., Wolmer, L., Mayes, L., Gershon, A., Weizman, R. and Cohen, D. (1997) Israeli preschool children under Scuds: a 30-month follow-up. *American Academy of Child and Adolescent Psychiatry*, 36 (3), 349–55.

Levine, I. (1997) The protection of children in zones of conflict. *Refugee Participation Network*, 24, 6–8.

Lin, K.M., Tazuma, L. and Masuda, M. (1979) Adaptational problems of Vietnamese refugees: health and mental health status. *Archives of General Psychiatry*, 36, 955–61.

Lipson, J.G., Omidian, P.A. and Paul, S.M. (1991) Afghan Health Education Project: a community survey. *Public Health Nursing*, 12 (3), 143–50.

Loughry, M. and Nguyen, X.N. (1997) *The Reintegration of Unaccompanied Returnee Children in Thua Thien Hue Province*. A report for the Norwegian Refugee Council, Oslo.

McCallin, M. (1992) *Living in Detention*. Geneva: International Catholic Child Bureau.

McCallin, M. (1996) The impact of current and traumatic stressors on the psychological well-being of refugee communities. In M. McCallin (ed.), *The Psychological Well-being of Refugee Children: Research, Practice and Policy Issues*, 2nd edition. Geneva: International Catholic Child Bureau.

McClosky, L., Southwick, K., Fernandez-Esquer, M.E. and Locke, C. (1995) The psychological effects of political and domestic violence on Central American and Mexican immigrant mothers and children. *Journal of Community Psychology*, 23 (2), 95–116.

McInnis, K. (1991) Ethnic-sensitive work with Hmong refugee children. *Child Welfare*, 70 (5), 571–80.

Macksoud, M.S. and Aber, J.L. (1996) The war experience and psychosocial development of children in Lebanon. *Child Development*, 37, 70–88.

Masser, D.S. (1992) Psychosocial functioning of Central American refugee children. *Child Welfare*, 71 (5), 439–56.

Miller, K.E. (1996) The effect of state terrorism and exile on indigenous Guatemalan refugee children: a mental health assessment and an analysis of children's narratives. *Child Development*, 67, 89–106.

Moss, N., Stone, M.C. and Smith, J.B. (1992) Child health outcomes among Central American refugees and immigrants in Belize. *Social Science and Medicine*, 34 (2), 161–7.

Muecke, M. (1992) New paradigms for refugee health problems. *Social Science and Medicine*, 35 (4), 515–23.

Punamäki, R.-L. (1996) Can ideological commitment protect children's psychosocial well-being in situations of political violence? *Child Development*, 67, 55–69.

Raundalen, M. and Dyregrov, A. (1991) War experiences and psychological impact on children. In C.P. Dodge and M. Raundalen (eds), *Reaching Children in War*, pp. 21–37. Bergen: Sigma Forlag.

Ressler, E.M., Boothby, N. and Steinbock, D.J. (1988) *Unaccompanied Children*. New York: Oxford University Press.

Rousseau, C., Corin, E. and Renaud, C. (1989) Conflit armé et trauma: une étude clinique chez des enfants réfugiés latino-américains (Armed conflict and trauma: a clinical study among Latin American refugee children). *Canadian Journal of Psychiatry*, 34 (5), 376–85.

Sack, W.H., McSharry, S., Clarke, G.N., Kinney, R. *et al.* (1994) The Khmer Adolescent Project: I. Epidemiologic findings in two generations of Cambodian refugees. *Journal of Nervous and Mental Disease*, 182 (7), 387–95.

Schapiro, A. (1988) Adjustment and identity formation of Lao refugee adolescents. *Smith College Studies in Social Work*, 58 (3), 157–81.

Schwarzer, R., Jerusalem, M. and Hahn, A. (1994) Unemployment, social support and health complaints: a longitudinal study of stress in East

German refugees. *Journal of Community and Applied Social Psychology*, 4 (1), 31–45.

Straker, G., Moosa, F., Becker, R. and Nkwale, M. (1992) *Faces in the Revolution: The Psychological Effects of Violence on Township Youth in South Africa*. Cape Town: David Phillip.

Strober, S.B. (1994) Social work interventions to alleviate Cambodian refugee psychological stress. *International Social Work*, 37 (1), 23–35.

Terr, L. (1991) Childhood traumas: an overview. *American Journal of Psychiatry*, 148 (1), 10–19.

Tolfree, D. (1991) *Refugee Children in Malawi: A Study of the UNHCR Guidelines on Refugee Children*. International Save the Children Alliance.

Tolfree, D. (1996) *Restoring Playfulness: Different Approaches to Assisting Children Who Are Psychologically Affected By War or Displacement*. Stockholm: Radda Barner.

Tran, T.V. and Wright, R. (1986) Social support and subjective well-being among Vietnamese refugees. *Social Service Review*, 60 (3), 449–59.

UN (1996) *Study on the Impact of Armed Conflict on Children* (The Machel Study). New York: UN.

UNHCR (1994) *Refugee Children: Guidelines on Protection and Care*. Geneva: UNHCR.

UNICEF (1996) *The State of the World's Children 1996*. New York: Oxford University Press.

Van Haren, L. (1997) Towards implementing guidelines for protection and assistance of adolescents and youth. Report of a mission to Rwanda, April. Programme Policy Unit, UNHCR, Geneva.

Zivic, I. (1993) Emotional reactions of children to war stress in Croatia. *Journal of the American Academy of Child and Adolescent Psychiatry*, 32, 709–13.

10

Containment and validation: psychodynamic insights into refugees' experience of torture

Susan Levy

IF THIS IS A MAN

You who live safe
In your warm houses
You who find, returning in the evening
Hot food and friendly faces:
Consider if this is a man
Who works in the mud
Who does not know peace
Who fights for a scrap of bread
Who dies because of a yes and a no

Consider if this is a woman
Without hair and without name
With no more strength to remember
Her eyes empty and her womb cold
Like a frog in winter

Meditate that this came about
I commend these words to you.
Carve them in your hearts
At home, in the street,
Going to bed, rising:
Repeat them to your children,

Or may your house fall apart,
May illness impede you,
May your children turn their faces from you

Primo Levi, 1987

This remarkable poem is one of the many pieces Primo Levi offered to the world after his release from the Nazi concentration camp, Auschwitz. The poem conveys some compelling themes and images to me that I repeatedly witness in my work with survivors of torture and which will form the basis of my discussion in this chapter.

It seems to me to be Levi's powerful wish to communicate, through his poem, his experience of the concentration camp to another person, as if they were in fact there, to allow somehow for the reader to enter the mind and body space of 'he' and 'she' who is no longer a man or a woman. When I read Levi's poem (and indeed his work in general) I feel this intense communication and am drawn to him in sorrow and compassion. There is a part of me which would like to reach out to this poet, not as a fellow human confirming and validating his experience, but in denial of the horror he describes.

Therapists working in this field often feel the need to deny the terribleness of their client's experience. There is a strong desire to replace the experience with something more comforting or easier to bear. We are confronted with the painful question of whether, indeed, we can hear and contain the memories of the atrocities our clients describe to us.

It is not only the pain of these experiences that is so disturbing. In the final stanza of Levi's poem, he curses those who do not, or who are not able, to carve the Holocaust onto their hearts. He visits upon them a terrible punishment and one is left feeling the hugeness of his rage and hatred. Bruno Bettelheim (1979) wrote in his paper 'Owners of their faces' that 'when one is forced to drink black milk from dawn to dusk. . . a living soul has death for a master'. In my opinion this is indeed so. The greatest difficulty in working with survivors of torture is managing and containing their powerful feelings of hatred and death. The death and hatred in the survivor is often experienced by the therapist as an attack on him or her. Therapists can often feel savagely cursed in the way Levi curses his unknown betrayers.

It is the overall tone of Levi's poem, however, which is most moving and perhaps also the most resonant for therapists working with survivors. The whole poem is a plea, both powerful and poignant, for the world never to forget the Holocaust. This seems to be different from the attack against those who do or may forget. Levi's anger is a part of the poem but not its essence. It is the poet's attempt to validate his experience which is the major theme of the poem. Levi uses both his intensity of communication and also his vengeful rage to frame his plea; that survivors can survive only if their experience is validated – if it is reflected politically, socially and economically in the external world.

In many countries today the validation of the experience of refugees is largely absent. Instead, refugees are accused of lying about their experiences. In Britain it is common for refugees to be detained in prison and then deported back to the countries from where they fled. Those refugees who do remain often face poverty, alienation, loss of language, family, culture and, of course, home country. In addition to these burdens survivors often have to live with the memories and experiences of trauma and torture. It is the task of the therapist to address these many different conflicts and problems of the refugee survivor; to attempt both to contain and to validate them. An exploration of these two themes, containment and validation, forms the core of this chapter.

Containment and validation

Containment can be understood as the therapist's attempt to manage the survivor's internal, feeling states of mind. Central to this concept are two factors; first, the provision of a holding environment, a safe physical and emotional space for the client. This safe and holding environment refers both to the reality level (providing a quiet and contained physical space for the client) and also to the level of fantasy (providing a mental holding environment for the expression of what occurs in the mind of the client; Winnicot, 1965).

Second, containment also refers to the capacity of the therapist to manage the disturbed and distressed feelings that the client puts into him or her in the course of their work together. Bion described this form of containment as not so much the containment of the client but the containment of the feeling which the client puts into the therapist. In this way the therapist is required to hold or manage the feelings of the other person and to use his or her own mind as a container for these emotions (Britton, 1992).

By containing the thoughts of the client the worker hopes to remove some of the 'poisons' which the client believes or feels are inside his or her mind. In the course of this process the individual's intolerable feelings are held or contained by the therapist and then 'returned' in a less poisonous, worrying or disturbed form. The relationship which client and therapist have established together becomes the medium for this communication (Blackwell, 1992).

Validation refers to the therapist's acknowledgement of the client's actual experience and not simply the feeling state of the client. This is an essential part of working with survivors. Their external reality has been massively and brutally interfered with in an ongoing and intentional way. Like Primo Levi, many survivors struggle most with the experience or fear of their sufferings being forgotten or minimized or even disbelieved. This lack of validation can be seriously damaging both to individual victims and also to their broader communities. The suffering of the survivor is private to them but it is also public, a more generalized political experience which impacts terribly on their lives and those of their community.

Containment and validation in this context represent a union between the personal and the political lives of survivors. This union is crucial in the treatment of survivors of torture. The validation of a survivor's experience is probably the most containing therapeutic gesture a therapist can make to him or her.

Donald Winnicot (1965) wrote about the validation of the infant in the mother's eyes. By acknowledging the infant's existence in her look and gesture, the mother contains her baby as he or she struggles to make sense of life. According to Winnicot, the infant feels its existence because it is represented and validated through the mother. More recently, Peter Fonagy and colleagues have suggested that this form of validation ensures the development of resilient 'mental equipment' in an individual. They argue that resilience in children is a crucial determinant for their adult mental health (Fonagy, 1991). Like Winnicot, they propose that it is the mother's validation and representation of the child's mental state which provides the basis for the development of the child's psychological resilience (see Chapter 9). This resilience relies both on the mother's capacity to provide for her infant as a separate entity in its own right (e.g. to love and cherish her child) and on the mother's capacity to think and reflect on behalf of her infant (Fonagy *et al.*, 1993b).

Fonagy emphasizes that this relationship, in particular the relationship of attachment between mother and child, is crucial in the development of resilience. The fundamental aim of torture is to destroy such resilience and undermine attachment relations, not only in the individual tortured but in the broader community of which the individual is a part (see Chapter 5).

Torture: an attack on attachment

The act of torture is not, as is so commonly misunderstood, an isolated attack on a person. Torture is a highly sophisticated social construction used by many governments to control their populations. In many modern regimes (often with the assistance of Western democracies), 'specialist soldiers' are recruited from ordinary army and police ranks and refined for the job of torture. There is increasing evidence that these specially selected men, and sometimes women, are intensively and expertly trained in the work of torturing individuals. They do not come to this work 'naturally' or by 'chance' but are chosen with intention; that is, to root out and destroy those elements of society which threaten the *status quo* and to paralyse any further form of resistance or remonstrance from the broader community by these acts of terror (Amnesty International, 1984; Torture, 1996).

Under torture an individual's basic sense of trust is abrogated. This breakdown of trust occurs not only individually but within the community at large. Sections of communities may become alienated from each other, with people becoming hesitant, suspicious and ultimately hostile towards each other.

This terrorization of societies through torture and the threat of torture has long-term and devastating effects. If we understand resilience as Fonagy *et al.* (1992) do, then we can see that the experience of torture is an attack on human attachment. The intimacy and closeness of the original attachment to the mother is mirrored, in a perverse and distorted way, in the act of torture. Body touch, dependence, the constant presence of another human being, all essential aspects of a good mother–infant relationship, are repeated but perverted in the process of torture.

These repeated and 'perverted' acts of terror and violence against an individual and a society can result in a rupture of the system of defence, in an invalidation of the resilience which protects and maintains the self and identity of individuals and communities. The internal mother which Fonagy describes as providing basic mental resilience is now replaced by another representation which distorts and disfigures the nature of these earlier experiences (Fonagy *et al.*, 1993a).

If we understand the mind as a structural unit with a mental sheath, barrier or psychological skin protecting it, then we can understand the experience of torture as tearing or rupturing this psychological skin or mental sheath. In the same way as an individual's body can massively haemorrhage causing severe organic damage, so too can there be a psychological haemorrhaging (Krystal, 1976; Pines, 1986).

Clinicians working with survivors of torture have identified three important factors which, if present together, are highly likely to precipitate a rupturing of the mental stimulus barrier. They are:

- near-death experience in the presence of
- helplessness, and
- forced passivity/impotence (Solomons, 1989).

In these circumstances the flight/fight response, which is automatic in any human stress situation, is interfered with. The flight/fight energy which is aroused in a near-death situation is inhibited by the helplessness and forced passivity under torture. We hear again and again, for example, our clients' experiences of mock executions, when they absolutely believed they were to die, only to be cynically 'spared' while those 'less fortunate' were killed. This form of deliberate and repeated exposure to death (without the capacity to flee or fight) destroys the ability of the mind to prepare for and respond to disaster. The result is a collapse of mental resilience and death of the will to live (Weisaeth and Eitinger, 1993).

This collapse may be conceptualized as a regression to a state of ambiguity, where the individual is unable to distinguish between good and bad, self and other, and internal and external processes. In terms of such analysis, in primitive states of ambiguity antagonistic states of mind (for example, danger and safety) are confused and become interchangeable. It is this interchangeability, this absence of conflict which creates the ultimate existential and psychogenic death. The most extreme example of this form of ambiguity must be when the tension between the will to live and the threat of death is collapsed, when life and death have the same 'no meaning' status. It is at this point, then, that the 'rupture' or tearing of the mental shield or 'skin' occurs and there is a breakdown in the human defence system.

Such an assault naturally has many symptomological consequences. There are immediate responses and there are later, less conscious symptoms which haunt people and hold them hostage to their traumatic experiences (Bettelheim, 1991; Laub and Auerhahn, 1993). The most notable short-term symptoms which clients describe are flooding of the mind with intense and overwhelming anxiety, loss of the capacity to think outside of the experience, loss of the capacity to feel (in mind and body) and loss of the sense of the self as a living organism (psychogenic death).

Longer-term difficulties, however, are also part of the consequences of torture. Often these symptoms are more complicated and less evidently linked to the torture experience. In my experience of working with survivors of torture I have observed three broad descriptive modes of personality response. Although these categories are neither comprehensive nor discrete, they do provide some framework for understanding.

I have outlined the categories as follows: first, the most overtly disturbed group, regressed individuals with pronounced breakdown in personality functioning; second, a less overtly regressed group with the major feature being breakdown on the interpersonal level; and third, a more rigid and persecuted group who usually present with somatic symptoms.

Profound personality breakdown

In the first category, the smallest and certainly the most overtly disturbed group, there is pronounced breakdown in personality functioning. The dominant symptom in this group is that of repetition compulsion, where the individual constantly and relentlessly re-experiences the trauma. Depending on the severity of the symptom, there can actually be a delusional belief that the individual is literally in the traumatic situation. In such a group of survivors we see the breakdown of the mental barrier or shield and a regression to a more psychotic state of mental disintegration. There is limited capacity for the internal mind to create order and sanity and at times clients in this category will need to be hospitalized.

Often in this group of survivors we see that an external representation of order and sanity – the concrete building of the clinic, for example – comes to represent symbolically the validating mother who acknowledges the survivor's experience. Often clients in this condition do not have a coherent memory of their experience. They may have fragments of memory which they feel continue to torture them, but there is an overall absence of the facility to give meaning to the experience.

In this context, the 'brick mother', the actual hospital or clinic where the person attends for treatment, provides both a reality-testing validation of the survivor's experience and a containing environment where the client feels that he or she is safe and understood.

An example of this type of client is Mr A, a 24-year-old Iranian man, bereaved of his entire family and brutally tortured in Iran for a period of three months. When I first saw Mr A he was unable to function on a day-to-day level and under normal circumstances would have benefited from a period in hospital (part of his torture, however, involved being hospitalized, and it was therefore considered in his better interests not to hospitalize him).

Mr A presented with multiple trauma symptoms, most notably overwhelming and repeated re-experiencing of the traumatic events around his torture and the separation from his family. This would occur at all times of the day and night and would often result in his unintentionally losing control of his bladder, vomiting in his sleep and at other times smashing the walls of his bedroom and causing injury to himself.

In the early phases of treatment of this man, the most containing experience for him was the 'bricks and mortar' of the specialist centre for survivors where he was being treated. Although he later became accustomed and attached to me, his therapist, in the early stages of the treatment he seemed to feel as contained by sitting in the waiting-room with its many clients from all over the world. This man would always arrive for his sessions two to three hours early and would often remain in the waiting-room for some time after the session. He once described coming to the unit as 'the only safe place I know, because here we are all suffering from the same problem and I don't have to explain myself; at the centre we know we are safe because we are victims of torture'.

Here we see a client in whom the trauma has led to a massive breakdown of identity and sense of self. To use Fonagy *et al.*'s (1992) term, his 'mental equipment' has been fragmented. The client can no longer turn to his sources of internal resilience and instead relies on and feels contained by both the external identity of the organization and the collective identity of the other clients/survivors. The concrete 'brick mother' presence of the building (and all its 'clients') serves as a substitute mental apparatus and helps to metabolize the constantly repeated unthinkable and unbearable experiences.

In traditional psychoanalytic thinking the compulsive re-experiencing of the event, or, in Freud's terms, repetition compulsion, was understood by Freud to be the ego's defective attempt to master a traumatic situation. He understood the repetition compulsion to be a primitive defence mechanism aimed at predicting and controlling the traumatic experience. By re-creating the event in the mind, the individual attempts to re-experience the trauma in a more prepared fashion and thus reduce the assault on the mind's stimulus barrier. The failure of the repetition compulsion to reduce tension is ascribed to the failure of the ego to integrate the trauma experience (Freud, 1987).

In more recent thinking, however, there is increasingly the view that the repetition compulsion is not a skewed or failed defensive functioning but a breakdown of the entire defence system. Included in this overall breakdown of the defence system would be a collapse of memory modulation. Writers like Krystal (1976) argue that the ego's screening capacity is massively disrupted and that, in fact, in these severe circumstances the repetition compulsion represents flooding of the ego rather than an attempt to defend it. As suggested earlier, in extreme cases of trauma the individual may be so overwhelmed by stimuli that the result is psychogenic death (Weisaeth and Eitinger, 1993).

Mr F, a Zairean refugee whom I treated for one and a half years, related to me an experience of a series of mock executions where he had been forced to witness fellow prisoners being drowned. He described three occasions of being driven in a jeep with his cellmates to the banks of a river which he recognized from his childhood. There, he and one other person were forced to witness two prisoners being bundled and tied into two large sacks. He remembered their screams of terror and his own desperate screams as he watched the sacks being thrown into the river and slowly sinking. On each of these occasions Mr F would be informed that 'today will be your day to die'. On each occasion he was one of two prisoners spared.

Mr F described himself to me as a man who is 'a living dead man'. He said he could not imagine ever enjoying life again and that his only real experience was constantly reliving the above scenario. He described having 'no feeling' – either of sadness or of happiness – and was aware of being different from others in his responses to everyday life events. Increasingly he felt cursed with the burden of living and wondered aloud to me why he was alive.

I am aware that in describing this fragment of Mr F's story I am placed in the uncomfortable situation of both wanting to protect my audience from such horror and feeling a need to make known this man's terrible experience. Perhaps this can give us some little insight into how torn the client/survivor feels. Many of my clients feel deeply protective of the listener, fearing to share what in their minds is dirty and perverted, yet also, like Primo Levi, are powerfully compelled to say what has happened, to give testimony to their experiences and those of the dead.

I believe it is the responsibility of the therapist, as perhaps it is the responsibility of the reader of this text, to bear witness to this testimony. In my experience, individuals like Mr F are often contained by the telling of their story, in this case to the therapist. Although these testimonies are usually related with minimum affect, there seems to be a deep comfort in the knowledge that the atrocity is documented and regarded not only as the secret history of one person but also potential evidence against those responsible for the atrocities.

Hearing testimony can become a method of validating the experience of both the survivor and those who were killed. Bettelheim (1979) writes about the 'compulsion to bear witness' experienced by many survivors of the concentration camp. Although many people who have been tortured feel deeply ashamed to speak about what happened to them, those individuals who witnessed death and executions of others and who themselves feel internally dead often feel contained by describing their story in great detail and so to some extent sharing their unbearable burden (Bettelheim, 1991).

For the therapist, however, this form of containment and validation can be deeply disturbing and even overwhelming. Fischman and Ross (1990), working with South American torture survivors, describe the two most common defensive responses in therapists working with survivors as being over-identification with the client or over-distancing oneself and attempting to minimize the level of damage sustained by the individual. The danger for the therapist in relation to Mr F, for example, could be to try to inject him with life, and thereby to deny the validity of his experience.

In my mind the most important communication the therapist can convey to the client is that we can tolerate the testimony we hear. This is not to say that one must not respond or be moved or horrified. Indeed I believe that, like Primo Levi, clients at all times during testimony need to know that they are affecting their listener, that their words are having impact. The important issue is that the level of disturbance aroused by the memories does not overwhelm the worker. The function which is always threatened in these situations is the therapist's capacity for thinking. Thinking is replaced with horror for which there are no words. Horror has no language or formal structure and corresponds more to dream representation than to thinking processes. It is often the only communication some survivors can convey to others.

Interpersonal breakdown

Mrs G is a young Ugandan woman who was imprisoned and tortured as a result of her husband's political activities. She was raped and abused in prison and also witnessed the execution of others. In my work with Mrs G, I was struck by her many words in the sessions, her constant speaking and my equally constant failure to understand her. She would always tell me about her experiences in long and horrific detail and yet I could not comprehend her words. I began to notice how confused I became and how I was always stopping her and asking her to explain some obscure point. Sometimes I felt so confused that I believed she was lying to me and I felt angry with her. I also noticed that I used a pen and notepad in the session, taking everything down as if I were taking dictation.

It was not until I became aware of the level of horror she was trying to convey to me and my own deep reluctance to receive this communication from her that I was able genuinely to engage with Mrs G. I felt that in some profound and unconscious way I had become overwhelmed in my mind in the same way that Mrs G was overwhelmed in hers and that I was rather desperately trying to manage these feelings by writing them down. When I became able to communicate these observations to Mrs G, she told me that indeed she could not understand herself and that she felt as though her mind was 'broken up' inside her. We were then able to put into words how utterly horrific her story was and how she felt words had no meaning for her, no capacity to describe her experience.

Our acknowledgement of this breakdown in the communication process seemed to facilitate a deeper engagement. Mrs G began to describe some of her experiences in a more interrelated way to me. She told me that during her time in prison she had been subjected to violent beatings and rape. She spoke about being forced to stand naked for many hours with her hands stretched out in front of her. She was denied food or drink or any toilet facilities and humiliated herself in front of the guards, who used her sexually in a degrading way. Mrs G also told me that she had been constantly aware of other women screaming in the cell next to hers and had been convinced she would suffer the same fate as them.

In my mind Mrs G fits more into my second category mode, where disturbance on the interpersonal level is more prominent than personality breakdown. Mrs G was able to function on a fairly normal level. She attended school and, despite very serious difficulties, she managed to take care of her family, cooking and cleaning for her husband and two children and generally maintaining the domestic household. She knew who she was and also had an understanding of why she was coming to see me. The disturbance in her mind was expressed less as a confusion about her internal boundaries than in misunderstandings or complications in her relationships.

I became particularly aware, for example, of how skewed Mrs G's relationship was with her husband and later with me. Mrs G repeatedly told me that she felt a deep and venomous hatred for her husband. As he had been the politically active one she blamed him for her troubles and punished him in a number of ways. She refused to allow him to make love to her and would insult and abuse him when he asked her for sex. She seemed to experience some feeling of triumph and excitement when she was able to wound him in this way and would tell me in great detail how distressed he would become when she attacked and shamed him in his desire for her. Her pleasure in his pain was always accompanied by her assertion that she did not feel guilty for hurting him because he was to blame for her suffering and 'now it is his turn to suffer'.

Here we see an example of what Bamber and Shlapobersky term the 'perversion of intimacy', where the individual in his or her close relationships identifies with the former aggressor and repeats the torture experience (H. Bamber and J. Shlapobersky, personal communication, 1992). Although Mrs G understands that she is destroying her marriage, she feels compelled to pervert her intimate relationship with her husband in the way she experienced herself being perverted by her torturers. Mrs G told me that she was able to stop her attacks only when her husband became angry with her and returned the abuse. In her mind, however, he always remained the 'cruel' and 'evil' one deserving of a fate she could not express. A cycle of violence is thus set in motion which both mirrors the past and destroys the present.

These forms of communication are extremely difficult to manage as a therapist. I have often felt afraid to resemble the torturer in any way. In my work with Mrs G I identified with the shame and paralysis inflicted on her husband and have at times resented the subtle attacks I have felt I suffered at her hands. It has been difficult to remember that my uncomfortable feelings spoke the experience she could not yet put into words.

If we return to the section in Levi's poem where he curses those who do not or are not able to 'meditate that this came about', we can understand something about the dilemma of clients who do not and are not able to be heard. An Iranian woman, Mrs S, came into treatment filled with curses which she said were so great that she found herself shouting out loud to herself in the street. Mrs S had no English and I engaged to work with one of the Iranian interpreters working at the unit.

Mrs S presented with a history of imprisonment and torture for her political activities. She had witnessed her first husband's assassination and had herself been seriously wounded during this incident. On her release from prison, Mrs S, together with her small daughter, had fled to a neighbouring country where she had remarried a fellow exile and given birth to another daughter. Further intimidation and persecution in that country led to the whole family seeking asylum in Britain.

Mrs S did not wish to be in Britain. She could not speak English and felt isolated and trapped in her small council flat, so different from the flat-roofed, open houses of her home country. She expressed great difficulty with 'the English', who she said were silent haters of people from the Middle East. Like Mrs G, Mrs S felt rage and hatred for her husband. She also struggled to manage her youngest daughter, whom she described as demanding and badly behaved. Her chief concern with this child was that the child would constantly cling to her and attempt (often successfully) to bite her breast. This enraged Mrs S and she would retaliate against this 4-year-old daughter with great anger.

Mrs S seemed to feel safe working with me and the male interpreter. She understood that 'something is wrong in my head' and was able to ask for help with this serious concern of hers. She attended her weekly sessions very regularly and was clearly committed to her therapy. She was also deeply grateful to be referred, with her husband and children, to the child and family team, who directly addressed the problems presented in the child.

In my work with Mrs S, however, it became clear that the experiences of guilt, abandonment and loss relating to the death of her first husband had been 'perverted' by the violent nature of his death and also her own experience of imprisonment and torture. I believe that these experiences translated themselves into hatred and rage and were communicated to her youngest child, who was born from the second marriage. As the therapy developed, this 'perverse' and hostile thread came alive between the two of us.

Mrs S, although not a religious woman, came from a Muslim background and was very aware of my being Jewish. On one occasion, for example, fourteen months into our work together, she enacted two situations which I believe portray her own identification with her aggressors. It was our last session before the long Christmas break and she expressed quite openly to me how upset she was at my leaving. Instead of conveying my understanding of her distress I attempted to comfort her.

I told her that she was much better than the Christmas before and I proceeded to give her some examples of this improvement. I pointed out to her that although she was not Christian, she had told me that she would be buying a tree for her two little girls to celebrate the Christmas festivities. This, I believed, would give her and her family pleasure, and reflected how much better she was. Mrs S responded to my comments by agreeing with me and then (through the interpreter) went on to say with considerable intensity that when she walked down the streets and saw the Christmas lights, she felt goodwill to all humankind, even the Jews whom she hated.

I felt deeply upset and thrown by her remark, and before I could respond, Mrs S asked if she could smoke a cigarette, knowing that I had a no-smoking policy in my office. Again, before I could respond, she lit the cigarette and drew her chair close to me, ostensibly to blow the smoke out of the window. The effect was that she blew the smoke directly into my face.

Here we have an example of torture re-enacted in the session with the therapist. Mrs S had one desire in her mind, and that was to maximize my discomfort and rid herself of the painful and humiliating experience of being left alone in what she felt was a hostile and unfamiliar environment. I felt myself to be the victim of an anti-Semitic attack which aroused distressed and angry feelings in me. I also felt paralysed: if I reflected how viciously she wanted to hurt me then I feared I would assume the shape of the torturer. If I dismissed her comments as meaningless and harmless I would deny her intention.

John Steiner (1993) writes about moments in a therapeutic situation where clients are unable to acknowledge or feel responsible for their communications. He argues that at these moments clients need to feel understood by the therapist or worker even though they are unable to recognize their own part in the interaction. Steiner emphasizes the job of containment of the client through the therapist's understanding of the client's predicament rather than through the client's understanding. In this way the therapist neither denies the communication nor retaliates against it but attempts to offer some deeper understanding of the emotion that is conveyed.

In the case of Mrs S, her hostility and distress were alleviated only by my acknowledgement of how deeply she needed me to understand that I had not heard – or, in fact in her mind, not wanted to hear – how she felt about my going away for the Christmas break. When we focused on me and my 'failure' to listen to and validate her experience, we were then able to talk about the horrible and violent feelings that were awakened in her when she felt this 'invalidation'. Mrs S spoke openly about her anti-Semitic attack on me and conveyed her concern that I was hurt and damaged by this attack. She was also, however, able to acknowledge her deep desire to torture 'somebody', to enact a revenge that would 'somehow' release her from her suffering.

Identification with the aggressor is a common theme for survivors of torture. Dinora Pines (1986), in her work with Holocaust survivors, writes about the distorted internal identifications survivors have with their abusers. In particular she draws attention to the powerful somatic symptoms present in many of those who have survived atrocities.

Pines describes somatic pain as a 'masochistic submission' which protects the person from the more devastating emotions of triumph, guilt and despair at their survival. This 'masochistic submission', however, also represents a repeat of the torture experience. The attack on the body by the self (psychosomatic pain) represents both a refuge from a deeper psychological pain and an internalization of and identification with the torturer (Pines, 1986).

Psychosomatic illness

In my experience, those clients who present with psychosomatic pain are often the most rigid and persecuted in their defences, and fit into the third category of personality types. It is these clients who typically have a history of political activism in their country of origin. Often they have been members of a political party with a strong ideological identity. This is not to say that there is an inevitable correlation between political activism and rigid personality types, but it has been my observation that often the 'hard-line' ideologies which accompany many revolutionary movements serve to reinforce personalities who understand their worlds in black-and-white stereotypes. These personalities easily divide life into rigid 'good' and 'bad' categories, idealizing the good and denigrating the bad.

Melanie Klein (1988) identified this form of relating as a primitive defence mechanism which in early infantile development is crucial in protecting the individual from overwhelming negative stimuli. The individual 'splits' good and bad feelings, both internally (where the self is divided) and externally, where others become either good or bad. In this way the individual attempts to separate and protect 'goodness' (sanity, love, thinking capacities, etc.) from the overwhelming and destructive feelings of 'badness' (hatred and hostility, breakdown, insanity, etc.).

In normal development, 'healthy splitting' ensures that the individual is initially prevented from being overwhelmed by negative stimuli. Only when the infant has developed the adequate mental resilience to tolerate positive and negative stimuli in one object does the splitting become less intense and 'whole object' relating more apparent. As was discussed earlier, 'resilient mental equipment' is a product of healthy early attachment relationships (Fonagy *et al.*, 1992). 'Whole object relating' as opposed to 'splitting' can also be understood as an extension of good attachment relationships.

Individuals who have survived torture, however, will to some extent (depending on the nature of the individual and the circumstances of the trauma) have been divested of their capacity for attachment and resilience. Under torture, intimate attachment relationships are re-created in a perverse form which instead of reinforcing resilience and 'whole object relating' creates a regression towards primitive 'splitting' methods of self-protection.

I have often heard survivors describe this splitting as occurring not only in their minds but also in their bodies. Mr M, for example, is an Iranian man who had been imprisoned for eight years in Iran for his antigovernment activities. He had a range of serious somatic complaints and had been paralysed for two years while he had been in prison. He also suffered recurring pain in his body for which there was no obvious organic cause.

Despite a very difficult interaction between us, Mr M was eventually able to tell me that his pain came from a hateful, disgusting body which he said felt as if it did not belong to him. He had sustained many severe attacks on his body, most notably being sexually tortured and also repeatedly beaten on the soles of his feet and then forced to stand for long periods without sitting.

Mr M's method of managing these brutal assaults had been to split his own perception of his body into the body that was attacking him – his 'bad' body – and the body that remained faithful to him – his 'good' body. In this way Mr M was able to survive unbearable physical pain. He would similarly 'split' his feelings. He would have 'idealized' feelings for one person and very negative sentiments for somebody else. As our work together progressed, we came to understand that he had a 'nice' face which he believed he showed to the world and an 'ugly' face which he kept hidden to himself.

My difficulties with Mr M were less obvious than with any of the clients I have already discussed. He was not disintegrated like Mr A, nor openly vengeful like Mrs S or Mrs G. Instead, Mr M described himself as a man whose 'greatest love on this earth is humanity'. He would speak for minutes at a time about his concern for others, injustices in the world, the oppression of women and suchlike.

Despite his humanitarian concerns, however, I felt that there was a cruel and even perverse element in our work together which I struggled to manage. Mr M would, for example, often speak in great detail about other people's horrific sufferings. To my distress he would insist that I look at photographs he had compiled of dead and mutilated bodies. Unlike Mrs G and Mrs S, who were quite open about their hostility, Mr M always denied he had any feelings of anger or distress about these photographs and stories. Whenever we approached these subjects he would immediately return to the theme of his commitment to his people and his love of humanity.

I often attempted to reflect to Mr M that he may feel uncomfortable speaking about himself to me, a foreign, Western woman who he perhaps felt could never understand the horror of his experiences. He would always respond in the same way, smilingly and almost tenderly, saying, 'Ah, Susie my dear, why would I feel uncomfortable with you? I think you do have a lot to learn.' When Mr M spoke to me in this way I felt patronized and angry. I would struggle to stay in my position as therapist and would feel that Mr M wished I were in some subordinate daughter/lover relationship with him where he was the person in control.

In my experience, clients who present in this way have usually suffered an extraordinarily severe form of torture. Aside from their own actual trauma, they typically carry a heavy burden of guilt about survival and often have been forced to participate in atrocities to save their own lives. These clients remain haunted by their dead comrades. I believe, however, that they are also haunted by the empty shells of their own emotional lives, which were formerly protected by political action.

Perhaps the most important point about these clients, however, is that there appears to be a limited capacity to put any of these intense and painful feelings into words. Instead, physical pain and 'silky words' can substitute for the mental pain which the mind fails to articulate. Joyce McDougall (1992) describes alexythymia (the inability to put feelings into words) as a defence against catastrophic mental breakdown. The mental process is somehow bypassed, leaving true feelings deposited in secret, disguised forms.

In my mind, both Mr M's physical suffering and his denigrating behaviour towards me hid not only his unbearable guilt at survival but also his own deep despair at the meaninglessness of his existence. This existential predicament is very common in certain clients who have been passionately involved in their liberation movements. Many clients, like Mr M, deny that they have lost their commitment and insist on their love for their people. Others turn violently against sections of their party and engage in fierce political battles over fine ideological points. These clients, however, often convey the exact opposite to the love of freedom and humanity which they so ardently profess. Again and again I have experienced powerful and painful feelings of hatred and disgust in my sessions with these clients. I am always struck by the veneer of words which mask their deeper feelings of loneliness and despair.

Clients in this category are typically single or in failed relationships. Many will point to their passionate involvement with the struggle as a reason for this single status. They often describe their happiest memories as 'fighting in the mountains' or being 'on the run' with their comrades. Although they were not engaging in intimate relationships they describe having felt precious and vital as 'revolutionaries'.

In my experience many of these hard-line political activists felt deeply unloved and neglected in their primary relationships. The allegiance to a group with clearly defined political and humanistic aims may well have provided an alternative to this mental pain and loneliness. Feelings of need and vulnerability are denied by the individual, who often takes great risks on behalf of the movement or struggle. The individual replaces concern for the self with 'concern for humankind'. In these cases it may be appropriate to understand the passion invested in the political struggle as a substitute form of love.

The pain and shame upon realization of this more or less 'false' love can be overwhelming for many survivors, who become deeply depressed and despairing about what they suddenly consider to be their wasted lives. These men and women may turn as rigidly against their comrades and movements as they were previously for them. Often any attempt to address the feelings behind these political or 'moral' struggles results in a breakdown of the therapeutic alliance.

In the case of Mr M, for example, he became defensive and denigrating when any attempt was made to understand the meaning behind his words. He seemed to feel neither validated nor contained by my interventions and I was often left despairing about whether I could be of any assistance to him.

Pearson, in his 1992 paper 'Problems with transference interpretations in short term dynamic therapy', suggests that in cases where the client is clearly hostile to the therapist's ideas, the therapist should remain within the client's own metaphor, rather than comment on the client–therapist interaction. Pearson argues against the client–therapist interpretations aimed at facilitating insight and says that often clients feel persecuted and attacked by such insights. Pearson believes that the client's own metaphors provide rich and informative material about his or her internal states of mind. In this way Pearson argues for a validation of clients' experiences through their own narratives and methods of storytelling.

In the case of Mrs S, she was considerably relieved by the focus on the client–therapist interaction. Mrs S's experience was contained by my validation of her feelings in relation to me, her therapist. In the case of Mr M, however, he seemed to derive no support or understanding from my interpretations and I therefore made fewer client/therapist comments in my work with him. I attempted, as best I could, to remain within his own metaphors.

Mr M's metaphors, however, became increasingly difficult to listen to. Our work together became more painful and difficult as we laboured under his alternating 'torturing' and 'loving' communications. I noticed that during our sessions, instead of becoming angry and offended as I had previously done, I tended to drift off into my own private thoughts. After the sessions ended I would often be consumed with guilt about Mr M and would think about how I had abandoned him and left him to his own devices. I found that I spent more time thinking about Mr M than I did about many other, equally distressed clients. The thoughts were always around feelings of guilt and shame at what I had done to him.

Slowly I began to understand that Mr M was not only communicating his horrific experience of torture to me but also powerfully conveying his own unbearable feelings of guilt about his survival. I became conscious that Mr M needed me to feel the guilt and pain that were so intolerable for him to bear. I realized, however, that as powerfully as Mr M tried to let me know about his guilt, so I resisted receiving these communications.

Whatever the origins of the therapist, whether we are European born or Asian or African, or born from generations of refugees across continents, there is a level of identification with the survivor and also with those who did not survive, which can arouse unbearable feelings of guilt in both therapist and client. As a South African white woman I struggled to acknowledge my own guilt and stress about my own 'survival' and successful and contented life. Dinora Pines emphasizes the importance of the therapist's acknowledgement of not only the client's but also the therapist's survivor guilt. If this emotion is denied in the therapist there is a strong likelihood it will not be managed with the client. It is this shared identification which can facilitate but also potentially undermine a therapeutic engagement (Pines, 1993).

In my opinion, the acknowledgement of the pain and guilt of survival is the crucial validation of these clients' experiences. Their primary defence has been to deny their own needs and be absorbed into actions on the part of others. Their survival, when others have died, is therefore a rupture of this defensive mode. Often these clients feel directly responsible for the death of hundreds of youngsters whom they recruited. For them, there is considerable relief when the relentless feelings of guilt are addressed.

Bettelheim's (1991) moving account of his experiences in the concentration camps forcefully reminds us that there is a crucial difference between those who are destroyed by their internal states of mind, by their investment in the power of others to ruin them, and those who in reality have experienced destruction at the hands of others. For refugee survivors of torture this is their quintessential experience.

Although all the individuals I have presented in this chapter clearly brought their own personal 'psychopathology' to bear on their experiences, none of them considered themselves to have previously been dysfunctional in their societies. In their minds they had managed their lives and their difficulties up until the time when they were tortured and forced into exile. It is these external events, torture and exile, over which survivors have no control, which have skewed and distorted their functioning and which have remained in their memories to haunt them.

As therapists working with refugee survivors, we share with our clients the task of facing these memories. Their pain is twofold: on the one hand they must face the reality of the cruel and destructive forces of our world; on the other, they must make peace with the fact of their own survival.

From trauma to bereavement

Mr T is a young Iraqi man whom I treated in psychotherapy for a period of three years. Like Mr M, he suffered from severe somatic symptoms. He complained of heart pain and difficulty with breathing. He was convinced that his heart pain was going to kill him and on many occasions he found himself in the casualty department of his local hospital.

Unlike Mr M, Mr T allowed himself the right to his psychotherapy. As time went by he was able to tell me about his prison experiences. Mr T had been a serious political activist and had been responsible for recruiting a considerable number of young men and women into his movement. When he was arrested he found that many of these youngsters were with him in prison. Most of them did not survive.

Mr T spoke to me about his feelings of helplessness and powerlessness as he watched the younger boys (some as young as 13) disintegrate under interrogation. He described how he tried to be strong for them and encourage them not to give up. On one particular occasion Mr T told me that an even more important leader in the prison, a revered sportsman, was chosen by the guards for execution. This young sportsman was both a beloved friend of Mr T and a great source of support to him. At the moment of farewell, the friend said to him that he should not break down before the younger boys but should stay strong in their eyes. Mr T told me that at that moment his 'heart broke'. He felt he could not let either his friend or the younger boys down by weeping and instead he put a cloth over his face and stayed the tears inside of himself.

Although the above account is on one level utterly horrific, on another level it represents the beginning of the transition from trauma to bereavement. For Mr T it was the first time he was able to tell me about his experiences in prison without being overwhelmed by guilt or physical pain. He was able to express his grief in the session in a way that had not been possible in the prison. We understood that despite the pervasive cruelty and insanity of the prison, Mr T had found friends to love and care for and he mourned their loss.

This transition from horror to mourning reawakens many feelings and memories which have been blunted and disturbed. Torture often results in a profound sense of dehumanization in the individual. People typically feel that their experiences place them outside normality. In particular, clients describe being unable to feel 'ordinary' responses such as sadness or happiness (Pines, 1986).

For Mr T his tears for his friend reminded him not only of the terrible fate this friend suffered, but of how much he had cared for him and how grieved he himself was over this loss. By grieving for his dead friend Mr T reclaimed some of the ordinary human feelings he had lost through his trauma. Although on one level he remained persecuted by the fact of his own survival, his acknowledgement of the pain of his loss was also a validation of his own continuing existence.

Work with survivors is about both survival and death. Bettelheim (1979) describes the Holocaust as the triumph of the death drive over the life drive. For Mr T, his pain poignantly reflects the survivor's struggle to acknowledge the life drive and somehow find meaning in the world once again. The work of the therapist in containing and validating a survivor's experience can perhaps also be understood as a representation of this struggle, between the death drive and the life drive. The horror of the experience must be validated and contained for the person to begin to feel their existence once again. Equally, however, the knowledge of survival must have its place.

I conclude this chapter with a quotation from Bettelheim, whose courageous struggle to find meaning in his survivorhood, despite his tragic suicide, must remain an inspiration to all the life-giving forces in ourselves and hopefully in our clients.

> Our experience did not teach us that life is meaningless, that the world of the living is but a whorehouse ... it taught us that, miserable though the world we live in may be, the difference between it and the world of the concentration camps is as great as that between death and life. It taught us that there is meaning to life. (Bettelheim, 1979)

References

Amnesty International (1984) *Torture in the Eighties*. London: Amnesty International.

Bettelheim, B. (1979) Owners of their faces. In *Surviving and Other Essays*. New York: Vintage Books.

Bettelheim, B. (1991) *The Informed Heart: A Study of the Psychological Consequences of Living under Extreme Fear and Terror*. London: Penguin.

Blackwell, D. (1992) Holding, containing and bearing witness: the problem of helpfulness in encounters with torture survivors. Unpublished paper.

Britton, R. (1992) Keeping things in mind. In R. Anderson (ed.), *Clinical Lectures on Klein and Bion*. London: Routledge.

Fischman, Y. and Ross, J. (1990) Group treatment of exiled survivors of trauma. *American Journal of Orthopsychiatry*, 60 (1), 135–42.

Fonagy, P. (1991) Thinking about thinking: some clinical and theoretical considerations in the treatment of a borderline client. *International Journal of Psychoanalysis*, 72, 639–49.

Fonagy, P., Steele, M., Steele, H., Higgit, A. and Target, M. (1992) The Emanuel Miller Memorial Lecture: The theory and practice of resilience. *Journal of Child Psychology and Psychiatry*, 35 (2), 231–57.

Fonagy, P., Moran, G.S. and Target, M. (1993a) Aggression and the psychological self. *International Journal of Psychoanalysis*, 74 (3), 471–85.

Fonagy, P., Steele, M., Moran, G., Steele, H. and Higgit, A. (1993b) Measuring the ghost in the nursery: an empirical study of the relation between parents' mental representations of childhood experiences and their infant's security of attachment. *Journal of the American Psychoanalytic Association*, 41 (1), 957–89.

Freud, S. (1987) *On Metapsychology: The Theory of Psychoanalysis*, tr. J. Strachey, vol. 11. Harmondsworth: Penguin.

Klein, M. (1988) On the theory of anxiety and guilt. In *Envy and Gratitude and Other Works 1946–1963*. London: Virago.

Krystal, H. (1976) *Massive Psychic Trauma*. New York: International Universities Press.

Laub, D. and Auerhahn, N. (1993) Knowing and not knowing massive psychic trauma: forms of traumatic memory. *International Journal of Psychoanalysis*, 74 (2), 287–302.

Levi, P. (1987) *If This Is a Man/The Truce*. London: Abacus Books.

McDougall, J. (1992) *Theatres of the Body: A Psychoanalytic Approach to Psychosomatic Illness*. London: Free Association Books.

Pearson, M. (1992) Problems with transference interpretations in short term dynamic therapy. Unpublished paper.

Pines, D. (1986) Working with women survivors of the Holocaust: affective experiences in transference and counter-transference. *International Journal of Psychoanalysis*, 67, 178–204.

Pines, D. (1993) *A Woman's Unconscious Use of Her Body: A Psychoanalytic Perspective*. London: Virago.

Solomons, K. (1989) Untitled unpublished paper written in collaboration with the Johannesburg Detainees Counselling Service, Johannesburg.

Steiner, J. (1993) *Psychic Retreats: Pathological Organizations in Psychotic, Neurotic and Borderline Patients*. London: Routledge.

Torture (1996) *Quarterly Journal on Rehabilitation of Torture Victims and Prevention of Torture*. Supplementum 1.

Weisaeth, L. and Eitinger, L. (1993) Post traumatic stress phenomena: common themes across wars, disasters and traumatic events. In J.P. Wilson and B. Raphael (eds), *International Handbook of Traumatic Stress Syndromes*. New York: Plenum Press.

Winnicot, D. (1965) *The Maturational Process and the Facilitating Environment*. London: Hogarth Press.

Index